1985

Publications on Asia of the
Institute for Comparative and Foreign Area Studies
Number 21

Modern Chinese Poetry: An Introduction

by
Julia C. Lin

University of Washington Press
Seattle and London

This book is one of the volumes assisted by the Asian Literature Program of the Asia Society, New York.

Library of Congress Cataloging in Publication Data
Lin, Julia C.   1928–
    Modern Chinese poetry.
    (Publications on Asia of the Institute for Comparative and Foreign Area Studies, no. 21)
    Bibliography: p.
    1. Chinese poetry—20th century—History and criticism. I. Title. II. Series: Washington (State). University. Institute for Comparative and Foreign Area Studies. Publications on Asia, no. 21.
    PL2307.L56   895.1'1'509   70-152330
    ISBN 0-295-95145-1
    ISBN 0-295-95281-4 (pbk.)

Publications on Asia of the Institute for Comparative and Foreign Area Studies is a continuation of the series formerly entitled Far Eastern and Russian Institute Publications on Asia.

With deep gratitude and affection
this book is dedicated
to my two professors,
Vincent Shih and Hellmut Wilhelm

Preface

The first significant collection of modern Chinese poetry was Hu Shih's *Experimental Verses*, published in 1919. A series of events in the second half of the nineteenth century had brought China into direct contact with the outside world; the painful experience of military defeat by foreign forces resulted in a popular realization of China's comparative backwardness and a desire to modernize the country by emulating certain aspects of Western civilization. The Literary Movement of 1917 urged a break with tradition and an exploration of new forms of expression.

This process of reform was given direction and stimulation by Hu Shih, whose numerous essays established the principles of new poetry. Following Hu's instructions to avoid the forced, artificial, and monotonous elements of traditional verse and to use the vernacular language in treating more commonplace themes and emotions, subsequent poets turned the years 1917–37 into a period of extremely active experimentation. Poems were written in such Western verse forms as the sonnet, limerick, and free verse. Works of certain Formalist poets echoed the Western Romantics, Keats and Shelley, while Baudelaire, Verlaine, and Mallarmé gave rise to the Chinese Symbolist school. But the second Sino-Japanese War brought experimentation to an end by turning Chinese poets to patriotic, war-oriented themes; and the Communist regime has molded current poetic expression into a rigidly proletarian literature.

The purpose of this book is to make the new poetry more accessible to readers in the West. The material currently available on the subject consists mainly of a few introductions in poetry anthologies and brief surveys in studies of Chinese literary history. This study examines the rise and development of the new genre, from 1919 to the present, by focusing on the period's major poets, and lesser talents when they are significant. In my discussion of each poet, I have tried to convey a sense of his style, themes, characteristic techniques, faults and virtues, major concerns, and important contributions. The main sources for my study were necessarily the works of the poets, for few biographical or critical essays, English or Chinese, exist. As few English translations of the works have been published, almost all of the translations are my own; I hope that these poems and my analyses of them will serve the twofold purpose of both introducing and evaluating modern Chinese poetry.

It has been common for scholars of modern Chinese poetry to regard every instance of similarity to Western poetry as a sure sign of indebtedness to the West. To my mind this is an oversimplification, ignoring the possibility that such parallelism could result simply from the affinity of poetic minds, whereby similar characteristics could develop simultaneously in two different cultures. In fact, it may well have been the nostalgically familiar elements in Western poetry that attracted the young Chinese poets. This is by no means to deny the tremendous influence of the West on modern Chinese poetry, but it is an argument for a more balanced critical stand in our evaluation of it. Indeed, to insist on the singular dominance of one source of influence is not only to ignore the fruitful interplay of diverse literary influences, but also to rob the poets of their own sensitivity and creative power.

I wish to thank the following publishers for permission to quote from copyrighted material. The portions of "On Encountering Sorrow" from *Ch'u Tz'ŭ, The Songs of the South: An Ancient Chinese Anthology*, by David Hawkes, are reprinted by permission of the Clarendon Press, Oxford. "The Laundry Song" and "The Iron Virgin" from *Twentieth Century Chinese Poetry* by Kai-yu Hsu, copyright © 1963 by Kai-yu Hsu, are reprinted by permission of Doubleday & Company, Inc. The selection from Rainer Maria Rilke's *Duino Elegies* from *Rilke Duino Elegies*, translated by C. F. MacIntyre, originally published by the University of California Press, are reprinted by permission of The Regents of the University of California.

I am grateful to the Social Science Research Council and to the American Council of Learned Societies, as well as to the Far Eastern and Russian Institute of the University of Washington and to the Asia Society, for the support they have given this study. I am indebted to the University of California, Berkeley, for kind permission to use its library facilities. My special thanks go to Dr. Ruth Krader and Mrs. Frances Wang, formerly of the Far Eastern library, University of Washington, and to Miss Catherine Nelson of the Ohio University library for securing necessary material for my research. Thanks are also due Mrs. Jocelyn Harvey and Miss Ruth Erwin for their help. I wish to express my warm thanks to Paul Kendall, Regents Professor of English at Ohio University, and to K. C. Hsiao, professor of Chinese history and political thought, Vincent Shih, professor of Chinese literature, and Arnold Stein, professor of English, all at the University of Washington, for their valuable suggestions, corrections, and criticism. I am also deeply grateful to Hellmut Wilhelm, professor emeritus of Chinese literature, University of Washington, for his constant encouragement and sustained help throughout the preparation of the present volume. My warm appreciation to Miss Gladys Greenwood for her expert advice, and my heartfelt thanks to my dear friend Siggy (Mrs. Paul Kendall), who has given most generously of her time and talent in improving my book and getting it ready for publication. Finally, my loving thanks to my husband, Henry, and my children, Tan and Maya, for their sacrifices, inspiration, and moral support that made possible the completion of this book.

J. C. L.

Contents

Part I: Before 1917

1

Tradition

Modern Chinese poetry provoked more hostile criticism and fierce opposition than any other form of modern Chinese literature. But this abuse was not without justification. The new poetry, especially in its early days, was disappointing: when compared with the great legacy of the traditional poets, it appeared awkward, crude, and immature. However, one must bear in mind that the new poetry was not built directly upon the old, as were modern Chinese fiction and drama, both of which had a long and remarkable vernacular tradition in their favor. The new poets, in rebellion against tradition, had rejected not only the literary language, *wen-yen*, as their poetic medium, but all the conventional verse forms and prosodic rules as well. *Pai-hua*, the vernacular, was elevated to being the only acceptable means for the new verse. And so apart from the usual problems faced by any poetry in revolt, these poets were further confronted with the predicament of mastering a new medium in order to create a prosody suitable to it.

During the early decades of the present century, when the impact of the West was beginning to be felt in China, poets naturally turned in that direction for inspiration and instruction. Western influence, however, did not mean that Chinese traditional poetry ceased to play a significant role. On the contrary, it continued as an important force throughout the development of the new verse.

Wen-yen, unlike the literary languages of many countries, is far from being only the artificial tongue of dead poets. Since the sixth century B.C. it has been the common written idiom for all the dialects in China. It is a language with a rich and extensive literature, "a language which has played in eastern Asia a part comparable to that of Latin and Greek in Europe."[1] By no means dead, it continued to be used in government documents, news dispatches, and business or personal correspondence long after *pai-hua*, the vernacular, was officially proclaimed as the "national language" by the government in 1921.[2]

The most striking surface feature of the Chinese language is the character, whose pictorial and ideographic nature has long piqued the imagination of Western writers. In fact, while it is true that some Chinese characters were originally direct representations of objects or ideas, they are not strictly ideographs or pictographs. Even as early as the Shang dynasty (1766–1123? B.C.), many characters were already symbols of particular words in the language. Moreover, a great number of the pictographs have been so reduced in strokes for convenience' sake through the years that they are now past recognition. Other characters, even in modern form, remain expressive through the inherent concreteness and suggestiveness of their unique structure. The structure of Chinese characters has changed comparatively less than the sound of the language. The most ancient forms of writing are those found on shells and oracle bones of the Shang dynasty, to be followed then by the Chou (1112?–256 B.C.) inscriptions on bronzes and stones. By the Ch'in dynasty (221–207 B.C.) writing was standardized, and since that time there has been little basic change in structure.

The evolution of Chinese characters produced four main categories, or methods, of formation.[3] The earliest characters are simple pictographs representing concrete objects, such as *jih* 日 "sun" (ancient form ☉), *yüeh* 月 "moon" (ancient form

---

[1] Bernhard Karlgren, *Sound and Symbol in Chinese*, p. 1.

[2] *Encyclopaedia Britannica*, 1967, s.v., "Chinese Language."

[3] Originally there were six principles, two of which were concerned not with the formation of new characters but with their extended use. These two are omitted here. See James J. Y. Liu, *The Art of Chinese Poetry*, p. 5.

⺼), and *mu* 木 "tree" (ancient form ⽊). Next come the simple ideographs, or symbols of ideas: *i* 一 "one" (ancient form 一), *shang* 上 "above" (ancient form 二), *hsia* 下 "below" (ancient form 二), *chung* 中 "middle" (ancient form ⊕). In the third group are the compound ideographs. These are formed by linking together two or more simple characters, the combined meaning of which suggests the quality or condition to be expressed. Thus we have *lin* 林 "woods" (ancient form 林), denoted by two trees; *ming* 明 "brightness" (ancient form 明),[4] sun and moon; *tsou* 坐 "sit" (ancient form 坐), two men sitting on the ground.

By far the largest category is that of the phonetic compounds. A phonetic compound consists of a simple character (called the phonetic) suggesting the sound and another (called the signific) indicating the meaning of the new compound. For example, *k'u* 枯 "wither" has two constituents—the phonetic, *ku* 古 "ancient," gives the approximate sound; the signific, *mu* 木 "tree," suggests its meaning. Frequently a phonetic also contributes to the meaning of the new word. The character *p'ing* 評 "to discuss, to criticize" has *yen* 言 "to speak" for the signific and *p'ing* 平 "level, equal, fair" for the phonetic, which further implies that "to speak fairly" is "to discuss or criticize." Again, when the same phonetic, *p'ing*, combines with *t'sao* 艸 "grass" and *shui* 氵 "water," the result is *p'ing* 萍 "duckweed," a water plant noted for its level leaves.

The Chinese written language is undoubtedly more concrete and suggestive because of its imagistic potential. An abstract word like *ming* 明 "brightness," with its latent images of sun and moon, is at once more tangible and buoyant than its English counterpart. It is natural then that traditional Chinese poets often display a strong visual imagination. The very architecture of the language fosters the concrete, the suggestive, the concentrated; it is an invitation to pure imagism.

Aurally, the Chinese language is distinguished by its tones

---

[4] The original form of the character *ming* 明 "brightness" is composed of two pictographs—window and moon—instead of the sun and moon components in the present form.

and "monosyllabic" nature; both are integral to Chinese metrical patterns. The common assumption that the language is entirely monosyllabic arises from a confusion of terms. A Chinese character contains only one syllable and appears more often than not as an independent word-unit. Many characters, however, have meaning only in combination, that is, as words. A Chinese word consists of one, two, three, or even more characters, or "syllables," and is therefore polysyllabic. The word *ying wu* 鸚鵡 "parrot," for example, is a disyllabic word of two characters. In *wen-yen* there are numerous disyllabic words, or compounds, many of which are alliterative (*ts'en tz'u* 參差 "uneven," *p'iao p'o* 漂泊 "wandering"), or rhymed compounds (*miao t'io* 窈窕 "graceful," *p'ai huai* 徘徊 "pacing back and forth"), or reduplicative (*ch'i ch'i* 淒淒 "sad," *ch'ing ch'ing* 青青 "green"). Disyllabic compounds are often onomatopoeic too and piquantly descriptive. They were lavishly used by the traditional poets for subtle verbal effects and descriptive force.

Every Chinese character has a specific "tone," so that characters otherwise phonetically identical can be distinguished by the rise and fall of the voice. In China the tone system, like the phonetic system, has undergone various changes with the result that the actual number of tones differs among modern dialects. Classical Chinese has four tones: (1) *p'ing* or "level" is fairly long and maintains the same pitch; (2) *shang* or "rising" is short and rises slightly in pitch; (3) *ch'ü* or "falling" slowly falls and then rises slightly in pitch, as in a doubtful, hesitating "Ye-es"; (4) *ju* or "entering" is short and abruptly arrested, like an emphatic "No!" in English.

For prosodic purposes the first tone is designated as "even" while the other three are "deflected." These tones, with their modulation of pitch and variation of duration and movement, are basic to the melodic patterns in China. In early Chinese poetry, writers depended only on natural modulation, but all the meters that emerged after the Tang dynasty (seventh to tenth century A.D.) demand strict adherence to fixed tone patterns. Two such patterns used in the regulated verse of this period are given in the chart below.[5] The symbol $(-)$ designates a level tone, $(+)$ a deflected tone, (R) rhyme, and $(/)$ pause.

Pattern 1: Five-Syllabic Regulated Verse	Pattern 2: Seven-Syllabic Regulated Verse
$--/-++$	$--/++/+--$ R
(or, $--/++-$ R)	(or, $--/++/--+$)
$++/+--$ R	$++/--/++-$ R
$++/--+$	$++/--/-++$
$--/++-$ R	$--/++/+--$ R
$--/-++$	$--/++/--+$
$++/+--$ R	$++/--/++-$ R
$++/--+$	$++/--/-++$
$--/++-$ R	$--/++/+--$ R

The basic principles involved here are repetition and contrast of tone sequences within the poem. The resulting tone patterns invariably decide the verse movements, which are predominantly musical. This innate musical quality of the language is the basis for the remarkable sense of tone color and musical nuance developed by traditional poets, and may explain why there is so much exquisite lyricism in traditional Chinese verse.

The Chinese language, especially the literary language, though it possesses inflexible elements, is basically uninflected. It is grammatically organized into a regular structure of word formation and word order: verb-object, subject-predicate, adjective-noun. A Chinese poet, therefore, enjoys greater freedom from the linguistic fetters of tense, case, number, and voice. Even connectives, prepositions, auxiliaries, and articles can be dispensed with readily, so that the poet can concentrate on essentials while ridding his verse of irrelevancies. The literary language is unquestionably a perfect means to secure compression and concision of form. It is no accident that traditional poets favor the short forms and that some of the best traditional poetry is written in these forms.

[5] Liu, *Art of Chinese Poetry*, pp. 26–27.

A Chinese word seldom has one arbitrary definition: it is surrounded by clusters of meanings, some of which may even be mutually exclusive. The ensuing obscurities and ambiguities in works of expository prose have kept research scholars in rice for centuries. For the poet, however, dealing as he is with a nebulous world of implication and association, the complexities of meaning are a treasure-trove.

In a traditional Chinese poem, it is the number of characters, not stresses, in each line that determines its meter. The earliest verse in China is in the four-character (or four-syllable) form used in the *Book of Odes* (ca. twelfth to seventh century B.C.), the first anthology of Chinese poetry. Generally believed to have been edited by Confucius himself, the *Book of Odes* was sanctioned in 136 B.C. as one of the Five Classics of the Confucian canon. The anthology contains poetic narratives celebrating the heroic founding of the Chou House, elegant court songs, ceremonial hymnals of great dignity, and numerous folk songs of astonishing vigor and simple lyric charm. Many of these verses, religious or secular, were originally sung or recited to the accompaniment of music and dance. This musical affiliation was to remain a vital spark in the subsequent period of poetic development.

The four-character verse form is so called because its lines consist of a standard number of four characters. These metrical lines are arranged in stanza units, with end rhymes commonly occurring in even-numbered lines (i.e., lines 2 and 4). Although there is no prescribed tone pattern, musical effects are preserved by devices like alliteration, assonance, internal rhymes as well as end rhymes, and a natural modulation of tones.

Generally, verse forms having a fixed number of characters produce a staccato rhythm which becomes mechanical and tiresome. The monotony is the more conspicuous in longer poems and in poems with few characters in the lines. When handled right, however, such forms create remarkable incantatory effects especially apposite to poems that are liturgical in character. Their formal regularity adds an air of austere grandeur and at the same time conjures up a visual beauty of perfect symmetry and balance rarely surpassed by any other verse form.

Following are some samples from the *Book of Odes*.

THE PEACH TREE
Fair, fair is the peach tree,
Bright, bright are the blossoms.
The young bride departs,
May she order her new house well.

Fair, fair is the peach tree,
Rich, rich are the fruits.
The young bride departs,
May she order her new house well.

Fair, fair is the peach tree,
Lush, lush are the leaves.
The young bride departs,
May she order her new house well.

YELLOW ARE THE GRASSES
Yellow are the grasses.
Day after day we march.
Our men are taken
Defending the frontiers.

Dark are the grasses.
Day after day the men are taken.
Alas for us soldiers
Who alone receive such treatment!

Not buffaloes, nor tigers.
Yet we are abandoned in this wild.
Alas for us soldiers:
Day and night we have no rest.

The bushy-tailed foxes

Roam among the deep grasses.
Our bamboo wagon
Rumbles along the ancient paths.

DEAD DOE IN THE WOOD
In the wood a dead doe lies,
White rushes over her.
Maiden's thoughts wander in spring,
Fine knight upon her lies.

In wood of oakenshaws,
In the wasteland sleeps the doe.
White rushes bury her,
Maiden fair as jade.

Touch me not sir, please.
Remove not my sash.
The dogs might bark.

As the *Book of Odes* represents the ancient poetic tradition of
Northern China, so *Ch'u Tz'u* (Songs of the South, ca. 340 B.C.)
embodies that of the South. *Ch'u Tz'u* is a collection of poems
written by Ch'ü Yüan (ca. 340–277 B.C.)—the first major
Chinese poet known by name—and his imitators. These southern songs are characterized by their Sao meter, believed to have
been created by Ch'ü Yüan for his major poem, "On Encountering Sorrow." The Sao lines, compared to those in the *Book of
Odes*, are longer (they usually contain an average of six or seven
characters) and more irregular, and are commonly distinguished
by a strong caesura in the middle with an unstressed syllable.
End rhymes and internal rhymes are both extensively used, as
are alliteration, assonance, apostrophe, parallelism, and repetition. Whereas the verses in the *Book of Odes* are simple, compact, and straightforward in style, the southern songs are
highly inflated and rhetorical. Their elegiac mood, erotic overtones, luxurious verbal texture, lush imagery, and recurrent use
of symbolic motifs project a sensibility that is unmistakably

romantic. Both the *Book of Odes* and the southern songs are of immense importance to the later development in traditional Chinese poetry: they establish the two main strains of poetic tradition and sources of influence in the centuries to come.

From "On Encountering Sorrow" by Ch'ü Yüan (ca. 340–277 B.C.):

> The days and months hurried on, never delaying;
> Springs and autumns sped by in endless alternation:
> And I thought how the trees and flowers were fading and
>   falling.
> And feared that my Fairest's beauty would fade too.
> 'Gather the flower of youth and cast out the impure!
> 'Why will you not change the error of your ways?
> 'I have harnessed brave coursers for you to gallop forth
>   with:
> 'Come, let me go before and show you the way!
>
>   .   .   .   .
> Truly, this generation are cunning artificers!
> From square and compass they turn their eyes and change
>   the true measurement,
> They disregard the ruled line to follow their crooked fancies:
> To emulate in flattery is their only rule.
> But I am sick and sad at heart and stand irresolute:
> I alone am at a loss in this generation.
> But I would rather quickly die and meet dissolution
> Before I ever would consent to ape *their* behaviour.
>
>   .   .   .   .
> I made a coat of lotus and water-chestnut leaves,
> And gathered lotus petals to make myself a skirt.
> I will no longer care that no one understands me,
> As long as I can keep the sweet fragrance of my mind.
> High towered the lofty hat on my head;
> The longest of girdles dangled from my waist.
> Fragrance and richness mingled in sweet confusion.
> The brightness of their lustre has remained undimmed.
>
>   .   .   .   .
> I will follow my natural bent and please myself;

I will go off wandering to look for a lady.
While my adornment is in its pristine beauty
I will travel all around looking both high and low.
Since Ling Fen had given me a favourable oracle,
I reckoned a lucky day to start my journey on.
I broke a branch of jasper to take for my meat,
And ground fine jasper meal for my journey's provisions.

. . . .

Long was the road that lay ahead and full of difficulties;
I sent word to my other chariots to take a short route and
    wait.
The road wound leftwards round the Pu Chou Mountain:
I marked out the Western Sea as our meeting-place.
There I marshalled my thousand chariots,
And jade hub to jade hub we galloped on abreast.
My eight dragon-steeds flew on with writhing undula-
    tions;
My cloud-embroidered banners flapped on the wind.

I tried to curb my mounting will and slacken the swift
    pace;
But the spirits soared high up, far into the distance.
We played the Nine Songs and danced the Nine Shao
    dances:
I wanted to snatch some time for pleasure and amusement.
But when I had ascended the splendour of the heavens,
I suddenly caught a glimpse below of my old home.
The groom's heart was heavy and the horses for longing
Arched their heads back and refused to go on.[6]

In the Han dynasty (206 B.C.–A.D. 219), ancient verse evolved
and later became one of the two main verse styles in traditional
China, the other being the modern-style verse of the T'ang
dynasty (A.D. 618–907). The ancient verse form is distinguished
by its lines of either all five-character or all seven-character
meters, though occasional liberty in the line length is per-
mitted. In these verses, as in the *Book of Odes* and the southern

---

[6] David Hawkes, *Ch'u Tz'ŭ, The Songs of the South*, pp. 22, 25, 33, 34.

songs, there are no fixed rules about the use of rhymes, nor are there rules concerning tones. However, rhymes—both end and internal—as well as alliteration, assonance, onomatopoeia, and reduplication, were widely employed; and so were the syntactical devices of parallelism and repetition. Like the Confucian odes, these ancient songs deal with universal themes. Mostly based on folk songs, they have a strong folk flavor and spontaneity of spirit.

> Marching, marching, forever marching.
> In life I'm separated from you
> By a distance of over ten thousand miles.
> Each at a different horizon.
> The way is difficult and long.
> When shall we meet again?
> The Tatar horse loves the north wind,
> The Yueh bird nests on the south branch.
> The day since we parted has long passed.
> My sash is getting looser every day.
> Floating clouds now hide the bright sun,
> Wandering man holds no more thoughts to return.
> Thinking of you ages me.
> Time becomes old suddenly.
> No need to speak again of your deserting me.
> Please make an effort to eat more.

Contemporary with the ancient verse are the *yüeh fu* ballads collected by the Music Bureau—an institution founded by the Emperor Wu (157–87 B.C.) of the Han dynasty. They differ from the ancient verse in that they were set to music. These song ballads, whose source may also be traced to the *Book of Odes*, share the homely realism and simplicity of treatment prefigured in the earlier poetry. Like the *Book of Odes*, the *yüeh fu* ballads contain a large body of "social protest" verses disclosing with pathos the social injustices suffered by ordinary people. Ballads like "The Orphan" and "The Peacock Eastward Flies" reveal a narrative skill rarely surpassed in later times.

From "The Orphan":

> Born to be an orphan,
> Fated to be an orphan.
> How bitter is my lot indeed!
> When my parents were alive,
> I rode a sturdy carriage
> Driven by four fine horses.
> After my parents died,
> My brother and sister-in-law forced me to be a
>   tradesman.
> I traveled south as far as Nine Rivers,
> As far east as Ch'i and Lu.
> At the end of the year I returned home.
> I dared not voice my miseries:
> The lice in my head,
> The dust in my eyes.
> My brother told me to cook meals,
> My sister-in-law wanted me to tend horses.
> I was always running up the hall
> And then down again to the hall below.
> The orphan's tears came down like rain.
> In the morning they sent me to draw water,
> In the evening I came home with the buckets.
> My hands were full of sores,
> My feet were bared of shoes.
> Sadly I walked on the cold frost,
> Treading on thorns and brambles;
> The thorns broke off in my flesh.
> In pain I grieved my fate:
> My tears fell like running water,
> I could not stop their flow.
> In winter I have no warm jacket to wear,
> In summer I have no cool clothing.
> To be alive holds no joy for me.
> It is best to die and go early to the Yellow Spring.

The most popular traditional verse form is the modern-style

verse of the T'ang dynasty. In contrast to the ancient verse, this newer verse style has a definite number of lines and an elaborate tone system and rhyme scheme, although the number of characters in each line remains the same—either all five or all seven characters. Poems written in this style may be further classified as regulated verse and short-stop verse (*chüeh-chü*). Whereas the former is written in eight lines with the middle four lines consisting of two antithetical couplets, the latter is a quatrain. Both forms are highly compressed. It is in these modes that Li Po, Tu Fu, and Wang Wei wrote their most memorable poems of exquisite lyricism.

SORROWS OF THE JADE STAIRS
By Li Po
White dew grows on the jade stairs,
At night it wets her silken hose.
Still waiting, she lets fall the crystal screen
And through it stares at the autumn moon.

SPRING
By Tu Fu
Mountains and rivers rest under the sun,
Spring winds quicken the blooms.
Swallows fly in pairs to build their nests,
The doves drowse on the hot sands.
The blue stream mirrors the white birds,
The red flowers burn on the green mountains.
In silence I watch the march of spring.
My thoughts turn to home.

COLD MOUNTAIN
By Wang Wei
Cold mountain turns dark green.
Autumn stream flows gently on.
While I lean on my staff by the wicket gate,
The cry of an old cicada is heard amidst the winds.

Not all traditional meters are of uniform length. A popular

poetic genre called *tz'u*, or song lyrics, composed to fit particular musical tunes, has, necessarily, lines of irregular numbers of characters. This form first came into being in the T'ang dynasty and flourished during the Sung dynasty (A.D. 960–1278). Most of the original tunes have been lost, but the meters that evolved from them did survive. The *tz'u* meter, contrary to its appearance of flexibility, is even more constrained than the modern-style verse form in its complex rules for tones and rhymes. Highly personal and subjective in approach, a *tz'u* poem is noted for its mellifluous music, elegant diction, and supple imagery.

To the tune of "Yü Mei Jen" by Li Hou-chu (A.D. 936–78):

> Spring flowers, autumn moon, when will you cease coming?
> How much can one recall?
> Last night again the east wind passed the tower.
> It's unbearable to remember the lost kingdom in the
>   moonlight.
> The carved balustrade, the jade steps must still be there.
> Only the face is changed.
> Tell me, how much sorrow is there?
> A river of spring water endlessly eastward flows.

Finally there is the dramatic verse of the Yüan, Ming, and Ch'ing dynasties (thirteenth to twentieth century). Like the *tz'u*, from which it developed, the dramatic verse permits a wider variation in length of line at the same time that it insists on rigid patterns of tone and rhyme. The musical tunes to which the words were originally set, however, belong to a different repertoire; greater liberty is allowed in the interpolation of additional words. The words themselves are more colloquial than in *tz'u*, the conversational tone closer to ordinary speech. Following is a descriptive passage from the popular drama, *Sorrows of the Han Palace*:

> I see you now with your lovely painted brows,
> Your hair dark as the crows,

Your waist as slender as the willows;
Your face opens up like a colored cloud.
Which part of my palace is worthy of sheltering you?
Who would care to ask if your family plows fields for a
    living?
By your lord's favor you shall share his pillows.
Heaven that asks the dews to grow the mulberries has
    made you mine.
If not so, how could I have found you in this small
    thatched hut
Of my vast kingdom that stretches thousands and thousands
    of miles.

The brocade that these traditional poets had woven throughout the dynasties is an old and resplendent one. In spite of the
resistance on the parts of many new poets, its powerful influence
shines through the contemporary fabric of much of their verse
as we examine its texture more closely in the following chapters.

2

Transition

In 1842 the Opium War between Great Britain and China ended with China's shattering military defeat by the British, and the signing of the Nanking Treaty with Great Britain forced the formal opening of China to the Western powers. In 1858 English and French troops advanced on Peking; within two years Anglo-French military forces had invaded Tientsin, captured the capital city of Peking, and compelled China to sign another treaty. Before the founding of the Republic of China in 1912, China endured yet another major loss at the culmination of the Sino-Japanese War (1894–95). Reviewing the events of this stormy era on the eve of revolution in 1911, one witnesses a succession of humiliating defeats suffered by a rapidly declining dynasty at the hands of foreign powers whose military and technological dominance posed a serious threat to the very existence of the nation itself. China was shocked out of its complacency to face the painful realization of its national weaknesses and backwardness. With this realization came an acute awareness of the urgency of the numerous problems— political, economic, social, and cultural—that confronted the nation. To solve these problems various individuals in China took different attitudes and approaches. Some were in favor of a slow and gradual reform, trying to preserve as much of tradition as possible.[1] Others, fiercely opposed to the moderate stand, preferred the drastic approach of making a radical break

[1] See C. T. Hsia, *A History of Modern Chinese Fiction, 1917–1957*, pp. 3–27.

with the past. Both moderates and radicals, however, shared the same awareness of the problems and the same desire to modernize the nation. They also shared the conviction that there was much to be learned from Western civilization.

What followed was a period of seething activity in translating Western works—philosophical, scientific, political, literary. This activity was to exert an important influence on the emerging literature in subsequent decades. Among the translators was Yen Fu (1853–1920),[2] who after having studied in England, in 1898 brilliantly rendered Thomas Huxley's *Evolution and Ethics* into classical Chinese prose style. His other translations include Herbert Spencer's *Principles of Sociology*, John Stuart Mill's *On Liberty*, William Stanley Jevons' *Elementary Lessons in Logic*, and Montesquieu's *L'Esprit des lois*. These works became exceedingly popular among the intelligentsia. What Yen Fu did in the field of philosophy and the social sciences, Lin Shu (1882–1924) did equally well in the field of literature. He, too, used the *wen-yen*, the literary language, in his many translations of European, English, and American novels. Though Lin Shu knew no foreign languages, with the help of oral interpreters he turned out the staggering number of 170 titles of Western fiction, including works by Dickens, Dumas, Scott, and Tolstoy.

In poetry, Su Man-shu (1884–1918)[3] elegantly translated nineteenth-century English Romantic poetry into the familiar classical verse forms. This poetry's popularity was to inspire an enduring interest in Western Romanticism among the young aspiring Chinese poets. The translations not only kindled interest in Western literature but made the translators conscious of the need for a more flexible and suitable instrument for their tasks. They found *wen-yen* too far removed from ordinary speech and too rigid a medium for disseminating modern ideas adequately. To reach a wider audience, K'ang Yu-wei (1858–1927) and Liang Ch'i-ch'ao (1873–1929), two leading

[2] For Yen Fu's translations, see Benjamin Schwartz, *In Search of Wealth and Power*.

[3] For Su's translations of English poetry, see Henry McAleavy, *Su Man-shu, 1884–1918*.

liberal scholars during the Reform Movement, modified the *wen-yen* into a semiclassical prose style that was grammatically more flexible and more satisfactory for expressing Western ideas and incorporating Western terms.

In the tradition-bound field of poetry, the first ripple of change appeared when a small number of scholar-poets, headed by T'an Ssu-t'ung (1865–98) and Hsia Tseng-yu (1865–1924)—contemporaries of K'ang and. Liang—launched a movement hopefully labeled "new poetry." The newness of their style consisted mainly of the injection of new terminology —mostly transliterations of foreign words—into traditional verse: "The laws of human relations suffered under *caste*./The Assembly of laws prospers within the *parliament*."[4] The other new feature of this poetry was its use of references to foreign literature. In one of Hsia Tseng-yu's poems we find the line "thrice denied, the cock crows"; in another is a reference to the tower of Babel; in still another the strange beasts of Revelation appear. Such Biblical allusions were employed mostly for exoticism and imaginative appeal. It is obvious that these "new" elements were surface novelties only, as Liang Ch'i-ch'ao pointed out:

> At those times, the so-called new poets loved to drag in new terms in order to show that they were different. . . . At a transitional time, revolution is inevitable. But, in revolution, it is the spirit rather than the form that must be revolutionized. Our party lately is fond of talking about revolution in poetry. Still, if one calls piling one's poem with new terminology revolution, then it is no different from the Reform Movement launched by the Manchu government. Only when one can provide new situation to old style can it be called a true revolution.[5]

Though these endeavors failed to produce a true modern poetry, they unquestionably signified the poetry that was to come.

[4] Liang Ch'i-ch'ao, *Yin-ping-shih ho-chi* [Collected works], 16:40.
[5] Ibid.

Huang Tsun-hsien (1848–1905)

Among the poets cultivating this new poetic style, Huang Tsun-hsien was its most successful exponent and practitioner. Liang Ch'i-ch'ao, a friend of Huang's, was impressed by his works and frequently referred to them in his *Shih-hua* (Talks on poetry). His praise was lavish: "Among the recent poets, one who is able to forge new ideas into old verse is no other than Huang Kung-tu. . . . The poetry of Huang has created a new horizon, uniquely established in the poetic world of the twentieth century. All have unanimously praised him as a true master; these opinions are not to be proven false."[6]

Huang Tsun-hsien, a native of Kwangtung province, was a man with versatile talents and a wide range of interests. An accomplished poet, classical scholar, folklorist, and reformer, he was also a diplomat whose official duties took him to Japan, England, France, Malaya, and the United States. These travels abroad furnished many cosmopolitan settings and varied material for his poetry; they also fired the patriotic feeling and social consciousness that permeate his works.

Like his reform-minded colleagues, Huang was enthusiastic about the Reform Movement of the nineties and he actively participated in the movement in Hunan in 1897. He was particularly concerned about the current conservative attitudes toward poetry. He felt the pressing need to free poetry from the conventions of the past and was one of the few who dared challenge the ancients, arguing that "the world today differs from that of old. Thus, the men today need not be the same as the ancients."[7] He determined to liberate himself from the shackles of convention by refusing to specialize in any writing style of the past—such specialization being a standard practice of poets of his day—and by boldly innovating his own brand of poetry. His poetic credo is best summed up in his famous statement: "My hands write what my mouth speaks,/How can

---

[6] Ibid.
[7] Huang Tsun-hsien, *Jen-chin-lo shih-ts'ao ch'ien-chu* [Collected works], Preface, p. 1.

antiquity curb me?"[8] Huang never actually repudiated the traditional verse. Most of the poems in his collection are in the fairly relaxed ancient-verse form, whose prosodic rules permit the poet to write at any length he wishes. This was a freedom that Huang favored since many of his poems dealing with contemporary events are descriptive narratives that require detailed treatment.

Huang Tsun-hsien's enthusiasm for folk songs, both ancient and contemporary, inspired him to compose his own versions, which he called *shan-ke*, or mountain songs. These derivative songs are mostly allegorical satires on human nature and behavior. They reflect the writer's astute comment on society and men.

> Difficult is my mother-in-law!
> Difficult is my mother-in-law!
> Sister-in-law adds her vicious slander,
> Complaining that I idle too much.
> The wicked slaves and the crafty maids daily add
>   their tyranny.
> For ten years I have borne no child.
> I can only sigh for my fate,
> The nest remains unbuilt.
> I can only pray for punishment;
> Wholeheartedly I offer my gratitude to my
>   mother-in-law.
> Why is she still displeased with me?
> Oh, difficult is my mother-in-law, difficult is my
>   mother-in-law!
>
> Ah-p'o has burned the cake!
> Ah-p'o has burned the cake!
> Ah-p'o when young
> Was expert in making soup.
> Now she has become old and haughty.
> "None of you know anything!" she said.
> Ah-p'o had to do everything herself.
> The eldest daughter-in-law arrived:

[8] Ibid., 1:15.

She argued and wrangled.
The youngest daughter-in-law arrived:
She hustled and bustled.
But everyone praised the talent of Ah-p'o.
Frying too fast, the dried bean husks are burned.
Hands are scorched, cries are heard.
Ah-p'o's cake got burned.

Like the folk songs, these verses are simple in construction, direct and unpretentious in expression. The anecdotal tone and the idiomatic language of the common people invest the pieces with an earthy, unaffected charm that gives them great popular appeal.

If Huang made no radical attempt to introduce a new prosody, he tried to shake off clichés and stereotyped poetic diction by insisting on a plainer medium. His efforts in this direction are not always successful. Instead of displaying a natural ease, his lines sometimes are trite and dull, as in the poem written on a visit to the United States in 1884:

Alas, Washington,
By now one hundred years old:
You American people have raised the flag
    of independence,
You no longer suffer from oppression;
Races of red, yellow, black, and white
Now are all considered equal.
All men have obtained freedom;
All things are benefited by you.
The wisdom of the people has increased,
The nation's wealth has doubled.
Oh, great are the ways of this nation .

. . . .

But when it comes to electing a president
One sees so many strange doings:
The candidates angrily point their weapons
And bitterly fight for the nation's seal.

. . . .

> If only there were no party battles,
> One could still hope for a peaceful world.

Some of the flat phrasing seems to derive from Huang's over-anxious attempt to make the poem colloquial in tone while adhering to the traditional meter.

As for poetic devices, Huang used much that is inherent in the traditional poetry: alliteration, rhyme, reduplication, allusion, and quotation. His use of the first three devices is restrained, especially in poems dealing with current incidents, but less so in those of more conventional theme. Huang made ample use of the last two devices. His works are studded with allusions ranging from the Confucian classics through legends and myths to current issues. Although the indiscriminate use of allusions by poets in the past frequently resulted in pedantry, artificiality, and obscurity, Huang handles the device with discretion. In his descriptive poem about the Suez Canal, he alludes to the accomplishment of the legendary Emperor Yü (second century B.C.), who was given the throne by his predecessor, Shung, after he curbed the disastrous floods plaguing the country. By comparing the completion of the Suez Canal with an occasion whose importance and impact were familiar to native readers, Huang was able to convey the significance of an international achievement.

The other traditional device that Huang favored was the incorporation of lines or parts of lines from other poets' works into his own verse. This was a legitimate practice encouraged in classical poetry.

1. Huang's line:	Tsung chi wu ting so
	蹤 跡 無 定 所
	The footprints have no permanent place.
From a line by Pao Chao (ca. 414–466):	P'iao p'iao wu ting so
	飄 飄 無 定 所
	Wandering, wandering with no permanent place.

2. Huang's line: chiao chiao huang niao t'i

                                   交　交　黃　鳥　啼

From the   "Chiao, chiao," the yellow bird

Book of Odes: cries.[9]

                               chiao chiao huang niao.

                                   交　交　黃　鳥

                                 "Chiao, chiao," the yellow bird.

Huang's poetic collection contains a miscellany of occasional verse celebrating a specific event or addressed to a particular person. Poems like his "On the Departure of a Student," "The Birth of a Daughter," and "For My Wife" usually appear in any anthology of traditional Chinese poetry. The themes are as conventional as their modes of expression. Huang's quatrain to his wife is a perfect specimen:

> Ten years happily together, I knew no sorrow.
> Today, flying apart, I alone journey far.
> I know not if my wife is watching for me on the bridge.
> Light smoke, a thin willow—a few lines of autumn.

One of Huang's most admired contributions is his conscious exploration of new subject matter. Many critics and readers eulogized Huang's poetry as a remarkable mirror of China's recent history. Wang Yao, a recent reviewer of Huang's work, assessed the value of his poetry in this way: "His poems truly revealed the countenance of China's recent history, especially the history of the imperialistic encroachments and the poet's patriotic spirit."[10] In "Song of Tung-kou," Huang recorded the Japanese invasion of Darien Bay in the 1890s, as describing how the Chinese navy became so cowed after their initial defeat that they dared not venture again to defend their country. In another piece, "Song of Taiwan," Huang voiced his grief over the loss of Taiwan to Japan:

[9] Ibid., p. 7.
[10] Wang Yao, "Wan-Ch'ing shih jen Huang Tsun-hsien" [Huang Tsun-hsien, a poet of late Ch'ing], *People's Literature*, 1951, no. 20, p. 68.

On top of the city wall thunder the rolling drums,
Heaven sheds its tears like rain;
The short men have cut away Taiwan in the end,
What of old was within our map now belongs to the
    imperialists.

The poet's indignation over the unequal treaties signed with
foreign nations in the latter part of the nineteenth century is
eloquently translated in the poems lamenting the loss of Port
Arthur, Weihaiwei, and other places. The same impassioned
outcries resound in the poems describing the burning and loot-
ing of the capital by the Allied army during the Boxer Rebellion
in 1900. In 1882, when the United States Congress prohibited
further entry of Chinese labor to the country, adding more insult
to the chronicles of national humiliations, Huang wrote the
satirical "On Driving Out the Visitors." Starting with a nostalgic recalling of the country's glorious past, he then compared
it to the backward and weakened state of the present. Huang
bitterly denounced the inability and unwillingness of the
Chinese government to protect its citizens abroad when they
received rude treatment and injustice.

During his trip to the South Seas, Huang was moved by the
hardship suffered by the Chinese who, like their countrymen
in the United States, obtained no protection from their own
government. Worse still, when they returned to their homeland
after achieving success abroad, they enjoyed no welcome from
their fellow countrymen. On the contrary, they were ridiculed,
discriminated against, and even mercilessly robbed. Huang
compared these "homeless" and mistreated people with the
wandering Jews. Despite an overall embittered tone, his poem
about these returned immigrants closes with a note of optimism
as the speaker anticipates a day when these people can return
with their families to their native land and live in peace.

Huang Tsun-hsien's poetry combines the extravagance of
traditional poetry with a diction that foreshadows the trend
toward a plainer and freer medium. There is no straining of

effect, no burning ambition to parade virtuosity. He says what he wants to say, then stops. His patriotic poems, written in a highly charged style, show a similar preference for colloquialism and directness, which gives them immediacy and power. A poet of social consciousness, Huang in his poetry not only illuminates his own personality but embodies the emotional and historical meanings of a stress-filled era. His best poems transcend the private emotion of an individual to encompass a nation's impassioned cry of shame and frustration. If his use of the conventional forms and techniques belongs to the past, his insistence on writing "what my mouth speaks" and his daring departure from the conventional attitudes have distinguished his works from his predecessors and from many of his contemporaries. His poetry has served as an important bridge between the classical poetry of the past and the new poetry of the future.

Part II: 1917-37

3

The Pioneers

The Literary Movement of 1917 was more sociopolitical than literary, but its antipathy to tradition and passion for reform wrested Chinese literature from its age-old wrappings. Poetry was the last to be disentangled from the tradition-bound cocoon. It was Hu Shih, the father of modern Chinese poetry, who unwound the strangling silk with his eight cardinal tenets of literary reform.

The period that followed (to 1937) saw the most exciting and diverse experimentation in the history of modern Chinese poetry. Hu Shih's elevation of the vernacular to a literary language fired young aspiring poets to take up the challenge of the new verse. To sever themselves from the past, these pioneering poets eagerly experimented with a wide range of Western forms, from free verse to sonnet. Unfortunately, in their determination to create poetry of a modern temper, they often indiscriminately incorporated scientific terms, foreign words, and new "bold" imagery in their works. Their crude attempts to achieve contemporaneity often fell short of their admirable intentions.

Notwithstanding this dedication to modernity, tradition persisted. Consciously or not, the pioneers intermittently harked back to the familiar modes of the past. Echoes of earlier masters reverberate through their lines; colloquialism sits uneasily beside traditional motifs. The silkworm had emerged, but it had not forgotten the coziness of its snug cocoon.

Hu Shih (1891–1962)

In 1917, while a student of philosophy at Columbia University, Hu Shih published an article in the influential *New Youth* review and thereby launched a literary revolution. "A Modest Proposal for the Reform of Literature" actually consists of the eight cardinal tenets of literary reform for which Hu Shih became famous:[1]

1. *Do not neglect substance in writing.* Hu Shih had in mind here the emotional and thought content of a work. To him, any literary piece devoid of these two basic elements was like "a beauty without brain and soul." One of the main weaknesses of modern poetry in his opinion was its lack of "lofty ideals and sincere emotion."

2. *Do not imitate the ancients.* According to Hu Shih's theory of evolution, literature is constantly changing. It would be wrong to assume, as had been done traditionally, that all writings of the ancients are superior to those of modern writers and therefore must be emulated. Each period should create its unique literature.

The literary movement in China has been compared with the vernacular movement of the European Renaissance because both advocated the use of the "vulgar tongue" as the new literary medium and both cultivated nationalistic sentiments. But in Europe the movement led back to the ancients, to revivals of the classics; whereas in China it meant renunciation of orthodox Confucian classicism. The antitraditionalism in the Chinese movement was partly due to the new consciousness of the nation's backwardness and to a feeling of inadequacy, even inferiority, on the part of the more radical revolutionaries. In their youthful ardor at welcoming Western learning, they rejected out of hand their own tradition, bound up as it was with that authority beyond criticism, Confucianism. Father O. Brière, the well-known Sinologist, observed:

[1] Hu Shih, *Hu Shih wen-ts'un* [Collected works of Hu Shih], 1:7–23. These eight tenets were reduced to four in later years.

For the partisans of the Republic the fate of Confucianism was tied in with the Empire. Its moral and political philosophy was the firmest ideological support of the old regime, and because of this fact it shared in the general reprobation involving the fallen dynasty. Furthermore, "Confucianism" was synonymous with conservative, backward, stereotyped thought; it was an enemy of progress and anti-scientific. Therefore it was necessary in the name of science and democracy [the two dominant slogans of the period] to destroy this emblem of obscurantism and despotism.[2]

On the other hand, most of these reformers were reared and tutored in this very tradition. If they seemed to abandon the old in order to advance the new, the tradition was far from being lost. Like a river dammed by a rockfall, it continued to seep through the stony barriers. Ironically, the most energetic innovators and experimenters, including Hu Shih, were often those who dipped the deepest into the ancient waters.

3. *Do not neglect grammar.* In this tenet, Hu Shih complains about the lack of concern for grammar in the prose and verse writing of his day. He does not elaborate.

4. *Do not moan without being sick.* Hu Shih deplores the melancholy poses, the languorous and sentimental attitudes of romanticism prevailing among the new poets. He urges them to assume a healthy and optimistic outlook more in keeping with the new revolutionary era.

5. *Do not use stilted language and outworn poetic diction.* He admonishes writers who cling to old clichés and refuse to forge their own expressions.

6. *Do not use allusions.* Hu Shih considered the use of parables, proverbs, and historical allusions legitimate in writing. What he objected to was the narrow and limited kind of allusion which distracts rather than directs the reader's attention. The use of allusion should not be merely a display of erudition; it should be a means rather than an end in itself.

7. *Do not use parallelism.* He admits that it is natural to have

[2] O. Brière, *Fifty Years of Chinese Philosophy, 1898–1948*, p. 23.

parallelism in writing; but he cautions writers not to carry the practice too far, lest they sound forced, artificial, and monotonous. In poetry, he advocates the abandonment of couplets and rhymes, which he regards as "literary stunts," not to be pursued seriously.

8. *Do not avoid colloquialism.* By drawing a parallel to Dante's defense of the vernacular, Hu Shih sanctions his own *pai-hua* movement. He reviews the splendid vernacular tradition in Chinese popular literature and states his conviction that *pai-hua* should be the only medium for the future literature. He also urges the new poets to make use of the vivacity of colloquialism.

Hu Shih's proposals were not strictly new. More perceptive and daring critics in past ages had defended the "moderns" against the "ancients," attacked the overuse of allusions and parallelism, and even championed the use of a plainer and more speechlike idiom. Hu Shih's "revolutionary" theories, therefore, are more rediscovery than discovery. Nonetheless, these practical suggestions disclosed Hu Shih's serious concern with the literary situation of his day and his attempts to solve basic literary problems.

The effect of this early treatise on his own work and on that of others in subsequent decades was far-reaching. Echoes of his words reverberated in writings of other "revolutionaries." Chen Tu-hsiu (1879–1942), the editor of *New Youth* and a strong supporter of Hu Shih's program of literary reform, expounded the same theories and arguments in a much more radical vein. Like Hu, Chen looked toward the West for exempla. He credited the recent triumph of Western civilization to the various revolutions—political, religious, and literary—it underwent after the Renaissance. He, too, centered his attacks on the three specific types of traditional literature. His alleged purpose was:

(1) To overthrow the painted, powdered, and obsequious literature of the aristocratic few, and to create the plain, simple, and expressive literature of the people;

(2) To overthrow the stereotyped and over-ornamental literature

of classicism, and to create the fresh and sincere literature of realism;

(3) To overthrow the pedantic, unintelligible, and obscurantist literature of the hermit and recluse, and to create the plain-speaking and popular literature of society in general.[3]

Chen was far from being alone in his support of this literary reform. The overall response to it was very encouraging despite the noisy warfare waged by conservative literati like Lin Shu and other die-hard classicists. In the fateful year of 1919, the reform movement suddenly gained tremendous impetus. After the government submitted to Japan's demands for economic and territorial rights in China, the May Fourth student movement broke out in protest. Papers and essays in the vernacular appeared all over the nation, written by students and published by student organizations that mushroomed all across the land. These publications in turn greatly accelerated the adoption of the vernacular by many important literary reviews. Articles written in *pai-hua* were being accepted by some of the major daily newspapers in metropolitan cities. This enthusiastic response, combined with pressure from the public, especially the intelligentsia, forced the government finally to act. In 1920 the Ministry of Education announced the adoption of the vernacular in all elementary schools. The following year the term *pai-hua*, the vernacular language, was officially changed to *kuo-yü*, the national language, thus bestowing on the "vulgar speech" a dignity and respect it had hitherto lacked. By 1922 all classical texts used in schools had been supplanted by texts written in the vernacular, and the future success of the literary movement was further consolidated.

As early as 1916, four years before the publication of his *Experimental Verses*, Hu Shih gave the reason for his use of the vernacular in poetry: "I feel *wen-yen* is decidedly not an adequate instrument for our literature in the future. Shih Nai-an,

---

[3] Tse-tsung Chow, *The May Fourth Movement*, p. 276. I quote Mr. Chow's translation here.

Ts'ao Hsüeh-ch'in [two famous novelists] and others have already proven the fact that the *pai-hua* should be the medium for the novel. At present, there remains an urgent need for someone to explore the possibilities of using the *pai-hua* as our poetic medium."[4]

This cautious attitude within four years had turned to rebellion. In his essay, "On Modern Poetry" (1919), Hu vigorously calls for a poetic revolution in language, meter, and technique:

> The language of the new literature must be that of *pai-hua*, its meter free from any formal restrictions. The relation between form and content is an intimate one. To acquire a new content and new spirit, liberation of their constraints is an absolute necessity. The poetic movement, therefore, may be considered as a "liberation of poetic form." Once this emancipation is actualized, rich subject matter, lofty ideas, astute observation, and complex emotions can henceforth enter poetry.[5]

In the same article Hu Shih attacks the traditional meters as too artificial and binding to accommodate different subjects and complex emotions and ideas. He promotes the use of free verse and exhorts the new poets to exploit natural speech cadence, musical phrasing, and colloquialism.

Although *pai-hua* verses had appeared from time to time in literary magazines or newspapers before Hu Shih's collection was published, it remained for Hu Shih to publish the first volume of poetry in *pai-hua*. Though the artistic merit of his verse is questionable, one cannot deny that Hu Shih proved the potentiality of the vernacular as a new poetic medium.

Hu Shih classified his experimental verses as those written before 1918 and those after. The former are marked by traditional elements in theme, form, and means of expressions, as exemplified in the poem, "Mid-Autumn" (1916):

The small stars have all hidden, the large stars

---

[4] Hu Shih, *Ch'ang-shih chi* [Experimental verses], p. 1.
[5] Hu, *Hu Shih wen-ts'un*, 1:227–28.

are few.
Indeed, there is much clear light tonight!
The moon passes over the river at midnight,
The river is transformed into the Milky Way.

The four seven-character lines can be easily traced to the *chüeh-chü* meter of the T'ang dynasty, and the poem is as rhyme-ridden as its antecedents, in spite of Hu Shih's repeated denunciation of rhyme as being unimportant. The three nature images (stars, river, and moon) are stereotyped enough, but Hu Shih's fusing of the three in the concluding line is fresh. The dramatic metaphor of the Milky Way absorbs and blends all the coolness and brightness of the celestial bodies and the long moonlit waterway. The reader is left with a vivid impression of a mid-autumn night when the moon, according to tradition, is at its most resplendent.

THE BUTTERFLIES (1916)
Two yellow butterflies
In pair fly to the skies;
I don't know why
One suddenly returns
Leaving the other one
Lonely and pitiful.
It too has no heart to fly into the skies,
For heaven is too lonely a place.

Traditional elements are again apparent in this piece. The choice of butterflies, a favorite with earlier poets, strikes a familiar note that prepares the traditional setting of the verse. The use of the standard five-character line is again a derivative of the five-character regulated verse of T'ang times, and the description of heaven as a lonely place adds yet another familiar echo from the past. There is also a conscious preoccupation with rhyming. Both end rhymes and internal rhymes are employed: *t'ien* 天 with *lien* 憐 in lines two, six, and seven; *me* 麼 with *ke* 個 in lines three and seven; and *hu* 蝴, *h'u* 忽, *ku* 孤, and *wu* 無 are internal rhymes that contribute to the subdued tone and mood of the poem.

Hu Shih's adherence to rhyme persists in most of his poems. On the other hand, the equally conscious cultivation of more colloquial expressions and diction such as *pu chih wei shen me* 不知為什麼 "not knowing why," *nei ike* 那一個 "that one," and *kuai k'e lien* 怪可憐 "rather pitiful" is just as conspicuous. Despite this added new trait, the verse is still very much like "the suddenly freed bound feet of an old-fashioned Chinese woman," as Hu Shih candidly confessed all his early verses to be.

The vestiges of the past, though still apparent, are less dominant in the second phase of Hu Shih's verse. There is a definite change in both form and content: the stanzaic form is borrowed from Western versification; the verse length is more varied, the rhythm more flexible; new themes are introduced; and an increasing use of ordinary speech idiom is noticeable.

YOU MUST   (1919)

Perhaps he loves me, perhaps he still loves me,
But he always advises me not to love him any more.
He often blames me;
Today, with tears brimming in his eyes, he looks at me
And says: "Why do you still think of me?
Thinking of me, how could you face him?
If you truly love me,
You must give him the heart that loves me,
You must treat him with the feelings you hold for me."
Every phrase of his speech is right:
God, help me!
I *must* act this way!

The above poem, according to its preface, was based on the content of two poems written by Hu's deceased friend. Convinced that the emotions of the original works were obscured by classical diction, Hu Shih felt compelled to rewrite them in the vernacular, to better express the "complex psychology and emotional reaction of the protagonist": "The thought and spirit of this poem cannot be fully conveyed in a traditional verse. Take, for instance, the lines, 'perhaps he loves me, perhaps he still loves me': the several levels of meaning in these words can hardly be conveyed by a traditional verse."[6] Despite Hu's ingenious explication, "You Must" reads more like a play on words than a poem. It is emotionally unrealized and thematically confused, a failure as the aesthetic projection of the psychological motives behind it that Hu claimed it to be. Nevertheless, the poem survives as an early effort to explore and analyze more complex aspects of love.

Perhaps this failure was partially responsible for the last two lines of "Dream and Poetry," written the following year:

> All is commonplace experience,
> All is commonplace impression.
> By chance they rush into a dream
> They are transformed into many new patterns.
>
> All is commonplace sentiment,
> All is commonplace word,
> By chance they meet a poet
> They are transformed into many new poems.
>
> Only after being drunk does one know the wine is
>   strong,
> Only after having loved does one know the depth
>   of love.
> You can never write my poems,
> I can never dream your dreams.

In his note to this verse Hu Shih explained: "This is my 'poetic empiricism,' which simply means: even dreaming needs experience for its basis, how much more so does verse-writing. At present, a serious problem with many people is that they love

[6] Chu Tzu-ch'ing, ed., *Chung-kuo hsin-wen-hsüeh ta-hsi* [Compendium of modern Chinese literature], 8:1.

to write poems without actual basis in experience."[7]

In "One Thought" (1920?), Hu Shih departed further from the conventional motifs of his earlier verses:

> I laugh at you, earth, who revolve around the sun.
>   You can only go around once in one day and one night.
> I laugh at you, moon, who revolve around the earth
>   But can never remain full.
> I laugh at you, radio, who can travel five hundred thousand
>   miles per second,
>   But can never catch up with the thought in my mind.
> This thought in my mind:
>   It has barely started from Bamboo Lane,
>   It is already arriving at Bamboo Tip.
>   Suddenly it is on the Hudson River,
>   Suddenly it is on Cayuga Lake.
> If I am truly stricken with deep thought,
> It will certainly speed around the earth three thousand
>   million times per minute.

A fresh impulse and new sensibility enliven the poem with a buoyancy hitherto absent in Hu's verse. The deliberate choice of a more flexible framework of metrical irregularity, the material derived from a contemporary scene, and the assimilative use of scientific knowledge are all in perfect consort with the poet's new accent.

Less boldly innovative but more characteristic of Hu's general style is "One Smile" (1920).

> Over ten years ago
> Someone gave me a smile.
> At the time—I did not know why—
> I only felt that he smiled well.
>
> I don't know what happened to that man,
> But his smile remained;
> Not only could I not forget him,

[7] Hu, *Ch'ang-shih chi*, pp. 63–64.

> But the longer the smile lasted, the more
>   lovable it became.
>
> I have written many love poems on it,
> I have made many different settings for it;
> Some felt sad reading the verse,
> Others felt gay reading the verse.
>
> Gay or sad,
> It is only a smile.
> I have never found that man who smiled,
> But I am grateful for his lovely smile.

Here is a felicity in the mastery of the vernacular and its cadence of natural utterances previously lacking in Hu Shih's verse. Simple, spontaneous, and entirely conversational, the poem moves with ease and lyrical grace.

The general reaction to Hu Shih's volume of experimental verse has been unfavorable despite its acknowledged significance in the subsequent development of the new poetry. The conventional poets had scorned Hu's poems as vulgar, inelegant, dull, or simply "not poetry at all." The new poets' criticism was no more complimentary. Chu Hsiang, a poet-critic, labeled Hu's "Dream and Poetry" as "sheer nonsense" and decided that *Experimental Verses* was "shallow in content and juvenile in technique."[8]

It is true that many of the poems in the volume are a curious blend of native and foreign elements. True too, some of the poetry has little intrinsic value. Nonetheless, Hu Shih was the first to make a conscious effort to elevate and popularize the use of the vernacular as a poetic medium and he created an awareness of the potentiality of *pai-hua* as an artistic means. His endeavors were partly responsible for the increased interest of the young generation in the new verse. Hu Shih was also among the first to introduce Western poetic patterns into the

---

[8] Chu Hsiang, "Ch'ang Shih Chi" [Experimental verses], *Chung shu chi* [Collected essays] (Shanghai: Sheng-huo shu-tien, 1937), pp. 358–64.

country. Many of the rules that he advocated were at least partially carried out: the use of a plainer, more colloquial idiom; the introduction of new, meaningful content; and the adoption of a positive attitude toward life. Some of his poems demonstrated an inventiveness and originality rare even in the works of many later poets. Hu Shih was a pioneer in his day; his poetry, though limited in aesthetic worth, is important in indicating some of the directions modern Chinese poetry was to follow.

K'ang Pai-ch'ing (?)

Although in his prose Hu Shih promoted free verse, he wrote most of his own poetry in highly regular stanzaic patterns and it remained for his contemporaries to explore the new verse form. K'ang Pai-ch'ing, striving for the utmost laxity and liberality in metrics and expression, was among the first to use this form extensively. His efforts in writing free verse, however, were not always successful. Structural slackness and prosaic banalities are persistent weaknesses of his works.

LATE CLEARING   (1920)

The great wind and sleet storm have passed;
The whole world is laughing.
Beyond the Gate of Heavenly Peace is displayed a skyful
    of somber colors:
Red shot past from the western corner,
A huge piece of blue jade is baked by it.
On the ground that can hold five hundred thousand men
    are reflected many-patterned red shadows:
The red-faced, red-handed soldiers, wearing red caps,
    very solemnly stand in line above the red shadows;
All around, red walls, red bricks, red balconies, and
    green bricks all correctly face the red sun emitting
    light in the northwestern corner.
Over the arch on the Tung An Street are two very long
    rainbows encircling the great city balcony above the
    Cheng Yang Gate.
All along the road, the red-capped acacia flowers are gilded

a reddish gold color by the golden smoke of the chimney
of the Peking Electric Light Company.
Oh ho! The whole world is laughing!
The great wind and sleet storm are over.

The laboriously long lines weigh the verse down and invite
metrical monotony. Inconsistency of tone and mood adds yet
another faltering effect to the piece. The opening picture of the
whole world laughing suggests joy and relief at the clearing after
the storm, but the mood that follows is unexpectedly grave.
Despite the central red image, which is compatible with a
buoyant mood, one encounters the stress of words like *chuang yen*
莊嚴 "somber," *yen shu* 嚴肅 "solemn," *tuan tuan cheng cheng* 端々正々
"orderly" ("in line")—words that connote a serious setting and
atmosphere. Perhaps K'ang intends an effect of austere grandeur, since the color red has been associated with occasions that
are formal and ceremonious. Even so, it remains inharmonious
with the speaker's emphatic proclamation that "the whole
world is laughing."

K'ang Pai-ch'ing was among the first to reintroduce the old
popular subject of travel in a thoroughly unconventional way.
His longest and most ambitious work is a sequence of verse
called "Travel to Lu Shan" (1920). Its thirty-seven sections are
a loosely connected composition of dialogues, lyrical and descriptive passages, and straight prose comments on religion,
government, and education. The writing is very uneven and
lacks control. Ineffective adaptations of cadence to rhetorical
and colloquial rhythm fracture a large part of the work, and its
language and imagery are generally undistinguished. The
better parts of the poem are the simple descriptive moments,
marred though they are by monotonous repetition:

Going up the mountain! Going up the mountain!
All along the path are the white streams,
All along the path are the stone bridges,
All along the path are the red houses,
All along the path are the glistening green pines,

> All along the path are the reddish yellow day lilies,
> All along the path are the paulownia trees.

But K'ang's insistence on parallelism did not necessarily lead to dull uniformity:

> The black shining hair,
> The sleeves with the gold-threaded border,
> The sedate spirit;
> The orderly advancement and retreat,
> The metaphysical beauty!

Here the repetition seems appropriate and in harmony with the placid tempo and leisurely pace of the lines.

"Travel to Lu Shan," though basically descriptive in style and lyrical in impulse, frequently lapses into lengthy comment on a variety of prosaic subjects. In these aberrations, K'ang clearly feels compelled to combine description with his engrossment in the revolutionary modernization of China. Caring more for overt didactic statements than artifice, he inevitably reduces the poem to tedious sententiousness. Yet K'ang's idiom is unmistakably his own. His speech, though clumsy, is authentic:

> I feel it is indeed fortunate to be these mountains and
>   streams!
> Their masters are actually willing to indulge them this
>   much.
> There are so many monasteries yet no schools.
> There is a huge waterfall yet no electric generator.
> There is wealth of mineral reserve yet no excavation.
> There is a wide expanse of tall trees yet no cultivation of
>   forestry.
> Their masters actually are willing not to disturb them to
>   this extent!

The obtrusion of the speaker's views is characteristic of the violence K'ang inflicts on his work. The same obtrusion occurs in another poem when, in the midst of rhapsodizing over the beauty of Hangchow's famous West Lake, K'ang interrupts himself with flat expository diction and bland profundities:

> I've always wanted to ask the god of the West Lake:
> "If the electric tram is built all the way to T'ien Chu,
> Will it really vulgarize these hills?
> If there are steamboats in the West Lake,
> Will it really remove the antique bronze hue of the
>   water?"

Fortunately not all of K'ang's works are marred by faults like these. He has more success in shorter pieces, where he is content to let well enough alone, such as "In Peaceful Spring" (1920):

> All the country north of the river has greened.
> The willows have greened.
> The wheat stalks have greened.
> The slender grass has greened.
> The ducks' tails have greened.
> The rooftops of the thatched huts have greened.
> The hungry eyes have greened.
> In this peaceful spring a few balls of country fires
>   are burning in the distance.

The world of modern Chinese poetry, like that of its Western counterpart, has been predominantly governed by a metropolitan consciousness. K'ang's poems of rural scenes with their personae of simple country folk offer the reader a refreshing change. His lyrical and realistic repossession of the rural world is simple, direct, and often baldly folksy:

> MORNING (1920)
> The paper windows are white now.
> The mirror box is bright now.
> The old man is up,
> The children are up,
> The women folks are up, too.
> Ya, what fine colored clouds!

Ya, what fine dews!

Shouldering a hoe,
Back carrying a bag,
Hand clutching a basket,
Together up the slope go.

The rocks are moved,
The weeds are cut,
All the waste is turned around.
Dig up the dirt
Sow down the wheat.

Bunches of wheat blooms,
Turfs of wheat.
Something to look at.
Something to eat.

Yü P'ing-po (1889–)

In the preface to his first volume of collected verse, *Winter Night* (1922), Yü P'ing-po gave his intention of writing a "true and free verse": "I have no wish to be concerned with the metrical rules of poetry. Neither do I wish to be confined by any isms. I have no intention to imitate. Nor am I willing to initiate any school of poetry. All I want is to express myself, to express the 'I' in the world of men, the 'I' that lives for love. I aim to express it naturally and by means of contemporary idioms. . . ."[9]

In order to write unencumbered by rules, Yü chose free verse for most of his poems, but it is a more patterned free verse than that used by contemporaries such as K'ang Pai-ch'ing. Yü made a conscious effort to vary the verse lengths or the syllables in the lines, with the result that his poems have a tighter organization while obeying a freer meter. There are, too, a purer lyricism and a sensitivity to verbal melody which K'ang's works lack. Yü's poems, however, suffer from a relative absence of technical daring and emotional intensity. Even in his finest

[9] Yü P'ing-po, *Tung-yeh* [Winter night], p. 2.

work the conventionality of rhythm, diction, and tone conveys a certain tedium. Content and form in Yü's verse seem, therefore, weaker and more timid than in that of his contemporaries. Despite his insistence on a more modern medium, Yü favors words that are considered poetic in the traditional sense. Not only his diction but his themes, setting, imagery, and devices are strongly derivative from traditional poetry.

THE EVENING MOON   (1920?)
Sparse, sparse are the stars,
Sparse, sparse are the woods,
Beyond the sparse woods, sparse are the lamp lights.

In the night cold as ice,
In the night clear as ice,
Who has inked these few strokes of tree shadow?

The moon turns her back on me.
The north wind greets me
And on my face silently strikes.

The lamp lights slowly grow dim,
The moon sends over her radiance;
But my eyes are growing tired.

The year already is near its passing,
The moon already is near its rounding,
And I am already near my departing.

A prime example of traditional influence in Yü's works is his poem "Small Kalpa" (1921). "Small kalpa" is a Buddhist term which means, according to one definition, a period of time that lasts 16,800,000 years—in other words, infinity.

The bright clean clouds are my costume,
The splendid colored clouds are my skirt and robe.
Throughout antiquity I roam and soar,
Following the vast expanse of the great vapor.
Why this lowering of head?

For lamenting the loss of our friends?
Go and lower your head! Lower your head and behold—
     behold below:
Behold below, oh, my heart trembles;
Beholding below, oh,
The lotus fragrance on my body is dispersed.
The high wind has felled my cap,
The cold hail beaten loose my clothes,
And they, like the mottled moths, flutter in a throng.
All the fairies have left to greet the sun;
They have lost their voices singing to the Eastern Lord, the
     singing has provoked the Sky Wolf.[10]
The Sky Wolf bit their wings to pieces!
Now alone in this long night, above the world of men,
The heaven is deserted, the earth aged, and I have reached
     the end of time.
Only the stark naked "I" remains, Oh, why such infinite
     vastness? Why such infinite vastness?

Yü's indebtedness to *Ch'u Tz'u* is exceptionally pronounced
in this piece. Of particular interest is his adaptation of rhythmic
devices of the *Ch'u Tz'u* poems, as in the use of the contrasting
stressed and unstressed syllables to create an incantatory effect.
Yü does not employ a single *hsi* (兮), the unstressed archaic
particle that studded the *Ch'u* poems; but he has substituted for
it some similar unstressed colloquial words (*le* 了, *te* 的) to secure
the same effect and rhythm:

Ssu	hua	hua	*te*	hu	t'ieh,
似	花	花	的	蝴	蝶
Ke	ya	*le*	tung	chün	
歌	啞	了	東	君	
Je	nao	*le*	t'ien	lang.	
惹	恼	了	天	狼	
Ch'ih	lo	lo	*te*	wo.	
赤	裸	裸	的	我	

[10] The Eastern Lord is the sun deity in Chinese mythology, and the Sky Wolf is
the star Sirius.

This rhythm is sustained throughout the poem with some calculated modification that admits a variation of movement at
once apt and musical. This variation appears in Yü's use of a
stressed syllable, usually the verb of the line, in place of the unstressed syllable:

Chung	ku	*ch'ü*	ao	hsiang.
終	古	去	敖	翔
Kang	feng	*lo*	wo	mao.
罡	風	落	我	帽

The diction here is a mixture of the archaic and the colloquial
that is almost a mannerism with Yü. Other echoes from *Ch'u
Tz'u* are the theme of human distress and solitude, the elegiac
tone, the supernatural setting, and the lyrical sensuousness. It
is Yü's ingenious blend of the vernacular with the resounding
motifs from his heritage that is his version of "newness." In this
sense his poetry is very much in the classical tradition.

Apart from the poems steeped in classicism, Yü wrote some
captivating mini-poems about his childhood and adolescence.
These are fittingly collected under the title of *Reminiscences*
(1922). Written in free verse, these simple and spontaneous
verses with their spare diction come closest to the "contemporary idiom" that Yü strove to achieve.

I

There are two oranges:
One is mine,
One is my elder sister's.

She gave me the pocked one,
Keeping the smooth-faced one for herself.
"Little brother, yours is better.
It is embroidered."

Indeed, it is good!
Good orange! Let me eat you up.
It is truly a good orange!

XX

Before the lamp glowing bright with its two
    grass wicks,
I spread open the Book of Rites,
Let me for a while chant it like a mountain song.
Suddenly I hear chatterings and laughter in the next
    room.
"Is she here?"
Now the Book of Rites is filled with her.
"Mother, I have finished studying my book."

Yü P'ing-po's poetry lacks originality and power. His contribution lies not so much in introducing fresh elements into the new verse as in his often successful adaptation of conventional themes and techniques to the vernacular. Rhythmic effects from classical meters have enriched his verse and at the same time opened the way to new possibilities for old subject matter and techniques.

Ping Hsin (1902–68)

One interesting poetic phenomenon of the twenties was the immensely popular *hsiao-shih* 小詩, or mini-poem. Although short verse existed from the beginning of the new poetry, it became popular only with the surge of interest in Japanese tanka and haiku and the short lyrics of Tagore.

While the Indian and Japanese influences undoubtedly promoted the writing of *hsiao-shih*, its roots go deep into Chinese poetic tradition to the T'ang dynasty's *chüeh-chü* or short-stop verse. The *chüeh-chü* consists of four lines, each line having either all five or all seven characters, and is the most compressed of all traditional meters. Looking back through the history of traditional Chinese poetry, one cannot fail to discover the predominance of short lyrics. James Liu has pointed out:

Another trait of the Chinese mind which is in favour of short poems is its concentration on the essence of an object or experience rather than its details. The Chinese poet is usually intent on capturing the spirit of a scene, a mood, a world, rather than depicting its multifarious manifestations. In view of what I said in the last paragraph, the Chinese mentality presents something of a paradox; as far as individual experience is concerned, the Chinese mind is inclined to concentrate on the essence rather than the appearance, and is therefore "essentialist"; but in its attitude towards life as a whole, it is more "existentialist" than "essentialist" in so far as it concerns itself with actual living experience rather than with Platonic ideals or abstract categories.[11]

This dedication to the essence of things led poets to revere those techniques that have since characterized the Chinese lyrics: suggestion, compression, and concreteness of expression. The emergence of *hsiao-shih* or short verse only reillustrates this vital aspect of Chinese poetic sensibility.

Although Ping Hsin is better known for the short stories and letters she wrote during her college days in America, her two volumes of short lyrics—*Star* (1921) and *Spring Water* (1922)— won her a place among modern Chinese poets. When *Star* was first published, Ping Hsin apologetically announced that this was not poetry but just "a collection of fragmentary thoughts." Her personal opinions about the new verse were equally modest: "I don't understand modern poetry; I am skeptical about it and I dare not try writing it. I feel that the heart of poetry lies in its content not its form. . . . I wrote the *Stars*, just as I said in its preface, after I read Tagore's *Stray Birds*. By using his form, I tried to collect my fragmentary thoughts. . . ."[12]

Ping Hsin is the pen name of Hsieh Wan-yin, the only woman poet of wide recognition in a field dominated by men. Though a native of Fukien (a southern province), she was brought up in Shantung, in Ch'iloo, a northern coastal town of great natural beauty. Memories of happy childhood days spent here with an

[11] James J. Y. Liu, *The Art of Chinese Poetry*, pp. 153–54.
[12] Ping Hsin, *Ping Hsin shih-chi* [Collected poems of Ping Hsin], p. 9.

unusually close and loving family furnish the material and inspiration for her poetry. Affection for her brothers and father, a
deep attachment to her mother, sympathy for the young, and
compassion for mankind in general—all these are an integral
part of Ping Hsin and her work.

The majority of Ping Hsin's poems are either in free verse or
stanzaic forms, with occasional rhymes for emphasis or em-
bellishment—the forms in which Tagore's poetry appears in
translation. Her poetry, like much of Tagore's, is characterized
by its lyricism and romantic idealism. Most of her verses have
the same tone of gentle, almost naïve simplicity and sadness, as
shown in these two examples:

> O mother!
>> Throw away your sorrows
>>> And let me soundly sleep in your bosom,
>>>> For you alone are the shelter of my soul.

> O Creator—
>> If in an eternal life
>>> There is only one promise of perfect bliss,
>> I would earnestly pray:
>>> "I in my mother's bosom,
>>> Mother in a small boat,
>>> Small boat in a moon-bright ocean."

Ping Hsin favors the apostrophe as an opening for many of her
verses. She is fond of paradox, usually emotional rather than
intellectual.

> O childhood!
>> You are the reality in dream,
>>> The dream in reality,
>>>> The faint tear-stained smile in remembrance.

A rueful nostalgia permeates many of her poems of childhood
memories.

O friends of childhood!
  The sea waves,
    The shadow of the hills,
      The splendid evening clouds,
        The somber and lusty bugle calls,
Have you truly grown apart now?

The little child as a symbol of purity occupies a special place in her affection.

Host of angels
  Sing praises of a small child.
O small child!
In your small frail frame
  Is held a great soul.

A great many of Ping Hsin's verses are epigrammatic.

Truth
  Is in the silence of a babe
    Not in the arguments of the wise.

When the flower of speech
  Blooms larger,
The fruit of action
  Grows smaller.

Ping Hsin's concern with the mission of the poet is reflected in many of her poems:

O poet!
  Be careful with your pen!
    The miseries of men
      Depend on you for comfort!

Compassion and love for mankind is the subject of the verse below:

O young men!
　Within this white expanse on earth,
　Seek out sympathy and love.

Human solitude is another recurrent theme:

It is only a solitary star
　In a boundless darkness.
　How it has written all the loneliness of the universe.

Her loneliness finds relief and solace in various ways:

O God!
　Even when the sky is dark,
　Humanity is hushed;
If there is but one soul
　who watches over your clear solemn night,
The sorrow of solitude
　Will vanish from the universe!

What is "home"?
　I do not know;
But loneliness, sorrows—
　All is dissolved within it.

In the gentle smile of nature
　Are dissolved
　The regrets of mankind!

Like many romantic poets, Ping Hsin is preoccupied with the passing of time, the meaning of existence, and the imminence of death:

How I wish to hold back the past,
　But in the warp and woof of time
　Is already woven the silk of the present.

The unborn babe
From beyond the sphere of life
Climbs to the window of birth
And dimly sees
The caverns of death before him.

The more successful parts of Ping Hsin's two collections are those that concentrate on the evocation of a specific scene or mood. Often they are little more than visual impressions or metaphors, reminiscent of the traditional short lyrics or Japanese haiku:

The fishing boats have returned!
Behold the specks of red light above the river!

The evening rain,
Strand by strand is woven into the thought of the poet.

This ancient courtyard,
This twilight,
This silken thread of verse
Closely binds the departing sun and me.

The accent of Ping Hsin's verse is thoroughly feminine, not only in subject material but also in technique. It is regrettable that this element frequently leads to an overindulgence in the use of "O's" and exclamation points, an excessive languor and mellifluousness of tone and rhythm, and, above all, sentimentality. At best, however, it lends an unusual grace, tenderness, and a quiet, nostalgic lyricism that are especially appealing to the adolescents who are her chief admirers. It is undeniable that her range of experience and expression is limited and narrow; her short verses are not poems of wide horizon nor of deep emotional intensity. Nevertheless, within this slim range, this small intimate world of hers, she moves with delicacy and sensitivity, a serene ease, and a classical grace.

Wang Ching-chih (1903)

The modern reader today is more likely to be amused than shocked by the "daring" love poems of Wang Ching-chih that roused so much passion and outrage when they were first published. Conservative critics condemned them as a bad moral influence on youth; but liberal-minded reviewers like Chou Tso-jen, Chu Tzu-ch'ing, and Hu Shih praised their freshness of approach and their spontaneous charm. Chu Tzu-ch'ing's comments on Wang's poetry best sum up the nature of Wang's verse: "His poems are mostly in praise of nature and love. The nature that he glorified is one that is beautiful and vital, not grand or mysterious. The kind of love that he versified is simple, spontaneous, and unsophisticated. His mode of expression is both obvious and direct. There is a lack of profundity and subtlety in treatment. . . ."[13]

Chinese poetic tradition has always placed high value on convention and decorum, an inclination perhaps largely due to the compelling impact of Confucianism on the society that produced it. Traditional love lyrics invariably lean toward generalization expressed in the conventional imagery, diction, and styles deemed appropriate by the age. It is therefore understandable that conservatives should denounce confessional outbursts of passionate attachment as not only indecorous and unpoetic but crude, ugly, vulgar, and in poor taste. On the opposite side, the youth in their revolt against dull conformity hailed the "daring" spirit behind these stanzas with their unabashed display of eroticism, as in these lines from "Parting Sentiment" (1921):

> Last night I dreamed I kissed you.
> Oh what a sweet mouth!
> When I awoke I found no mouth of yours.
> I wish you would send me your budlike mouth in a dream.
> . . . .
> When I sleep, I see only you inside the mosquito net;

---

[13] Wang Ching-chih, *Hui-ti-feng* [Orchid wind], p. 1.

When I drink, I see only you in my cup;
When I read, I see no words but you;
When I am in class, I see no diagram on the board but you.

Such is Wang's "bold" confession of love. Completely conversational, the lines move in the natural cadence so strongly advocated by Hu Shih.

Less adolescent and more sophisticated in technique is "The Wind's Arrows" (1922):

The wind's arrows endlessly strike out,
    Arrow after arrow piercing my heart;
Why do they wish to strike me?
    Because they want to quash my hope.

The sun is a revolving iron wheel,
    Day after day crazily rolling above my head.
Why does it wish to crush me?
    Because it wants to wreck my youth?

By no means a major performance, "The Wind's Arrows" is nevertheless a good exemplum of the new poetic temper. The poem not only marks a further departure from traditional themes and imagery but a realization that violence is a condition of existence. The brutal force of nature is here powerfully transmitted by the images of the arrow and the iron wheel. The sun conceived as "crazily rolling" seems not arbitrary but right. The strong key verbs of *kun* 滾 "roll," *nien* 碾 "crush," and *nien sui* 碾碎 "crush to pieces" ("wreck"), with their repeated sounds of *"un"* and *"en"* impart a sense of oppressive weight.

In "Time Is a Pair of Scissors" (1925), Wang uses another set of violent metaphors in an almost identical structure, which seems particularly congenial to his subject material:

Time is a pair of scissors,
    Life a bolt of silk brocade.
Piece after piece is cut away;
When the cutting is done,

Throw that pile of scraps to the burning torch!

Time is an iron whip,
　Life a tree of many blossoms.
Flower after flower is slashed away;
　When the lashing is done,
　　Trample the wasted red into mud and sand!

This propensity for explicit analogy is a dominant trait of Wang's; he uses the technique deftly and extensively in his works. It seems especially appropriate to poems constructed on parallel syntax. The same scissor motif recurs in the love lyric, "Her Eyes" (1922).

Her eyes are the warm sun;
If not, why, once she looks at me,
Is my frozen heart aflame?

Her eyes are the scissors that sever the knot;
If not, why, once she glances at me,
Is my shackled soul freed?

Her eyes are the key of happiness;
If not, why, once she gazes at me,
Do I feel I am in paradise?

Her eyes have become the fuse of sorrow;
If not, why, once she stares at me,
Am I drowned in the sea of sorrow?

Like the previous poem, "Her Eyes" achieves its unity by the parallelism that controls each stanza. In this way the poem resembles the classical odes or the ancient ballads. The same rhymes occurring in the second and third lines of each stanza (*wo* 我 and *ne* 呢, respectively) further strengthen the patterned effects of the verse. To avoid the monotony of repetition Wang uses the verbs *wang* 望 "look at," *ch'iao* 瞧 "glance at," *ch'ou* 瞅

"gaze," and *ting* 盯 "stare." These four verbs also suggest the various emotional conditions, that is, the stages of the speaker's relationship with his beloved. The scissors motif that appears in the second stanza is no longer the destructive agent of "The Wind's Arrows" but a powerful, elemental force that frees the imprisoned soul. In the concluding stanza, there is the baffling image of the fuse, which ought to ignite rather than to drown someone in the sea.

A quiet whimsicality characterizes "Song without Title" (1923).

> Sorrow is the boundless sky,
>   Joy is a skyful of stars.
> My love, you and I are
>   The bright moon in that starry wood.
>
> The deep, deep wood is sorrow,
>   The dark green foliage is joy.
> My love, the flowers that grow on top
>   Are you and I.
>
> The water in the sea is joy,
>   The shoreless sea is sorrow,
> The fish that swim in the sea
>   Are you and I, my love.
>
> Sorrow is the countless beehives,
>   Joy is the sweet honey,
> My love, those busy bees
>   Are you and I.

Aside from the love lyrics, which constitute his major contribution, Wang Ching-chih wrote a small body of nature poems. These pieces, though written in a descriptive vein, are often imbued with the subjective consciousness of the speaker. "The Beach" (1921) begins with a leisurely tempo:

Countless yellow grains of sand,
Smooth and sloping, they spread out.
I stroll on the sand,
The sand lightly covers my feet;
I take it as a coverlet.
Lying down, I pretend to be asleep.
The sand is as fine and soft as a sofa.
I feel inexpressibly restful
Nestling in the cradle of loving Mother Nature;
She sings lullabies to lull me to sleep.
Listen!
Chien chien, ch'an ch'an, p'eng p'eng, pai pai, ho ho, he he—
    these many voices of the sea fill my ears—
Is this not the splendid music of nature?

With irregular line lengths and natural cadences of speech, Wang
here tries for a more flexible colloquial framework. The tone is
appropriately casual. The inclusion of the six sets of onomatopoeic words—a feature common in traditional descriptive
verse—at the close of the stanza strikes a daring note.

The poem takes on erotic overtones in the second and concluding stanzas:

The wave stretches his arms;
Repeatedly hugging and embracing
The sand, he kisses her.
After one kiss,
He is pushed back by the wind.
He roars in anger.
He again rushes forward willfully
To embrace the small pagoda near the beach!
And even more passionately he kisses her.
He climbs up that small pagoda;
The snowlike sprays disperse, spattering all over.
He laughs, he laughs aloud in joy,
But again the wind pushes him back.
O wave!
Rest yourself awhile.

You have already left her
The remembrance of your love.
Continuing like this,
Aren't you a bit wearied?

The shift from a natural to an erotic theme occurs when the natural images take on qualities of human emotion and action. The effect of this anthropomorphism is novelty, and an indefinable earthiness. The inclusion of the speaker presents a more complex state of mind and emotion, for the use of transferred metaphors can be applied to him as well. Wang's response to nature here, at least, is at once descriptive and personal.

More explicitly descriptive and direct is the highly compressed and experimental exercise, "The Tides" (1922). A genuine creative spontaneity lurks beneath these thrashing lines:

The tide, rising, rising over, rising up;
Mounting, mounting, mounting up, charging forth;
Boiling, boiling, busting, busting, spurting;
Leaping, leaping, leaping, dancing;
Powerfully surging, surging, powerfully surging forth!

Despite the obvious faults that impair Wang's verse, one occasionally encounters flashes of genuine talent in his new themes and unconventional imagery. His love lyrics, too often tainted by juvenility, impart a youthful exuberance and charm that are his special contribution to the new verse.

Chu Tzu-ch'ing (1898–1948)

Primarily known as an essayist and short-story writer, Chu Tzu-ch'ing started his literary career in 1919 as a new poet. A few years later he found himself poetically sterile and turned to prose as a form more compatible with his abilities. Eventually he became a leading interpreter of the new poetry. A year before his death, his critical essays were collected and published in a volume entitled *Talks on the New Poetry* (1947), one of the few critical works on this little-explored subject. Chu's interpretation and evaluation of modern Chinese poetry are generally sound.

Chu is known too for his editorial talent. He compiled the first comprehensive anthology of Chinese new verse, published in 1937, which remains one of the best collections of its kind, encompassing more than fifty poets of various schools: the Free Versers, the Formalists, the Symbolists, and the Independents. The volume has great value because many early works of these poets are extremely difficult to locate; most of them are long out of print and inaccessible to us today.

In an introduction to his poetry, Chu categorized it as free verse, the form that dominated the earliest stage of this new poetry. But like many "free versers" of this period (such as K'ang Pai-ch'ing and Yü P'ing-po), despite his endeavor to rid himself of strict metrical rules, Chu maintains a degree of order and uniformity within the flexible framework of free verse. This uniformity is best illustrated in the recurrent lines of equal length within the stanza and repetitive use of certain rhymes, mostly approximate, within the poem.

Most of Chu's poems are short pieces characterized by their personal lyricism, fluent imagery, and felicitous use of the vernacular. They escape the awkwardness of cadence and phrasing that flaw much of the work of this period. In "Small Grasses" (1920), Chu adds a touch of novelty when he departs from the outworn motifs of spring—the willow or the more exotic blossoms of the favorite season—to use instead ordinary grasses as the central image of this simple lyric. The piece has a freshness and lucidity distinctive of Chu's style.

> The sleeping small grasses
> Now awaken,
> Standing in the sunshine,
> Stretching, they rub their eyes.

The dried yellow grasses
Now are greened,
Bowing before the fragrant breeze,
They smilingly greet each other.

The vanished small grasses
Now freely grow.
The birds cheerily sing,
"Friends, we have been apart long!"

How strong the feel of spring!
Lovely small grasses, our friends,
Has spring brought you?
Or is it you who have brought her?

Chu favors personification in many of his verses, such as "New Year" (1920?):

Dark, dark is the tent of night
Encircling the vast land.
New Year flew down from mid-air.
Oh what splendid crimson wings!
Her mouth held the yellow golden grain—
The seeds of the future.

The flapping noise of the wings
Startled the solitude.
Their radiance bright as blood
Pierced the tent of night.
The men in the tent awoke
To witness the joyous New Year!

New Year has entrusted to them
That round golden grain:
She spoke, "Make haste and plant it well,
This is the secret of your life!"

Though it may seem trite today to encounter the New Year as

a lovely female with crimson wings zooming down to earth to deliver the promise of future to mankind, the poem shows bold inventiveness in its thoroughly unconventional treatment of a familiar subject. Night, the prime image of darkness, provides the physical backdrop of the poem, at the same time suggesting the grimmer side of life. In direct contrast are the luminous images of crimson wings that radiate light "bright as blood" and the glow of the golden grain conveying hope and happiness. These vibrant sense impressions of sharp contrast give the poem drama.

In an introspective piece, "The Light" (1919), night again dominates the scene, a dark, stormy night during which the protagonist fearfully entreats God for light to guide him. God replies in a way Hu Shih would have applauded:

> Light? I cannot get it for you!
> If you want light,
> You must seek it yourself!

In contrast to the simple symbolism of "New Year" is a more complex treatment of the darkness motif, "Darkness" (1921):

> This is a dark lacquered night.
> I am alone in the corner of the vast field.
> In the distance the house sends out strands of lamplight;
> Like the pattern of lightning, they scatter upon the black
>   velvet carpet.
> These are the only lights.
>
> They wantonly
> Flutter with their feeble strength.
> Look wink after wink,
> These are the eye waves of the dark!
>
> In their trembling
> A few shadows hesitantly turn.
> The surrounding cypress trees speechlessly cry

The world's voice, the market voice, the human voice—
  the whole mass of voices is wafted over, near and far,
Clamoring, intermingling.
These are the heart waves of the dark!

  The vast field has indeed widened,
So wide that it cannot be any wider.
The wings of darkness have spread.
Who can envision their boundaries?
They are both loving and warm;
Everyone wishes to be sheltered by them.
The entire "I" is completely forgotten.
All is darkness.
"We are one!"

In his poetry Chu again plays off darkness against light. He appreciates the drama of the visual contrast, but he seems even more concerned with a mental, or symbolic, import that develops from the interplay of light and shadow. Darkness, the conventional symbol of hopelessness, ceases to represent despair when it acquires a new, affirmative quality that stands for hope and fellowship. It loses its frightening guise as men find brotherhood under its cover. The "I" is forgotten because "we are one," and loneliness gives way before warmth, love, and boundless joy.

Darkness is the subject of yet another poem, "Coal" (1920):

  You are asleep deep within the earth.
How ugly, how dark!
Those who look at you,
How they hate you and fear you!
They say:
"Don't get close to it."

  But in a second, when you start dancing in the Fire
    Garden,
Out from your black naked body
Dart red heat waves.

Oh everything has become red and heat,
Beautiful and bright!

They have now forgotten the matter just passed.
They all open their smiling mouths
To sing songs of praise to you;
They swing their bodies
To harmonize with the rhythm of your dance.

A reader in the sixties might seize upon this poem as a sociological piece about the Negroes—a tribute to the poet's metaphor; but this interpretation was scarcely likely in China in the early twenties.

Like Wang Ching-chih's, Chu's imagery is startlingly unconventional for his day. The choice of coal as a poem's chief image is daring. The original physical state of the coal—its repellent dark exterior—rouses fear and distrust, but this hostile attitude is transformed into one of adulation with the realization of coal's true potential. Out of ugliness and darkness, beauty and strength come into being.

Chu's warm feeling for humanity, as well as his optimism, is reflected in many of his poems, perhaps best in "The World of Men" (1921). This poem consists of two stanzas, each dealing with a chance encounter of the protagonist with a stranger. The first stanza presents a peasant, wearing a blue cotton jacket and with straw sandals on his bare feet, walking toward the speaker, who has obviously lost his way in this countryside. The kind peasant calls out warmly and offers assistance, and the speaker reflects:

I feel the touch of his pure and true heart
Though we have never met before.

In the second episode, instead of a simple-hearted adult there is a shy little girl walking behind her mother. The scene suddenly flashes across the car window through which the speaker of the poem is idly looking. In that instant his eyes meet the child's, and he experiences another surge of instinctive warmth.

A complete reversal of tone and temper to this touching yet somewhat sentimental picture of warm humanity is a provocative piece called "The Modern Age in a Small Cabin" (1921). This is one of Chu's few lengthier narrative poems. Cast in his favored free-verse form, the narrative first sets the stage—the inside of a passenger ship just before it sails. During these last few minutes of increasing confusion and mounting tension, the curtain rises on a frantic battle for existence. Small peddlers make a last desperate try to sell their merchandise: noodles, dumplings, pears and peanuts, newspapers, wine, and ear-wax removers. Their "yellow faces smeared with dust and perspiration/And eyes glazed with hunger," the vendors are like a herd of "hungry beasts [that] instinctively crave blood and flesh" because, in their mortal eyes, all they see is "the cabin filled with piles of coins and dimes"—the unattainable means of their pitiful existence.

Following this disturbing scene comes a swift metaphorical transformation of the small cabin into the battleground of a desperate struggle for survival in modern society.

> The small cabin has become the battlefield:
> They are the warriors,
> We, their enemies!
> From their deafening shouts,
> I hear the call, "Kill! Kill!"
> But looking into their eyes,
> I see panic and pain.
> And from their screams for help,
> I see their wounded struggle;
> The greediness of desire
> And the cruelty of treatment
> Are darkly seen.
> They are the soldiers on the battleground,
> And this is another Great War.

The poem concludes with the realization that

> I, a member of this War,
>
> .   .   .   .
>
> Have quietly come to know these stifling times.

By far the most ambitious work Chu attempted in verse is
"Dissolution" (1922); like most of his poems, it is in free verse.
In the prose preface, Chu gives a brief account of how he hap-
pened to write "Dissolution." The poem records an actual experience he had while vacationing one June in the famed resort city of Hangchow. After he had been boating on the West
Lake for three consecutive nights, an extraordinary sensation
came over him: "I felt that I was drifting like light smoke, like
a floating cloud, and I could hardly stand firm on my feet. At
that moment I was quite disturbed by a spellbinding tempta-
tion and desire for self-destruction."[14] "Dissolution" was considered not only a major personal triumph for its author but an
important poetic landmark as well. The work was the first to
explore a region which poetry in the past had completely
ignored, and although not without flaws, it is full of haunting
cadences, supple imagery, and provocative insights. In contrast to the faltering effects characteristic of this period's longer
poems (K'ang Pai-ch'ing's "Travel to Lu Shan" is one), the
mood and tone are firmly sustained, the movements sure, and
the phrasing incisive; Chu has remarkable control over his
material. Chu also shares with his good friend, Yü P'ing-po, a
feeling for the vernacular and a sensitivity to tone color that
may account for his graceful blending of lyricism and ordinary
speech idiom.

The poem begins with the dispirited poet stumbling along
the road. Suddenly lights beam, dazzling colors shoot past his
eyes. He is assailed by a pungent scent and a lingering taste on
his tongue. Whatever things touch him are all softness and

---

[14] Chu Tzu-ch'ing, *Chu Tzu-ch'ing shih-wen hsüan* [Selected works of Chu Tzu-
ch'ing], pp. 31–45.

smoothness. He has the sensation of being both pushed and held. An ephemeral atmosphere of unreality pervades the lines:

> The white clouds carry me,
> The winds waft by,
> The deep sea sustains me,
> The undercurrents surge forth.
> Only on the green, green earth
> Has there never been impressed, however lightly
>   and vaguely, my footprints.
> Roving, I drift along,
> Roving, I drift along.
> On tiptoe I step and step,
> But still cannot touch my native soil.
> I age midst wind and dust,
> I wither midst wind and dust.
> Only a sluggish and lumpish body remains,
> Heaps of black shadows!
> The curtain call of dissolution.
> I brood and brood:
> "So close, yet so far away
> Is my homeland, my homeland!
> Return! Return!"

Like Yü P'ing-po, Chu employs motifs from the past. The evocation "Return! Return!" echoes the similar refrain of the *Chao Hun* (Summons of the soul) poems in the *Ch'u Tz'u*. These ritualistic songs with their marked incantatory rhythm are invocations to a soul that has left a man's body because of death, temporary illness, derangement, coma, or simply a bad case of melancholia. In the two well-known *Chao Hun* poems, the shaman summons the departed soul of a sick king by frightening it with details of the perils awaiting him everywhere in the world and underworld. These terrifying descriptions are followed by a delicious depiction of sensuous delights with which the shaman hopes to lure the soul back to its mortal habitat. Chu's calculated references to these songs dramatize his theme of dissolution—especially of mental disintegration—and give it an added symbolic dimension. Chu is one of the few new poets who is able to mingle ancient motifs with his own immediate consciousness of the present and successfully bring them to a contemporary focus.

The haunting rhythm, the elusive imagery, and the trance-like mood continue in the following stanza. The setting shifts to a summer evening on a moonlit lake, where fireflies behave as if "they have lost their way in the fog," and the mournful sound of a flute floats across the water. The stanza ends with the same plaintive refrain, "Return! Return!" The elegiac mood deepens in the next section:

> Though there was snowlike raiment,
> Now it has drifted away
> Like the ashened paper money burnt for the dead.
> Those eyes like sprightly little rivers
> Holding so much thought, so many words,
> They too are dried now,
> As dry as the desert under the fierce sun.
> The lacquer-black hair
> Is changed to unruly autumn grasses;
> Once a delicate face,
> Now a yellow wax mold.
> There is no trace of a flowerlike smile,
> The pearllike throat utters not a single strain of sound;
> All is emptiness before the eyes.
> All is emptiness.
> Oh let go!
> What is there to let go?
> Return! Return!

Following the theme of physical disintegration with its grisly images of decay, the fourth stanza explores the changeable nature of men. The poet tells of a friend who used to compliment him, comfort him, and with whom he has spent many happy hours; but now

He turns away his face,
He backs away.
He no longer knows you!
It was only a passing amusement to him.
Is there anyone who truly cares?
To him, what remains is but a few vague names—
Now in this infinite blue,
Only you alone are left.

It is better to grope your way home;
There perhaps you'll find your brothers and sisters
Waiting anxiously for you.
Return! Return!

Stanzas five and six are perfect embodiments of Chu's obsessive motif of death, with its terror and its attraction. The passages become the projection of the death instinct or death wish.

Though there is the empty stomach,
Hooklike rheumatic hands,
Unruly long hair like weeds,
Sunken eyes,
Faltering feet,
And feeble heart
Pulling me downward,
Downward to the very bottom,
Asking me to smoke,
Asking me to drink,
Asking me to look at women.
In this bewildering spell,
I muddled through the hours.

He summons all his power to resist the tremendous magnetic pull of death, and finally asks himself:

Shall I allow myself to be destroyed so easily?
No! No!
Before you become maimed,

Use whatever strength there is left in you!
Return! Return!

The symbolic motif of death is recapitulated in the next stanza:

Though death is a white-robed maiden
Carrying a lantern, waiting ahead of me,
It is also a strong man clad in black
Clutching an iron club, bullying me onward.
When I am distressed over the impending family disaster—
A year of hostile relationships,
A time of angry staring at each other,
A time when life's burden on my shoulders
Weighs me down breathless,
A time when I see my harvest
Become as remote as the distant smoke cloud—
And when I face the dark uncertain future,
Not knowing which way to turn
But keep drifting as if in a daze,
During these moments, he and she would seem to appear,
Resembling something,
Again they seem to resemble nothing.
This unpredictable atmosphere
Is enough to urge me forward.
Go, go,
Go to her bosom, and his.
Well, she is beckoning me,
He is nodding at me too.
But—but
They are strangers.
I am wary.
Their hands float in the air,
Too remote,
Too hard to hold on to.
How could I get near them?
Even more so, the kingdom of Death is foreign.
Who knows what sort of place it is?

Only this plateau of life
Am I familiar with,
My homeland in memories.
Though already becoming faint,
I still can recall its outline.
Ah, isn't this my homeland stretching her arms to me?
The fruits are ripe and sweet,
The friends familiar and dear.
O little maiden,
O strong man clad in black,
I'd rather return to my native land,
I'd rather return to my native land.
Return! Return!

The poem ends with a spiritual awakening:

The returning me struggles and struggles,
Pushing away the dust to see my homeland.
All illusions dissolved,
All lights dimmed.
Freed at last of the harassing snare,
Back to an ordinary me,
I shall never lift my eyes to look at blue sky,
I shall never lower my head to look at white water,
I shall only watch my steps with care.
I want to step firmly on the ground,
Marking deep, deep footprints!
Although these footprints are small
And will be destroyed in time,
Although these slow steps
May not catch up with the long journey,
Still now an ordinary insignificant I
Can only see the distinct steps
And rejoice over the sight—
Those that are far, far away
Can never lure me now.
Oh, don't delay,
Go! Go! Go!

Poetic landmark it may be, but "Dissolution" is not without defects; the faltering rhythm and the occasional stiff phrasing are among the most conspicuous. Although Chu's deliberate use of ancient diction, phrasing, and motifs generally substantiates the atmosphere of unreality, at times the archaisms, especially the inversions, are disruptive. Lines such as *"che yang pei shuo tsai hsü to k'ou li/Pei chih tsai hsü to hsin li te"* 這樣被説在許多口裏,/被知在許多心裏的, "These uttered in the mouth / Known in the heart" sound awkward and inadequate. The rhythm in other lines, such as "Only on the green, green soil/Never imprinted, however lightly, faintly," is too strident and a bit strained. A common flaw that Chu shares with his fellow poets is the overreliance on the use of particles as end rhymes. *Le, te, che, me* (了, 的, 着, 麼) are too easy and intrusive, constantly calling attention to themselves.

From an examination of Chu Tzu-ch'ing's poetic work, one may safely conclude that though his output was slim, he has made an admirable contribution to the new poetry. He has used the vernacular as a poetic medium with an effectiveness encouraging to all the practitioners of this literary form. His constant concern for new subject matter and new ways of expression has given his verse an originality rare in the poetry of a period in which traditional themes and conventional treatments are still dominant. And, more than any other poet of his time, Chu succeeded in extending and enlarging the course that was first charted by Hu Shih.

4

The Formalists

Much of the experimentation initiated by the pioneering poets was carried on, extended, and at times completed with considerable success by the romantic Formalist poets Wen I-to, Hsü Chih-mo, and Feng Chih. With their excellent classical background and their knowledge of Western poetry they were able to profit from both Western tradition and their own heritage. In this highly productive period the liveliest action is to be found in poetic form: Wen I-to's well-known theories, published in 1926; Hsü Chih-mo's experiments with various stanzaic forms; and Feng Chih's special success with the sonnet. As a whole, the Formalists' poetry reveals a gradual mastery of the vernacular medium, a more felicitous exploration of complex themes and imagery, and a romantic lyricism expressing themes of human significance.

Wen I-to (1899–1946)

Born on November 24, 1899, in a small village in Hupeh province, Wen I-to began his education in the traditional manner by studying the classics. He preferred poetry to ethics and philosophy, and showed an early inclination toward art and a poetic sensitivity to color. At the age of eleven he was sent to a modern school, where he learned English and other modern subjects; a few years later he passed a special examination sponsored by the new government and entered Ts'ing Hua College (the predecessor of Ts'ing Hua University) in Peking to prepare for studying abroad. During his eight years at the college (1913–21) he followed a general, American-style curriculum from which he acquired an enthusiasm for the English Romantic poetry of the nineteenth century, especially the poetry of Keats. This new love, however, did not dampen his early admiration for traditional poetry or his respect for the classical language, which he continued to use up to this time. He engaged in many extracurricular activities, editing school papers and staging school plays. He was described as "enthusiastic, imaginative, eager for new knowledge, full of vigor and intense feelings."[1]

At the outbreak of the May Fourth Movement in 1919, Wen was swept into its powerful currents. Though he did not join the students' demonstration, he made posters and drafted and copied propaganda leaflets. After the movement subsided, Wen returned to his study of literature; but now he had come to appreciate the vernacular and wrote his first poem, "West Coast" (1919?), using this new medium. A fairly long verse by traditional standards, "West Coast" is introduced by lines from Keats's "The Human Seasons": "He has his lusty Spring, when fancy clear/Takes in all beauty within an easy span." The poem is a curious blend of foreign and native elements, with Keatsian and traditional echoes. Some of Wen's characteristic features— his preoccupation with the quest for beauty and his rich imagery —are already emerging. Such Images as the golden light being "sieved through the openings of fog" became favorites with Wen. Lines like "The whole sky is pasted with boundless bitter fog/Pressed down on the lake's eternal dead sleep" prefigure the synesthetic imagery that became the mark of his mature poetry.

In 1922 Wen traveled to the United States to study Western painting. He was first enrolled in the Art Institute of Chicago, but transferred to Colorado College in the summer of 1923. His nationalistic feelings sharpened when he first experienced the

[1] Kai-yu Hsü, "The Life and Poetry of Wen I-to," p. 137. I am indebted to Hsü's article for this section on Wen's biography.

"sting of racial discrimination." The result was his well-known "Laundry Song" (1925?), reminiscent of Thomas Hood's "Song of the Shirt," but an eloquent testimony to his bitterness at the situation of the overseas Chinese.

(One piece, two pieces, three pieces,)
Washing must be clean.
(Four pieces, five pieces, six pieces,)
Ironing must be smooth.

I can wash handkerchief wet with sad tears;
I can wash shirts soiled in sinful crimes.
The grease of greed, the dirt of desire . . .
And all the filthy things at your house,
Give them to me to wash, give them to me.

Brass stinks so; blood smells evil.
Dirty things you have to wash.
Once washed, they will again be soiled.
How can you, men of patience, ignore them!
Wash them (for the Americans), wash them!

You say the laundry business is too base.
Only Chinamen are willing to stoop so low?
It was your preacher who once told me:
Christ's father used to be a carpenter.
Do you believe it? Don't you believe it?

There isn't much you can do with soap and water.
Washing clothes truly can't compare with building warships.
I, too, say what great prospect lies in this—
Washing the others' sweat with your own blood and sweat?
(But) do you want to do it? Do you want it?

Year in year out a drop of homesick tears;
Midnight, in the depth of night, a laundry lamp . . .
Menial or not, you need not bother,
Just see what is not clean, what is not smooth,

And ask the Chinaman, ask the Chinaman.

I can wash handkerchiefs wet with sad tears,
I can wash shirts soiled in sinful crimes.
The grease of greed, the dirt of desire . . .
And all the filthy things at your house,
Give them to me—I'll wash them, give them to me![2]

This is not a typical Wen I-to poem, but it serves to introduce a quality inherent in most of his poetry: the acute awareness of reality. Even in his most lyrical moments Wen often brings this consciousness into the foreground, either by subtle juxtaposition or dramatic contrast. It is this sense of reality that allies him more with the modern poets than with Keats or Li Shang-yin. The poem is interesting too for its revelation of the poet's preference for a more orderly structure than the free-verse form favored by many of the earlier poets. The lines of ten characters are mostly end-stopped and rather heavily stressed, giving the poem an external formality and gravity that correspond with its somber tone and overt sarcasm.

After his return to China in 1925, Wen maintained his interest in the arts, but it was not so much as "a creator but as a promoter of art" that he now devoted his life. He became a cofounder of the Crescent Society, an association of new poets whose aesthetic stand on poetry for a while countered the sweeping current of sociopolitical verse. His poetry, together with that of other Crescent poets, was attacked as useless and ivory-towerish, but he continued to write; his second and last volume of poems, *The Dead Water*, was published in 1928. The verse in this volume retains much of his fertile imagination, his talent of weaving extravagant imageries, and his sense of balance in form. But the actualities of the world have marked him: the very title of his new collection, *The Dead Water*—symbol of contemporary life—indicates the direction of his mind.

Wen's growing concern for the health of the new poetry led

---

[2] Kai-yu Hsu, trans. and ed., *Twentieth Century Chinese Poetry*, pp. 51–52.

to his formulation of important theories on poetic form that were influential enough to turn the trend of free verse toward a more orderly poetic structure. His reviews of the poetry of Yü P'ing-po, Kuo Mo-jo, and others further reveal a critical intelligence not common in those days. From 1928 on, Wen wrote very little poetry; instead, he concentrated on teaching and scholarly research in Chinese classical literature. His numerous essays on Ch'ü Yüan, the *Book of Odes*, the poetry of the T'ang and Sung dynasties, as well as his studies on Chinese mythology and classics, won him recognition and prestige.

At the outbreak of the Sino-Japanese War in 1937, Wen fled Peking for Changsha, where Ts'ing Hua University was hastily relocated, and finally to Kunming when the university had to move farther west. With the horror of war constantly reminding him of the crasser side of reality, Wen's views on the arts underwent an inevitable change. He still upheld the importance of the aesthetic, but he now became convinced that the artist must project life, he must be the voice of his time. This shift of emphasis is best illustrated in his critical review of the poetry of T'ien Chien in 1943. A poet with a strong leftist strain, T'ien Chien claimed Mayakovsky as his chief source of inspiration. He innovated a thoroughly unorthodox "drumbeat" style that became extremely popular during the war. Wen I-to was generous with praise while admitting that the younger man's works were not completely successful. Wen felt that they fulfilled the fundamental prerequisite for poetry, "the lust for life: constructive and affirmative." He called T'ien Chien "the drummer of our age" and his verses the very embodiment of the "rhythm and emotion of the drum" whose vital beats are "unornamented. They offer no solace, nor do they intoxicate one with bewitching music to make one's fancy soar skyward. Theirs are the heavy drumbeats that incite you to love, to hate, and to live—to live with the greatest intensity and strength on this earth."[3] They represent the kind of poetry that is energetic and constructive, Wen continued, the poetry urgently needed to

[3] Wen I-to, *Wen I-to ch'üan-chi* [Complete works of Wen I-to], 3:57.

counter a trend that is but a continuance of the "fatigued, feeble half-note" of old poetry.

He concluded the article with a pronouncement which summed up his new conception of the arts: "This is an age that needs a drummer. Let us await the appearance of more "drummers of our age." As for the lute players, there is only a secondary need at present. Moreover, we have plenty of marvelous lute players today."[4] Wen never completely denounced the song of the lute; he was too much the genuine artist to do so. But he preached the social function of literature for the remaining years of his life. In 1946, as a result of his outspoken criticism of the government, he was assassinated.

Wen was writing at a time when most new poets were following the trend of writing free verse and adopting the more "natural rhythm" promoted by Hu Shih. The resulting hodgepodge was frequently unappetizing. Wen was appalled by the lack of discipline and the poor performance in the concoctions that appeared. Anxious about the future of the thriving new verse, he became more and more preoccupied with its problems and tirelessly sought solutions for them. The result was his well-known theories of form, which he eloquently defended in "The Form of Poetry," published in 1926.

In this essay Wen declared the inevitability of form in poetry. The poetic act is like playing chess, he maintained: "No game can be played without rules: no poem can be written without form."[5] He further asserted that the greater the poet, the greater pleasure he would receive dancing with chains on his feet. In his analysis of form, Wen I-to focused attention on the two basic patterns in poetry: visual and auditory. The visual pattern with its balanced grouping of characters and lines provides the framework and the structural symmetry of the composition, said Wen, while the auditory pattern with its metrical elements of foot, tone, and rhyme regulates the rhythmic movement of

[4] Ibid.
[5] Ibid., p. 245.

the poem.

Placing emphasis on structural symmetry, Wen urged the new poets to take advantage of their language's linguistic peculiarities to achieve a unique "beauty of architecture." This architectural beauty Wen defined as a visual structural beauty effected through a perfectly balanced and uniform arrangement of characters, lines, and stanzas. This, he pointed out hastily, does not mean a return to the regulated verse forms of the T'ang dynasty, although the latter do possess a limited sort of architectural beauty. "The regulated verse is a 'fixed form' which is forced to accommodate all kinds of themes, situations and emotions. . . . The new forms are infinitely varied, because every single form is created to suit its special content. Therefore, there is an intimate relationship between the form and its content. . . ."[6] What Wen was advocating here is simply the nonce form, which he regarded as ideally flexible, nonarbitrary, and inventive, because it is created to suit a single poetic occasion and experience.

During the early twenties, as in the West, it was the fashion for modern poets to reject conventional metrical schemes in favor of the natural speech rhythm proposed by Hu Shih. Needless to say, Wen was opposed to this "poetic license" and gave as his argument: "Certain poetic rhythm may be accidentally found in our natural speech. But, because of this, to claim that that speech *is* poetic rhythm and thereby determine to dispense with any regulated sound pattern is indeed committing suicide!"[7] Wen's poetic theories are crystallized in the meter he used for "The Dead Water" (1928), the poem he considered his most successful experiment. Following is the basic line that opens the poem:

che	shih	i	kou	chüeh	wang	te	ssu	shui
這	是	一	溝	絕	望	的	死	水

[6] Ibid., p. 250.
[7] Ibid., p. 246.

The metrical pattern of three two-syllable feet and one three-syllable foot within the line is observed throughout the poem, although the position of these metrical feet varies from line to line. The meter provides a compositional order of sorts, yet allows within that order a variety of sound arrangements.

This compact stanzaic pattern with its end-stopped lines proves particularly congenial to Wen's style, which is more sculpturesque and static than airy or fluid. It offers the structural integrity that Wen strives for. The end-stopped lines here are often deliberately employed to strengthen the syntactical patterns of parallelism in the line units. These stylistic devices produce effects of gravity and restraint, and convey a more formal atmosphere and rhythmic movement.

Wen's indebtedness to both Western and traditional prosody is unmistakable. His general principles are essentially derivative and conservative; nevertheless, they are sound. The meter of "The Dead Water," though it has an affinity with traditional verse forms, is designed to suit the vernacular's looser word order and grammatical construction. Wen's theories failed to solve all the prosodic problems, but they opened up new areas for exploration and at the same time offered a usable prosodic system for the new medium. They were especially meaningful at a time when modern Chinese poetry was desperately in need of order and new direction.

Wen I-to was not a prolific poet. Almost all of his verse was written during the mid-twenties when he was concerned with the problems of form, and his work inevitably reflects this concern. But it does much more. It opens up an extraordinarily lush world interwoven with dazzling colors, startling imageries, and a luxurious sensuousness worthy of his poetic mentors, Keats and Li Shang-yin. Wen attained sensuous effects by means of a richness and variety of imagery unsurpassed by his contemporaries. His poetry not only evokes the animated Keatsian world of "luxuriant vegetation," but also calls forth the inanimate world of sweet incense, red candles, and tinkling jewels that belonged to Li Shang-yin. An artist by instinct and training, Wen was fascinated by works of art whose man-wrought beauty he prized above that of nature. Images, symbols, and descriptive details in his poetry are frequently derived from or associated with the realm of art.

Wen's fondness for the tangible particular and the poised object is seen in the following lines from "The First Chapter of Spring" (1920?), in which he seeks to recapture an early spring scene:

> Over the bend of the arbor, there are a few lean hard
> Branches of elms that have not quite caught up with
>   spring.
> They are now imprinted in a sky of fish scales
> Like a page of light blue clouded writing paper
> On which monk Huai-ssu has scribbled his
> Cursive script of iron and silver strokes.

Blue clouds like fish scales, hard lean branches of elm, and angular script—these interpenetrating images weave a picture of staid repose in a cold, bleak, early spring. All is as serenely poised as a traditional landscape painting. There is no doubt that Wen relies largely on synesthesia to attain the fullest sensuous effects in his poetry. But, like Keats, Wen's pursuit of the sensuous is not an end in itself; it is a means to a more profound and complex poetic experience in which sense, intellect, and emotion are interfused. Again like Keats, Wen's synesthetic imagery holds up the mirror to his own awareness of the relations between nature and man.[8] It reflects, too, Wen's concern with the dualities in life. One feels an emotional, as well as an intellectual, tension in his constant juxtaposition of these opposing forces. It is this tension that distinguishes him as a modern poet, perceptive and deeply aware of the time and place that give his style its distinctive character and his works their special quality.

[8] See Richard H. Fogle, "Synaesthetic Imagery in Keats," in *Keats: A Collection of Critical Essays*, ed. Walter Jackson Bate, p. 42.

Synesthetic imagery is not alien to Chinese traditional poetry. In the poetry of late T'ang times (Li Shang-yin's era) and the *tz'u* verse of early Sung, this kind of imagery is especially abundant. Moonlight is often described as frost, as in the famous quatrain by Li Po that combines both visual and tactual senses in a single image: "Seeing the bright moonlight before my couch/I thought it was frost upon the ground." Here the coolness, the whiteness, and the brightness. of the moon are suggested in one image—the frost.

In his depiction of a deserted scene near a temple, Wang Wei, one of the greatest traditional nature poets, combines auditory sensation in one line while mingling the visual and the tactual in the next. The result is cool detachment—the state of mind of the protagonist projected through the synthesis of different sensations: "The sound of stream is echoed by the boulders,/The color of sun chills the green pines." A typical compliment to a beautiful lady is to poetize her as "soft jade and warm perfume," a description that embraces physical sensations of touch, sight, temperature, and smell. Such examples are a common feature in Chinese traditional poetry.

Wen often reinforces a sight or odor image with a kinesthetic one, giving the image added weight: "A patch of slanting sun hangs head down from the eaves." This line is reminiscent of Keats's exquisite blending of images in "Ode to a Nightingale": "Nor what soft incense hangs upon the boughs." It also recalls the line from Tu Fu: "The stars hang over the vast plains." In a love lyric entitled "Forget Her" (1926), Wen wishes he could forget his loved one as he would a flower: "That colored morning cloud on the petal,/That thread of fragrance in the heart of a flower."

On certain occasions Wen's interwoven images are the chief contributor to the emotional intensity of a poem. In "The Tears of Rain" (1922?), Wen compares the youth's tears with the "continuously falling gloomy rains," whose intensity is such that they have even "sprinkled the soil and bitter yellow plum to ripeness."

In still another verse, "The Red Candle" (1923?), Wen borrows Li Shang-yin's image of a candle melting into tears to suggest the self-consuming passion of the dedicated artist: "O red candle!/Every teardrop you shed has ashened a part of my heart." And in another poem the image is even more explicit: "The red candle ceaselessly sheds its tears of blood." In the first passage, blood is only implied by the color "red." This immediately calls forth a conceit popular in the old poetry when the lover's tears are said to be red because his eyes have been shedding blood. The instantaneous transference from a sight image to an emotional one is strengthened by another sense effect, the ashened heart. This last image, with its connotation of incense burning into ashes (another conceit of self-consuming passion in Li Shang-yin's poetry), completes the highly charged metaphor. Compression and association are the hallmark of Wen's synesthesia.

Like Keats and some traditional Chinese poets, Wen is equally successful at rendering sound more palpable by allying the sound image with some other order of sensation, usually tactual. "The bird sound is as round as a dewdrop." And every word of the song is "a drop of bright pearl/Every word is a drop of hot tear." Or, the children's laughter is crisp, "like a crystal pagoda crashing down."

Perhaps the best illustration of Wen's distinctive technique in fusing divergent sensations is his famous masterpiece, "The Dead Water," which may also serve as the supreme example of Wen's pursuit of stylistic and structural discipline:

This is a ditch of hopelessly dead water.
No clear breeze can raise half a ripple on it.
Why not throw in some rusty metal scraps,
Or even some of your leftover food and soup?

Perhaps the copper will turn its green patina into jade,
And on the tin can rust will bloom into peach blossoms;
Then let grease weave a layer of silk brocade,
And germs brew out colored clouds.

Let the dead water ferment into a ditch of green wine,
Filled with the floating pearllike white foam,
The laughter of small pearls turning into large pearls
Only to be pierced when gnats come to steal the wine.

Thus, a ditch of hopelessly dead water
May yet claim some small measure of splendor.
And if the frogs cannot bear the loneliness,
Let the dead water burst into song.

This is a ditch of hopelessly dead water,
A place where beauty can never live.
Might as well let vice cultivate it,
And see what kind of world it can create.

In this elegiac poem written in the late twenties, Wen expressed his feelings about the seemingly hopeless situation in China. It is a sad poem, but not a poem of despair. The formal structure and heavy stresses, the pregnant density, the ponderous movement—all contribute to the somber air and sculpturesque style characteristic of Wen. The use of end-stopped lines supports the syntactical patterns of parallelism and repetition, and thereby secures additional structural balance and unity within the poem.

It is true that Wen tends to overstress the visual at the expense of the auditory. Critics like Chu Hsiang who censured his slipshod use of rhymes would disapprove of Wen's loose rhyme pattern here, but there is justification for Wen's choice. Occurring in irregular order, the rhymes integrate the poem without calling too much notice to themselves; they direct the readers' attention to the content of the poem without being obtrusive. The predominant use of slant rhymes (such as *ming* 明 with *sheng* 聲, *lun* 淪 with *keng* 羹, *hua* 花 with *hsia* 霞, *tsai* 在 with *chiai* 界) is in perfect congruence with the colloquialism of the vernacular. The poem would risk the monotony of excessive symmetry if the rhyme were too orderly. Wen made abundant use of such devices as alliteration (*che* 這, *chüeh* 絕, *ch'ing* 清,

ts'ui 翠, *ch'i* 起), assonance (*ch'ing* 清, *tien* 点, *yeh* 也, *fei* 翡, *tieh* 鉄), and internal rhymes (*pu ju* 不如, *shuang* 爽, *wang* 望, *sheng* 瞳, *ch'eng* 成, *ts'eng* 層, *shang* 上, *jang* 讓) to achieve a subtle unifying effect, at the same time enriching the verbal texture of the poem. Wen's language is a masterful blend of the colloquial (*shuang hsing* 爽性 "might as well," *pu ju* 不如 "might as well" ["why not"], *yeh hsü* 也許 "perhaps") and the poetic (*i lun* 漪淪 "silken ripples," *yün hsia* 雲霞 "colored clouds"). The juxtaposition of the rigorous, the commonplace, and even the repulsive with the delicately sensuous and the desirable heightens the dualistic patterns as well as the emotional content of the poem.

"The Dead Water" is a prime example of Wen's synesthetic technique. In the third stanza the transformation of the ditch of dead water into luscious green wine produces a swift and exciting shift of sensation. The dead water is no longer stagnant but green— an association with spring which suggests the life force. This visual image is intensified by what it describes— wine, which at once evokes pleasant olfactory and taste sensations. In the next line Wen's favorite pearl image adds form, light, and weight. All these different senses undergo an instantaneous transmutation as the pearls, bursting into laughter, suddenly acquire human qualities. Personification reinforces the fusing of diverse sense images with the new organic feeling. The last line of the stanza brings us back to the initial images of the dead water and the green wine, thereby providing a final unity to the overall framework.

Wen shared with Keats not only the gift for synesthesia but a fondness for the luxurious world of plants, fruits, and flowers. As early as in his first poem, "The West Coast," one is led to "a small island wearing a headful of flowers and grass," where nature is envisioned in all her lush splendor. Like Keats, Wen favored the joining of the water image with a vegetative image. References to rain or its effects are frequent, as in "The First Chapter of Spring":

The rain that bathed men's souls has passed.

> The thin mud bites men's shoes everywhere.
> The cool breeze with its moist odor of earth
> Rushes forward to fill our nostrils.

A little later in the same poem, rain again appears:

> The east wind urges the stubborn rush roots
> To open up their newly awakened sprouts.
> The spring rain passes; the sprouts are just one
>   inch long.
> The water in the pond stealthily swallows them.

Wen's unqualified admiration for Keats is apparent in "The Loyal Minister of Art (1922?). By bestowing such a title on the senior poet, Wen paid him the greatest of compliments. Anyone familiar with Chinese culture will know that one of the highest forms of loyalty is that of a minister to his ruler. In addition to using this traditional symbol, Wen compares Keats's brilliance with the particular pearl on the emperor's robe that surpasses all the rest of the pearls. The piece ends with a couplet: "Your name has not been written on water./ It is cast on the imperial tripod of the sacred reign."

The choice of traditional Chinese symbols here is apt and imaginative; it deepens the sincerity of the sentiment. The inclusion of traditional motifs persists in many of Wen's works, whether they are poems inspired by a Western concept (the quest for beauty, love, and truth), poems dealing with a foreign subject, or descriptive verses. In the following passage Wen joins two old images associated with the moon in order to develop his own image, a device that was habitually cultivated by the traditional Chinese poets.

> O loyal descendants of the Great Cosmos!
> Younger sister of the moon!
> Are you the jade spittle splashed onto the sky?
> Or are you the pearls wept by the mermaid
> And washed up by the waves?

Wen combines here two common images of the moon (goddess and jade) with the verb *t'u* (吐, "to emit" ["splashed"]),
which is ordinarily associated with the moon. Tu Fu used the
same word to suggest the slow and graceful emergence of the
moon from the surrounding mountains in his famous line, "At
the fourth watch, the mountains exhale the moon." Wen uses
the familiar verb to describe the jade spittle emitted by the
moon goddess and splashed onto the horizon. The effect is a bit
strained. It needs to be pointed out here that both the words
for "emit" (*t'u* 吐) and "spittle" (*t'u* 唾) escape the unpleasant
associations they have in English. On the contrary, they are
considered poetically sophisticated in traditional Chinese
poetry. In the last two lines, a familiar allusion—the pearls of
the mermaid's tears—appears. (The mermaid who weeps tears
of pearls comes from a well-known Chinese mythological tale.)
Wen customarily employs conventional images in the traditional ways to set the tone or to create a desired atmosphere.
Sometimes these images embody a symbolic purpose. In Wen's
long narrative poem, "The Death of Li Po" (192–?), based on
the legendary death of the T'ang poet who, when inebriated,
drowned himself while trying to catch the image of the moon,
the moon becomes the central symbol of the poet's eternal
quest for beauty and truth. This quest is a theme important in
Wen's works and is traceable to Keats and/or Shelley.

Wen's fondness for the special effect of light filtering through
leafy openings is reminiscent of Keats's moon filtering through
"opening clouds" in "Endymion":

> And lo! from opening clouds, I saw emerge
> The loveliest moon, that ever silver'd o'er
> A shell for Neptune's goblet. . . .

Compare this with Wen's "The silver tide of moon/Trickled
through the leaves' openings to rush into the windows." And
his sun is "a laughing blaze—a ray of light/Filtered through the
trees' openings to be sprinkled on my forehead."

The moon is sometimes pictured in a more conventional way: "A jade plate hangs on a dark blue sky" has an instinctive rightness about it in a poem with a traditional setting. In the same poem ("The Death of Li Po," mentioned above), the moonlight is similarly depicted as "The dancing silver light sieved through the leaves' openings." The visual image here, enlivened by the blithe and graceful movements of the dance, gives a new personality to the moon. Something cool, precious, and yet quite out of human reach, the moon is now brought down to earth, dancing through the leaves. Toward the last part of the poem, it goes through yet another transformation: "Peeping out behind the shadow of the silken willows by the pond,/Like a beauty drying her hair by the window after her bath." Wen adroitly joins the attenuated image of silken willow strands with the implied vision of the moon's dark tresses, bodied forth by the special effect of the moonlight's being sieved through the willows and cast upon the pond. Here two related sets of descriptions are fused to create a unified vision of the moon that symbolizes not only beauty but love. It becomes a source of inspiration and an ideal to be intensely pursued. The ideal world of beauty and love, however, is illusory and destructive, for it is this very illusion that leads the drunken poet to leap into the water and ironically meet his death trying to save the drowning moon.

"The Death of Li Po" perfectly embodies the romantic awareness of the gulf between aspiration and actual fulfillment. The moon is not only an object idealized and pursued, but a symbol of unrealized yearning. Implicit from the beginning and growing in intensity throughout the poem is a sense of human mortality and futility. The ending has a climactic poignancy in the tragic death of Li Po, the great romantic idealist of his day. Li Po, seeing the round moon peacefully pressed against the sky, dies in ecstasy under the delusion that he has succeeded in saving his beloved, while the latter coolly and mockingly watches from above, as unattainable as ever.

The subject of love and beauty is treated more compactly in

a purely lyrical piece, "Beauty and Love" (192–?)

> The soft lamplight flickers through the window.
> Rows of saffron-colored squares are inlaid on the walls;
> The shadows of two jujube trees are like coiled snakes
> Spread in all directions and asleep beneath the walls.
>
> Oh that large star, the companion of Chang-o!
> Why do you come within my sight?
> The bird within my heart abruptly stops its spring songs
> When it hears your silent heavenly music.
>
> Listen, it has even forgotten itself,
> Determined only to fly away in search of you.
> It has crushed open the iron prison.
> But in an instant, you vanished.
>
> The chill wind at the corner of the house sadly sighs,
> Startling the sleepy snakes into motion.
> The moon has turned ghastly pale, perhaps annoyed.
> The window opens its large mouth as if it were laughing
>   aloud.
>
> Poor bird, he is back now.
> Muted, blinded, heart turned to ashes
> And wings dripping with fresh blood.
> Can this be the price of love, the sin of beauty?

It is difficult to discuss "Beauty and Love" without recalling Keats, who has influenced Wen in so many ways. One sees interesting parallels with Keats's "Ode to a Nightingale," the chief of which are a somewhat grim outlook on life and a questioning of the true nature of reality. Both poems close with irresolution: Keats asks, "Was it a vision, or a waking dream? . . . Do I wake or sleep?"; Wen's query is, "Can this be the price of love, the sin of beauty?"

But beyond these similarities the two compositions diverge widely. Keats's entire ode concentrates upon the nightingale's song, which seems to offer the only possible relief to "the fever, and the fret" of human life. In "Beauty and Love," although the bird is a prominent figure in its identification with the speaker, Wen centers on the dark and violent nature of reality. Many details are devoted to the mysteriously sinister, almost surrealistic world that confronts the escaped bird. The grotesque appearance of coiled snakes asleep on the ground suggests the potential evil inherent in nature and foreshadows the impending danger. The second stanza opens with an invocation to the large star, the symbol of beauty and love. The bird, hearing the ineffable music of the star, abruptly abandons his singing. The third stanza sees the bird—the human spirit—enthralled by the music, determined to venture forth in search of it. Bursting open its iron prison, it is instantly disappointed in its quest, for the star vanishes. The disconsolate mood deepens in the fourth stanza as the chill wind's sad sigh wakens the snakes by the walls. The window laughs maliciously with gaping mouth. The moon—the object of the bird's quest—turns phantomlike. The concluding stanza discloses the tragic aftermath of the bird's futile search and the speaker's despairing questioning of the experience. This awareness of violence as a condition of human existence is a particularly modern aspect of Wen's works.

One of Wen's early poems, "Death" (1921), deals with a theme recurrent in his later works:

> Soul of my soul!
> Life of my life!
> The failures and debts of my whole life
> Now demand their payments from you.
> Yet what do I have?
> What could I ask of you?
> Let me be drowned to death in your eyes' waves.
> Let me be burned to death in the melting stove of your
> heart.
> Let me be drowned to death in the sweet nectar of your
> music!
> Let me be suffocated to death in the fragrance of your

breath!
Otherwise, let your dignity shame me to death!
Let your cold freeze me to death!
Let that heartless poisonous sword stab me to death!
If you reward me with happiness,
I'll die of happiness.
If you give me suffering,
I'll die of suffering.
Death is my only respect from you.
Death is my ultimate offering to you.

This is a markedly inferior work. Rhetorical indulgences, banalities, and melodramatic gestures are some of its major faults. The word repetition and parallelism of line forecast, but in a relatively crude manner, the subtler technical devices of parallelism and antithesis in Wen's more mature works. The poem is interesting for its disclosure of Wen's concept of death, which he develops in his later verse, "The Last Day" (1926):

The dewdrops sob in the gutters,
The green tongues of banana trees lick at the window,
The chalk-white walls are receding from me.
I cannot fill such an enormous room alone.

With a brazier ablaze in my heart,
I await quietly the guest from afar.
I feed the fire with cobwebs and rats' dung.
I use the scaly snake skins for split wood.

The rooster continues its urging: a heap of ash remains
 in the pan.
A gust of chill wind steals over my mouth,
The guest is already before me;
I close my eyes and follow after the guest.

One notices a clear advance in Wen's art from the earlier practice to this present performance: the close-knit stanzas, the classical restraint, the dazzling images. The style is more polished too, and phrasings are less awkward and bland. Possibly the most striking surface characteristic is its astonishing empathic responsiveness to nature. Wen's consciousness of the perverse aspects of nature and his gothic sense of the macabre are vividly conveyed through images like snake skins, cobwebs, and rats' dung. Death is humanized as a guest calmly anticipated by the speaker. Despite its quiet air, the poem is tempered by a more formidable note: an ominous foreboding shrouds the closing lines as death inevitably arrives.

To Wen, as to Chu Tzu-ch'ing (in his poem, "Dissolution"), death has an aura of mystery that he finds hard to resist. Perhaps Wen's concept of death is akin to that of Keats—a "luxury" so "easeful" and seductive.

PERHAPS (A DIRGE)   (1927?)
Perhaps you are indeed too wearied from too much
    weeping.
Perhaps, perhaps you wish to fall asleep now.
Then ask the night owl not to cough,
The frogs not to croak and bats not to fly.

Let no sunshine pierce your eyelids,
Let no clear winds touch your brows,
And whoever he may be, let him not startle you.
With an umbrella of pine I shall guard your sleep.

Perhaps you hear earthworms turning the soil,
The grass roots sucking water.
Perhaps the music you hear now
Is lovelier than men's cursing voices.

Close tight your eyes then,
I shall let you sleep, let you sleep.
I'll gently cover you with yellow earth
  ⋅And ask the ashes of paper money to rise slowly.

"Perhaps" is a well-controlled poem; the elegiac tone and

gentle mood are consistent. The lyrical impulse is unusually
light for Wen. Implicit from the initial line is the speaker's
assumption that life is wearisome and full of woes (a further
reminder of Keats); only in death is ultimate ease achieved. To
secure this repose, however, it seems necessary to close out the
disturbing elements in life symbolized by the night owl's cough,
the frogs' croaking, the bats' flight, and the natural forces, the
sunlight and the winds. The serene atmosphere is enhanced in
the third stanza by a tranquil delineation of the underground
scene. Wen's extraordinary response to nature is here suggested
by his ability to hear earthworms turning the soil and roots
sucking water and music lovelier than that of the world above.
This amazing quality may explain why the poet is drawn to
death—he envisions the approach of death as opening up to him
a whole new realm of knowledge otherwise inaccessible to men.

Wen composed a number of nature poems, some richly dense
and elaborately wrought (such as "Autumn"), others spare and
taut, as is "Small Brook" (1923):

> The lead-gray trees' shadow
> Is a long chapter of nightmare
> Pressing downward on the bosom of
> The small brook in heavy slumber.
> The mountain brook struggles, struggles
> With no result.

This brilliantly compressed verse is as vivid as it is restrained.
The mood of stifling oppression is deftly imaged despite the
poem's extreme brevity. Like Chu Tzu-ch'ing, Wen often
imbues his descriptive verse with his subjective consciousness.
By a subtle transference of metaphor the poem is transformed
into a stricken vision of life's oppressive burden: in the purity
of Wen's lyrical voice is concealed a deep sense of human
pathos.

The range of Wen's poetry is quite wide. He has written
highly impassioned patriotic verse, in addition to nature poems,

occasional verse, and poems of social and political implications.
But the essential Wen I-to soars away from the topical and the
social to a realm of pure imagination. Behind his poems, be they
successes or failures, lies the intense dedication of a wholly
committed artist. It seems fitting to conclude here with an
earlier poem, "The Sword Box" (1921), which is probably the
clearest manifestation of Wen the poet.

As a prelude to "The Sword Box," Wen quoted the lines of
Tennyson's "Palace of Art":

> . . . I built my soul a lordly pleasure house,
> Wherein at ease for aye to dwell.
> .   .   .   .
> And while the world runs round and round, I said,
>   "Reign thou apart, a quiet king,
> Still as, while Saturn whirls, his steadfast shade
>   Sleeps on his luminous ring."
> To which my soul made answer readily:
>   "Trust me in bliss I shall abide
> In this great mansion, that is built for me,
>   So royal and rich and wide."

As Tennyson built his soul a "pleasure house," Wen in his poem
devotes himself to building a sword box so that his precious
sword may have a permanent place to rest.

The poem is not written in Wen's characteristic form, the
"Dead Water" meter, which evolved later. It is composed of
both short and long lines distributed in stanzaic units of unequal
length. Although end rhymes are profusely used for patterned
effects, the general mode of this verse-narrative is one of flexibility and freedom.

The style is less weighted though no less ornate or intense
than his later one. In one of his letters, Wen named this poem
together with "Remembering Chrysanthemum" (1922) and
"Autumn" (1922) as the three works most clearly influenced by
Keats and Li Shang-yin. The poem begins: "In the battle of
life/I was once a world-famous general." The speaker then

narrates how he came to a deserted island to "nurse his battle wounds" and "forget his enemies." In the stanza that follows, he announces his desire to live like a "nameless farmer drinking to the full the brilliant colors of the field," or a fisherman "casting his net of fancy" and dreaming all day long by the sandy beach, or just wandering in the woods collecting precious stones (these are familiar occupations of the recluse poets in traditional poetry). Having collected enough precious stones, he is determined to pursue the humble life of an artisan. He vows to build a box for his sword:

> I shall lay out all the treasures
> And display them before me.
> I shall carve, engrave,
> Rub and grind every single piece.
> Then I shall inlay them on the sword box,
> Using every chapter of my dream as the blueprint.
> I shall design all kinds of wondrous vistas.

The artist proceeds to carve four figures: T'ai I,[9] Venus, Buddha, and a blind musician. They are probably intended as symbols of harmony and permanence, beauty and love, Truth, and Poetry—the quintessence of life that Wen himself seeks in his ideal world of imagination. The four figures are wrought in the most elaborate physical details and sensuous images.

> I shall trace out the white-faced, long-bearded T'ai I,
> Asleep on the pink lotus petals
> And drifting amidst the white clouds of ivory.

The choice of T'ai I, the Supreme Sky God in Chinese

---

[9] T'ai I (太一), the deity known as the Supreme Sky God or Sky Emperor, was elevated to a central position in the state by Emperor Wu Ti of Han in 113 B.C. It was a specific divinity which was generally conceived as having a human form; it has also been described as a venerable old man in a yellow robe. Since this deity is presumed to dwell in a palace at the very center of Heaven, marked by the Pole Star, the term later also became the name of the Pole Star. Ch'ü Yüan used the figure of T'ai I (The Great One, Lord of the Eastern World) in *The Nine Songs*. See David Hawkes, *Ch'u Tz'ŭ, The Songs of the South*, p. 36.

mythology, to represent Great Harmony or Permanence is a masterful touch. Wen's personification of him as a "white-faced, long-bearded" old man caught reposing on lotus petals and borne on clouds of ivory imparts an atmosphere of calm and other-worldliness as well as the sense of tranquillity, harmony, and infinity so important to romantic poets of all ages. Wen's choice of Venus as his symbol of love and beauty strikes an incongruous note. Why did he not choose a more traditional Chinese beauty like Yan Kuei-fei or Hsi Shih? Venus certainly looks a bit odd and uncomfortable in the company of so many strangers!

> I shall use ink jade and gold threads
> To build an incense burner inlaid with lines of thunder.
> Over the burner a scriptlike smoke rises gracefully;
> It may be carved out of opaque cat's-eye.
> Above the half-dying smoke,
> A beauty of jade rises dimly.
> Oh how she resembles Venus in flesh:
> This piece of rose jade is just her color!

This dazzling tableau is immediately followed by an equally splendid presentation of the awe-inspiring Buddha:

> I shall carve the Buddha with agate,
> A Buddha of three hands and six arms,
> Riding on an elephant made of fish stone.
> Coral is the fire he holds in his mouth.
> Silver threads are plaited into pythons around his waist,
> And the halo over his head is a round disk of amber.

In all his earlier works, Wen tends to overload his lines with descriptive details. But even in these early attempts he demonstrates an astonishing capability for fusing diverse sense impressions and for attaining strong sensuous effects by transforming a visual image of weight. To invoke an impression of rich ornamentation here, Wen has selected a whole catalogue of precious stones—jade, amber, cat's-eye, coral. These sight images take on an added sense of touch and weight when enforced by words like "carve" or "plaited." The portraiture of the blind musician playing his ancient instrument on a bamboo raft in the river is just as impressive.

Once these four distinguished personae are carved, the artist-protagonist further embellishes his sword box with intricate decorations. When the project is finally finished, the artist rapturously kisses the sword and cries out:

> I kiss away its rust, its wounds;
> I wash its bloodstains with my tears.
> I cleanse away all traces of sin.
>
> .   .   .   .
>
> I then gently place it in the box,
> And singing a soft song,
> I urge it to sleep peacefully in this palace of art.

Having furnished a permanent abode for his cherished sword, the speaker declares that he now wants to "swoon to death in the radiance of the resplendent sword box." This state of swooning to death is repeated in the concluding stanza, when the artist-speaker is so overwhelmed with admiration for his completed masterpiece that he forgets to breathe, "and the blood forgets to flow,/The eyes forget to look." The poem ends in a romantic climax of triumphant death:

> Oh I have killed myself!
> I have killed myself with my self-made sword box!
> My great mission is accomplished!

Despite its seeming ambiguity, the violent ending has an immediate impact on the reader. Wen seems to seek romantic "rapture" in creative imagination and ecstasy, whose intensity is comparable only to that of death itself. Or is Wen thinking of Keats's lines: "Verse, Fame, and Beauty are intense indeed,/ But Death intenser—Death is life's high meed"? Wen may very well be attempting to express the tremendous conflict within himself, a conflict accentuated by his feelings of obligation to the modern world. Like other romantics Wen seems torn between an imaginative realm of art and the real world of suffering and pain. He tries to reconcile the two, but with little success. Very likely he feels that art, being useless because its world is an illusion, is ultimately destructive to life.

This feeling again leads us to one pervasive impulse in Wen's poetry: the profound awareness of reality and the preoccupation with the dualities in nature and art—beauty and ugliness, life and death. One senses an emotional, as well as an intellectual, tension in his constant juxtaposition of these opposing forces. It is this tension that distinguishes him as a modern poet, perceptive, sensitive, and keenly conscious of the time and place that give him and his works their special luster. He is a romantic poet living in the twentieth century, not the nineteenth or the tenth. Here is his own confession, in which, despite his disclaimer, he shows himself more a poet than many others of his generation:

CONFESSION   (1926)

I do not deceive you when I say I am no poet,
Even though I love the integrity of the white rocks,
The green pines and the vast sea, the sunset on the
    crow's back,
The twilight woven with the wings of bats.
You know that I love heroes and tall mountains.
I love, too, the national flag outspread in the breeze,
The chrysanthemums colored from soft yellow to antique
    bronze.
But remember that my food is a pot of bitter tea!
And there is another "I." Will you be afraid to know it?
The flylike thought crawling in the garbage can!

Hsü Chih-mo (1895–1931)

The name of Hsü Chih-mo is almost synonymous with modern Chinese poetry, for Hsü is undoubtedly the best-known and most admired, if not, as many of his contemporaries think, the greatest poet of his generation. His romantic personality and no less romantic life and death may have contributed somewhat to this adulation. But more than anything else, his popularity and importance are explained by the character and quality of his poetry.

A native of Chekiang and the only son of a well-to-do family —his father was a banker—Hsü was schooled in the classical tradition, but later studied at a Westernized college in Shanghai. In 1918 he left China to enroll at Clark University in the United States. His ambition then was to become a Chinese Hamilton; his major field of study was economics. Later he transferred to Columbia University, but before he had finished his doctorate he decided to study literature at Cambridge University in England. It was during his stay there that he transferred his allegiance from Hamilton to Shelley and Keats, and decided on a literary career. He become a great admirer of English literature, especially nineteenth-century Romantic poetry, an influence that was vital to his stylistic development in later years. In 1922 he returned to China to teach at the University of Peking. His first volume of poetry, *Poems of Chih-mo*, published in 1925, was an instant success and he was hailed the most promising young poet of his time. In 1926 he and Wen I-to launched the *Poetry Journal* to "encourage the development of a suitable form" for the new verse. Later, the two founded the *Crescent Monthly*, a magazine that was instrumental in shaping the course of the new poetry. In the meantime he had divorced his first wife and later, after a stormy romance, married Lu Hsiao-man, herself a divorcée. For these "scandalous" actions he endured the excoriation of his family and even that of his teacher, the eminent Liang Ch'i-ch'ao, who delivered a fierce diatribe against him at the wedding. On November 19, 1931, Hsü was killed in a plane crash, leaving behind him four collections of poems, three volumes of essays, one novel, one play, and a volume of his diary and letters.

Throughout his brief creative period (1922–31), Hsü maintained a high quality of performance and displayed a remarkable craftsmanship. His interest in metrics led him to the countless experimentations with stanzaic form that became one of his most meaningful contributions to the new verse. Though far from being a rigorous technician, Hsü was a serious practitioner of his art, constantly concerned with the finer details of structure and texture. His distinctive talent lies in his adroit blending of classical diction with the more vigorous colloquial; in his flair for combining the whimsical with the poignantly serious, the abstract with the concrete; and in his deft use of illuminating metaphors and symbolism. His lyrics alone sing out his gift. Hsü's passionate idealism and his belief that life must be taken "very positively" were the springs that nurtured his poetic vision. He wrote some of the most impassioned and memorable lines of his age.

Like his friend and colleague Wen I-to, Hsü was anxious for the future of the thriving new verse. Both were preoccupied with the problem of form: they were convinced that structural integrity should be enforced and new prosodic patterns developed. Although Hsü never formulated his theories as Wen did, his experimentations with Western verse forms were extensive and fruitful. His (and also Wen's) insistence on formal excellence and aesthetic aims awakened poets to a recognition of the intrinsic nature and function of poetry. The impetus for many of Hsü's experiments and innovations came largely, but not only, from his knowledge of Western poetry. Of his indebtedness to Wen's theories on form, Hsü confessed: "I-to is not merely a poet. He is deeply interested in poetic theories and art. I believe that during the last five to six years the few of us who write poetry have been influenced by the author of the 'Dead Water.' "[10]

On his own attitude, Hsü made the following comments: "My pen is a most unharnessable wild horse. When I read the meticulously executed works of I-to, I became aware of my own

---

[10] Hsü Chih-mo, *Hsü Chih-mo ch'üan-chi* [Complete works of Hsü Chih-mo], 2:344–45.

untamed nature, my independent spirit, which never allowed me to pursue any systematic studies on poetic theories."[11] Chu Tzu-ch'ing, in comparing the poetry of Wen and Hsü, pointed out that Hsü was not as "exact" a craftsman as Wen,[12] a judgment with which most readers would concur. This independent spirit of Hsü's, on the other hand, led him to more daring explorations in a wider field of verse forms and techniques.

Cyril Birch, in his article, "English and Chinese Meters in Hsü Chih-mo's Poetry," makes a detailed metrical analysis of some of Hsü's poems. His discovery of the two different types of meters is sound enough, but his basis for distinguishing them—by their stresses—is questionable. Any scansion of Chinese poems on the basis of stress is apt to be arbitrary because of the peculiar nature of the language itself. It is doubtful that Hsü, with his instinctive feelings for language and his "wild horse" temperament, ever seriously attempted, as Mr. Birch claims, to adopt a specific metrical pattern like the iambic meter used by Keats. What attracted Hsü was the external (the visual typographical shape) rather than the internal (the stress pattern) structure of stanzaic verse forms in the West. His indebtedness to the Western meters, then, lies not in a direct transplant of specific metrical patterns, but rather in the adaptation of stanzaic forms of unequal verse length and their accompanying rhyme schemes. Hsü's more Chinese meter usually contains equal verse lengths. It is most likely that these Chinese patterns follow Wen's theories of nonce forms based on the number of characters (syllables) rather than on stresses in a foot.

To understand better Hsü's process of adapting and modifying English stanzaic patterns, one should take a look at the English limerick form, which he seems to favor. The following short lyric, "By Chance" (1927?), is an example of Hsü's adaptation and modification of the form:

[11] Ibid.
[12] Chu Tzu-ch'ing, ed., *Chung-kuo hsin-wen-hsüeh ta-hsi* [Compendium of modern Chinese literature], 8:7.

I am a patch of cloud in the skies
That chanced to cast its shadow in your heart waves.
    You need not be startled,
    Still less overjoyed.
The trace vanishes in a wink of time.

We met in a dark night on the ocean.
You have your destination, I have mine;
    It is fine if you remember,
    It is best that you forget
The light that is brought forth by this encounter.

The original poem with its rhyme scheme of *a a b b a* is given below:

偶　然

我	是	天	空	裏	的	一	片	雲,	*a*
偶	爾	投	影	在	你	的	波	心	*a'*
		你	不	必	訝	異,			*b*
		更	無	須	歡	喜			*b*
在	轉	瞬	間	消	滅	了	踪	影。	*a*

你	我	相	逢	在	黑	夜	的	海	上,	*c*
你	有	你	的,	我	有	我	的,	方	向,	*c*
		你	記	得	也	好,				*d*
		最	好	你	忘	掉,				*d*
在	這	交	會	時	互	放	的	光	亮!	*c*

It is obvious that Hsü adapted here only the external frame of the limerick and its rhyme arrangement. Instead of adhering to the anapestic feet, he chose a less rigid pattern of three nine-character lines enveloping two short five-character lines in the first stanza. In the second stanza, there are ten characters in the longer lines, while the number of those in the couplet remains the same as in the first stanza. In place of full rhymes throughout the verse Hsü employs some slant rhymes.

The well-known "In Memoriam" stanza form (so named after its popularization by Tennyson) appears in Hsü's "For

Seeking a Bright Star" (1925):

> I ride on a limping blind horse,
>> Spurring it on into the dark night,
>> Spurring it on into the dark night,
> I ride on a limping blind horse.

Here Hsü honors the rhyming principle of enclosure (*a b b a*) to secure the effect of an exterior couplet enveloping an interior one. A variant pattern exploiting the same principle of enclosure is employed in this five-lined stanza from "News" (1924?).

> Thunder and rain ceased for a while,
>> Two rainbows like a pair of dragons
>> Emerge from the clouds of fog,
>> Lovely, radiant, and full of life—
> What a good sign! Tomorrow will surely be fine.

These compact stanzaic patterns (including the limerick), not unlike a musical structure in which the finale recapitulates the initial movement, are particularly congenial to the sort of lyrics that Hsü excels in, such as "A Snowflake's Delight" and "By Chance." They provide the structural unity he strives for, a structure that has balance and formality and yet escapes the rigidity of conventional metrical arrangement. Hsü's use of these patterns heightens his style and brings out the delicate grace of his poetic diction and rhythm.

The enjambed lines or rhymed couplets borrowed from Western models are used to great advantage in Hsü's longer works. Whereas the rhymed couplet is a common phenomenon in traditional Chinese verse, the technique of enjambment is absent; end-stopped lines have constituted the basic poetic structure since the *Book of Odes*. End-stopped patterns, when coupled with the monosyllabic nature of *wen-yen*, often produce a rectilinear, monotonous movement when used in a long poem. It is no accident that the great T'ang poet, Li Po, chose the more flexible ancient-verse form or the ballad form for many of his longer poems.

Kuo Mo-jo and others preceded Hsü in adapting this Western device to Chinese poetry, but it was Hsü who naturalized it in the vernacular language. The opening passage from his long poem, "Love's Inspiration" (1930), though mostly unrhymed, demonstrates his artful use of enjambment:

> It does not matter, you just sit down first,
> This moment is not light; I think it is
> Already done, already completely
> Departed from this world. Light and carefree,
> I know not where I am. As if there is
> A lotuslike cloud holding me
> (On her face floats a lotuslike smile),
> Holding me to a remotest land.
> Ah, I do not care to return again,
> Men speak of throwing off life's bondage, perhaps this is
>   it!
> I shall then be a bloom of cloud,
> A white, pure white cloud, completely
> Weightless. When the sunlight embraces me,
> I become light, a light-spirited orb
> Flying toward the distant land, flying farther, farther
>   away;
> Whatever the burden, sorrow,
> Love, pain, and regrets, now fade into the distance.

The easy run-ons, the casual tone, and the almost conversational yet somewhat heightened speech convey a relaxed and nostalgic mood essential to the poem. The casual but melodic colloquialism, far from vitiating the poem's lyricism, blends brilliantly with the sophisticated elegance of its poetic diction. The most delicate lyricist of his time, Hsü had an extraordinarily sensitive ear. His skillful play with the echoings and re-echoings of the same or similar sounds is a means of attaining organic unity and buttressing emotion and thought.

If the world evoked by Wen I-to's poetry is essentially that of the earth—richly varied, luxuriantly sensuous, and staidly concrete—the poetic world of Hsü is of the celestial realm, translucent, ethereal, and abstract. If Wen has claimed Keats and Li Shang-yin as his poetic mentors, Hsü with his aerial lyricism could easily claim literary and spiritual kinship with that "ineffectual angel" Shelley in the West and the "poetic immortal," Li Po, in his own background. This aerial quality in style, diction, and imagery is Hsü's hallmark.

Hsü's customary use of classical or stock poetic words may dismay modern readers, but it is an important element of his style, without which his poetry would lose a part of its classical flavor. Words like *ching mi* 静謐 "serene," *wu yin* 無垠 "boundless," *p'ang po* 旁礴 "extensive," and *k'ang k'o* 坎坷 "pitfalls" recall the elegance and refinements of classical poetry. Hsü's fondness for abstraction is reflected in the wealth of words dealing with abstract concepts or spiritual qualities:

1. time: *kuang yin* 光陰 "time," *shih chi* 時機 "time."
2. spirit: *shen hün* 神魂 "spirit," *k'ung ling* 空靈 "spirit," *shen ming* 神明 "spirit," *ching ling* 精靈 "spirit," *ling hun* 靈魂 "soul."
3. virtues: *ai* 愛 "love," *wen ts'un* 温存 "gentleness," *t'ung ch'ing* 同情 "sympathy," *ai lien* 愛憐 "pity."
4. vices and disagreeable sensations: *k'ung pu* 恐怖 "fear," *k'u t'ung* 苦痛 "pain," *ts'an k'u* 殘酷 "cruelty," *chien yin* 姦淫 "rape," *t'an hsin* 貪心 "greed," *ts'ai chi* 猜忌 "suspicion."

Apart from such abstract vocabulary, Hsü makes abundant use of conventional words or phrases that are light both in connotation and articulation: *ch'ing yin* 輕盈 "light," *p'iao yao* 飄遙 "floating in the air," *ch'ing ling ling te* 輕靈々的 "lightly," *mien mien te* 縣々地 "lingeringly," *ch'ing ch'iao ch'iao te* 輕悄々地 "quietly," *wu mang mang te* 霧茫々地 "vaguely," *ts'ang mang* 蒼茫 "vague," and *tang yang* 盪漾 "drifting." These favorites of Hsü's are usually alliterative, rhyming, or reduplicated compounds whose second or last syllable is lightly stressed (such as *ch'ing ch'iao ch'iao te*). His choice of the short vowel "i" in words like *ch'ing yin* 輕盈 "lightly floating," *mien mien* 綿綿 "lingeringly," and *i hsi* 依悕 "indistinct" occurs too frequently to be accidental. These words in both meaning and sound transmit an impression of airiness and evanescence.

A SNOWFLAKE'S DELIGHT   (1925)

If I were a flake of snow
Flitting light and free in the sky,
    I would make sure of my goal—
    I would fly and fly and fly—
On this earth, I have my goal.

Not to go to that desolate vale,
Not to go to those dreary foothills,
    Nor to feel sad on deserted streets,
    I would fly and fly and fly.
You see, I have my goal.

In the air I blithely dance,
Making sure that is her secluded place.
    I would wait for her in the garden—
    I would fly and fly and fly—
Ah, she has a clear scent of plum blossom!

Then with body airy and light,
I would gently press close to her robe,
    Pressing close to her soft bosom,
    I shall melt, and melt, and melt.
Melt into the soft waves of her bosom.

The light touch in diction, movement, and imagery harmonizes with the whimsical world of love and subtly suggests love's fragility, the joy as well as the transience of the romantic moment.

Hsü's elusive etherealism does not preclude sensuous imagery; he is capable of experiencing just as wide a spectrum of sense perceptions as Wen I-to. Even in his most abstract images, Hsü shares with Shelley the faculty of allying them with a strong tangible sensation (usually tactual), which gives a solid contour to the tenuous.

The visual images in Hsü's poems have extraordinary space and scope. His gaze is frequently directed toward the sky, and his favorite vantage point is the mountain peak, as in these two examples:

> Go away, world, go away!
>   I stand alone on the tall mountain peak.
> Go away, world, go away!
>   I face the sky's infinite azure canopy.

> I sit alone on the stone halfway up the mountain watching
>   The white clouds like steam ascending the peaks before
>   me.

At times Hsü's gaze is focused on the illimitable distance of the horizon: "That small star of blue at the sky's rim—It is an island. . . ." Hsü's visual images, like Ch'ü Yüan's and Shelley's, are often panoramic and dualistic in scope and comprehensiveness:

> I stretch out my enormous hands toward heaven and
>   earth, sea and mountain—greedily seek and demand.
> I snatch a handful of north wind and ask it for the colors
>   of the fallen leaves;
> I snatch a handful of southwest wind and ask it for the
>   luster of tender sprouts.
> I squat by the ocean's side, listening to the snoring
>   waves;
> I seize the glow of the setting sun, the dews of distant
>   hills, the radiance of autumn moon, and scatter them
>   on my hair, my bosom, in my sleeves, and under my
>   feet.
>   .   .   .   .
> Come, let me take you to the seaside to hear the stormy
>   waves shaking the great void.
> Come, let me take you to a secret chamber to hear the
>   low moan of a maimed soul.

> Come, let me take you beyond the misty clouds to hear
>   the sad solitary cry of a strange big bird.
> Come, let me take you to the world of common men to
>   listen to voices of the old and feeble, the sick and in
>   pain, the poor, the destroyed, the oppressed, the
>   frustrated, and the enslaved, the cowardly, the ugly,
>   the sinful, and the suicidal. Then harmonize these cries
>   with the sound of winds and rains of deep autumn in
>   order to sing a song of this ash-colored life of men.

This other side of Hsü reflects the influence of poets like Li
Po who excel in the more robust, masculine vein of romanticism. In spite of its considerable vitality, however, Hsü's verse
lacks both the control and the spontaneous lyrical abandon of
the T'ang master. In addition, elements such as sensuous in-
clusiveness, verbosity, and excessive cataloguing indicate the
influence of Walt Whitman. Hsü is not quite at home with the
more vigorous lyrical mold here. The rhetorical tone, feverishly
passionate, falls hysterical and grating on the ear. Overdepend-
ence on repetition and parallelism for the purpose of emphasis
only invites monotony. The ending is particularly weak with
its long, involved sentence and flaccid rhythm. The piece reveals, however, Hsü's awareness of actualities. Although he delights in the celestial realm and nature, he always returns to
earth, to the world of men. What Benjamin Kurtz said of
Shelley is equally applicable to Hsü: "He did not build a
philosophy of pessimism out of the unromantic lust and cruelty
of the actual world. Nor was he content to mourn because he
could not have life on his own terms. He did not use his dream
of benevolence and love as a way to escape captivity to the
lower reality. But he repeatedly tried to live his romantic
philosophy in the matter-of-fact world."[13]

The moon, one of Hsü's primary symbols of beauty, aspiration, and permanence, is frequently described as indistinctly
seen through a screened object: "A curve of jadelike moon

---

[13] Benjamin P. Kurtz, *The Pursuit of Death*, p. xvi.

peeps through the clouds' openings, / And through the gauze-curtained window is seen the lovely smile of Beauty." The idea of the veiled moon is essentially traditional though it is also reminiscent of Shelley's conception. Hsü uses the same effect in "Watching the Moon":

> Moon: through the gauze-curtained window in the
>   darkness,
> I watch her struggling out from behind the jagged
>   mountain crags—
> A disk of flickering, incomplete radiance.
> Like a virgin guarding her chastity,
> In fear, she struggles out from the claws of tyranny.

Hsü's harsh tactile imagery usually represents forces of evil, but he is also capable of a touch that is gentle and soothing:

> . . . in the desert,
> The tender fingers of the moonlight
> Gently stroke every grain of sand wounded by heat.

In many of Hsü's synesthetic images, the visual is combined with a water effect, with the whole being further strengthened by a motor image: "The bright moon streams down its shadow on the slumbering bosom of the rippled water," and, "The colored clouds at dusk overflooded the maple wood." Fog is like sea foam, "spouting, rushing, covering, / And drowning the green wood in the valley."

Among Hsü's motor images, flying is most frequent. He once wrote an essay on the subject that reveals a bit of his personality:

> Everyone wants to fly. It is so tiresome to be crawling on earth all
> the time, not to mention anything else. Let's fly away from this
> globe! Who does not dream of soaring up in the high sky to watch
> the earth roll like a ball in infinite space! . . . That alone is the
> meaning of being man the power of being man and the worthy

account of being man. If this fleshy carcass of ours is too heavy to be dragged along, throw it away. Wherever possible, fly away from this globe! . . . The greatest mission of mankind is to make wings. The greatest achievement in life is flying! It is the zenith of ideal, the end of imagination, and the transformation of man to God! Poetry is borne on wings. Philosophy soars in the sky. Flying is all-transcendent, all-inclusive, and all-consuming.[14]

Repeated references to images of flying, both literal and metaphorical, help to give Hsü's works their characteristic lightness, ethereality, and sense of life.

THE YELLOW ORIOLE   (1925?)
A streak of yellow flew into a tree,
"Look, a yellow oriole," said a voice.
Cocking its tail tip, it made no sound.
Its splendor brightened the dense, dark foliage
Like spring light, like flame, like passion.

The swift blithe movement of the bird is typical of Hsü; so are the buoyant images of light and flame dramatized against the background of "dense, dark foliage." "A Snowflake's Delight," quoted earlier, is another perfect example of his characteristic light touch.

Empathy, the natural projection of oneself into an object, finds expression in many of Hsü's works. Hsü had great admiration for the empathic powers of Keats and Shelley.

Keats once whispered to himself, "I feel the flowers growing on me." This means, "I feel flowers are growing on my body." This is to say, once he thinks about flowers, he himself becomes flowers, hidden in the grass, glistening in the sunlight. . . . This is the purest state of imagination: the monkey can undergo seventy-two transformations, the poet's transformation power is even greater. . . . Keats and Shelley are especially gifted in this ability to harmonize oneself with nature. In Shelley's "Ode to the Clouds," we don't know whether Shelley has become the cloud or the cloud has

[14] Hsü, *Hsü Chih-mo ch'üan-chi*, 3:430–32.

become Shelley; in the "Ode to the West Wind," whether the singer is the west wind or the west wind the singer! And in "To a Skylark" we don't know if it is the poet singing in the clouds or the skylark speaking to us. Likewise, when Keats poeticized on melancholy, he became melancholy incarnate. . . . When he praised autumn, he became the autumn leaves. . . .[15]

Hsü's response to this projection-of-self motif in Keats and Shelley is indicative of his own empathic inheritance from the traditional Chinese poets, especially the nature poets, who consciously seek union or communion with the objects of their contemplation. One characteristic feature of Hsü's empathy is his use of a mobile image, especially flying. Li Po employs the same means in his long poem, "A Dream of T'ien Mu Mountain," in which he one night

> Flew over the moon's mirrored lake,
> The moon reflecting my shadow on the lake,
> Carried me to the land of Yen Ch'i
>
> . . . .
>
> Shod with the clogs of Hsieh
> I mount the blue clouds' stairs.
>
> . . . .

And the same image appears in Shelley's "Ode to the West Wind":

> If I were a dead leaf thou mightest bear;
> If I were a swift cloud to fly with thee;
> A wave to pant beneath thy power, and share
> The impulse of thy strength. . . .

A notable example of Hsü's empathic experiences is his long prose poem, "The Babe" (1925), in which the physical and psychological states of a woman in labor pain vividly symbolize the creative process:

[15] Ibid., pp. 313–14.

Her usual composure, gentleness, and serene beauty are now transformed into unbelievable ugliness under the spasms of pain. Look at her veins exploding under her delicate skin. The terrible blue and purple colors are like frightened green water snakes anxiously swimming in the field ditches. The beads of perspiration like yellow beans standing on her forehead; her body and limbs in violent convulsion are now swirling as if her mat is woven with needles and her bed screen woven of flame.

Once a calm, poised, and beautiful young woman, now in the cruel seizure of spasmodic pain she has entered into a state of deathlike terror: her eyes one instant are tightly closed, the next, staring hollowly. The eyes that used to look like stars reflected in a winter pond are now shooting fierce flames, green and yellow. Her pupils, like burning red coals, reflect the final struggle of her soul. The once-scarlet lips are like cold ashes at the bottom of the stove. Her lips quiver, stick out, and twitch unnaturally. Death's hot kisses allow her not a second of peace. Her hair in utter disarray lies limply over her mouth like tangled hemp and in her hands are clasped a few strands. . . .

This strongly naturalistic piece with its violent synesthetic images—visual, tactual, kinesthetic, organic, and motor—is a rare exception to the habitual mode of Hsü's poetry, which, like Shelley's, "seldom localizes sensation and emotion within the individual body."[16] The poem projects, too, the repulsive and sinister strain in Hsü's most sinewy images.

This quality of violence and the recognition of brutality as an element of human condition (shared by Wen I-to) figures just as forcefully in "The Poison" (1925)—Hsü's symbol of evil. Characteristic passages from this long prose poem are:

Believe me, my thought is cruel and poisonous because this world is cruel and poisonous. My soul is dark because the sun has already destroyed the light. My tone is like the night owl among the graves because the world has killed all harmonies. My voice is

---

[16] Richard H. Fogle, *The Imagery of Keats and Shelley*, p. 182.

like the wronged ghost reprimanding his enemy because all
gratitude has given way to resentment.

But believe me, there is Truth in my words though my words are
like poison. Truth is never obscure, but in my words there seem to
be the tongue of the two-headed snake, the tail tips of the scorpion,
the antlers of the centipede. The reason is: my heart is filled with
mercy, sentiments, and love that are stronger than poison, more
poisonous than curses, more intense than fire, more mysterious
than death. Therefore, what I say is poisonous, blasphemous,
scorching, and empty.

Hsü's talent for rendering the abstract concrete is in evidence
when he says that all the faith one holds is "like a torn kite
rotting on the tree limb / Our hands still clutching its broken
thread." The disintegration of Confucian values in modern
China is as compellingly drawn:

Floating in the filthy streams of humanity, like drifting duckweeds,
are five mangled corpses: Benevolence, Righteousness, Propriety,
Wisdom, and Courage. They are now flowing down to the sea of
infinity. . . . Everywhere are the phenomena of Rape. Greed
embraces Righteousness; Suspicion threatens Compassion; Cowardice debases Courage; Lust flirts with Love; Tyranny intimidates
Humanity; Darkness tramples on Light. . . .

The poem ends:

The tigers and wolves are in the busy street, the thieves are in bed
with your wives, and sin is in the very depth of your own soul. . . .

Generally speaking, if one has read Hsü Chih-mo at all, it
will be his tender love lyrics, or nostalgic poems like "The
Snowflake's Delight" or "Goodbye, Cambridge," those peren-
nial favorites of the anthologists. Undeniably, these samples
represent his finest works, but there is more to Hsü's creative
imagination than might be indicated by the anthologists'

choice. Hsü himself claimed his "philosophical" verse to be his most satisfactory.

Although he was certainly aware of philosophical concepts, traditional or foreign, Hsü is by no means a philosopher: "My thought—if I possess any—is always unsystematic, for I do not have such talent. My spiritual activity is impulsive, even compulsive by nature."[17] Hu Shih, in tribute after his friend's tragic death, mentions Hsü's philosophical outlook: "His philosophy of life is truly a kind of 'simple faith' in which there are three words: love, freedom, and beauty. To dream that these three ideals will be harmoniously united in life is his 'simple faith.' His entire life was a history of the realization of this faith which constituted his central pursuit in life."[18]

According to Hu Shih, it was this simple faith that made Hsü embrace Carlyle's "everlasting Yea" and assert that he, Hsü, was an "undisciplined individualist" devoted to the perpetual "adventure of the soul." Hsü shared with his romantic peers, past and present, an intense individualism, a passionate yearning for spiritual freedom and self-revelation. His poetry is an expression of his romantic aestheticism. Seeking to discover himself through his private peephole into reality, Hsü explored a new world of his soul's adventure, where he recaptured the old familiar world of common human experiences. Love, beauty, and mutability weave the fabric of Hsü's thought.

The sense of impermanence has obsessed man since antiquity. Hsü, like many another poet, has felt sharply the inevitable encroachment of time and death, the transience of joy and beauty, and the unattainability of the Absolute.

FOR WHOM? (1925?)
In the last few days, the autumn wind has become notably
    sharp.
    I am afraid to look at our courtyard.
    The leaves, like wounded birds, wildly swirl,
    As if shot by invisible arrows—

[17] Hsü, *Hsü Chih-mo ch'üan-chi*, 3:12.
[18] Ibid., 1:358.

Gone, completely gone, are life, color, and beauty.

Only a few streaks of creeping vine are left on western
     walls.
          Its leopard-spotted autumn color still
          Bearing the beatings of the wind's fists,
          Lowly it moans a sound of sorrow.
"I endure for you!" it seems to tell me.

It endures for me! That splendid autumn vine.
          But the autumn wind mercilessly pursues,
          Pursues (Blight is its only act of grace!),
          Pursuing to the end of life's remaining radiance.
Now on the wall is no longer seen the brave autumn vine.

Tonight there are three blue stars in the sky,
          Listening close to the empty autumn courtyard,
          So quiet, not even a sigh is heard.
          The fallen leaves are asleep above the ground.
I am left alone in the deep night. Ah, for whom do I
     grieve?

Autumn, which forebodes the coming of winter and death,
has been a favorite subject with traditional Chinese poets from
the time Sung Yü (third century B.C.) wrote his immortal *Chiu
Pien* poems about this melancholy season. "For Whom?" opens
with the sharpening of the autumn wind, a symbol of nature's
destructive force. This prime image leads directly to the image
of "the leaves, like wounded birds," that, in swift motion so
typical of Hsü, swirl wildly. They subtly suggest the equally
helpless human lives driven before the onslaught of time. In the
second stanza the tenacious vine (with the added significance
of the Chinese name *p'a-shan-hu* 爬山虎 "mountain-climbing
tiger") is a contrasting symbol of resistance. Hsü's climber puts
traditional emphasis on the enduring quality of man—the Confucian virtue of fortitude. The poem ends in a scene of desolation. There is no note of triumph or sense of fruition as in

Keats's "To Autumn," nor is there the anticipation of spring's resurgence that is found in Shelley's "Ode to the West Wind." Only a deep sense of loss and melancholy remain as the poet wonders, "for whom do I grieve?"

In contrast to this gloom is Hsü's joyous celebration of the rebirth of spring, "Birth of Spring" (1929):

> Last night,
> And the night before as well,
> In the frenzied madness of thunder and rain
> Spring
> Was born in the corpse of winter.
>
> Don't you feel the yielding softness underfoot,
> The caressing warmth on your forehead?
> Greenness floats on the branches,
> Water in the pool ripples into tangled longing;
> On your body and mine
> And within our bosoms is a strange throbbing;
>
> Peach flowers are already in bloom on your face.
> And I more keenly relish
> Your seductive charm, drinking in
> Your pearly laughter.
> Do you not feel my arms
> Anxiously seeking your waist,
> My breath reflecting on your body,
> Like myriads of fireflies thrusting themselves into the flame?
>
> These and untold others,
> All join the birds in their ecstatic soaring,
> All join hands in praise of
> The birth of spring.

The verse has virtues to make up for its uninspired ending. The intimate linking of visual image with abstraction (the greenness on the branch with the endless "tangled longing") delicately evokes the emotion of the percipient—his sensuous response to the call of spring and its summons to love. The natural scene, initially a backdrop, becomes a visual projection of the protagonist's state of mind. The emotional intensity reaches its climax in one of Hsü's favorite metaphors, "fireflies thrusting themselves into the flame"—the symbol of love, beauty, and truth, to which the poet is irresistibly drawn, even though it costs him his life. A possible source of this emblem of supreme sacrifice is Shelley's glowworm—"the desire of the moth for the star."

In Hsü's prose rendering of Keats's "Ode to a Nightingale," he writes:

> Beauty is hardly ever there. And if it does reveal itself by chance, it only lasts for a moment, then vanishes like the fallen flowers in the stream. Spring light cannot be stayed. It isn't that there are no lovers of beauty. Beauty hardly remains in the world; we can only enjoy its fleeting visitation. We have barely closed our laughing mouths before the sad faces have already returned. Therefore, I only wish to follow your song and leave this world in order to dissolve the dark melancholy in my consciousness. [19]

This obsession with the passing of beauty is echoed in "Roaming in the Clouds" (1929?).

> That day you lightly roam among the clouds in the sky,
> Carefree, delicately graceful, you have no thought to tarry
> Along the sky's edge or the land's end.
> You have found your joy in infinite wandering.
> You are unaware that on this humble earth
> There is a mountain stream. Your radiant beauty
> In your passing has kindled his soul
> And startled him to awakening. He held close to your
>   lovely shadow.
> But what he held was only unending sorrow,
> For no beauty can be stayed in space or time.
> He yearns for you, but you've flown across many mountain

[19] Ibid., 3:322.

peaks
To cast your shadow in a yet vaster and wider sea.
He now pines for you, that one mountain stream,
Despairingly praying, praying for your return.

This fleeting visitation of Beauty may be interpreted as the "mysterious moment of sudden spiritual awakening and illumination" that Hsü strives to attain. His fundamentally Taoistic and Buddhistic vision of "ultimate truth" is reminiscent too of Shelley's "Intellectual Beauty," "the sudden vision of Platonic reality" which can "lift the human psyche into ecstasy."[20] In the limited scope of this modified sonnet, however, there are no detailed depictions of the exhilarating joy arising from a vision of Beauty nor of the deep gloom after Beauty's loss as in Shelley's "Hymn to Intellectual Beauty." Hsü's treatment is characteristically light in tone, the emotions are more subdued than Shelley's, and the dominant impulse of the poem is profound melancholy rather than ecstasy or despair. Hsü's expression of this elusive moment of sudden illumination in terms of symbolism is probably learned from Shelley.

One important theme of Hsü's philosophical poems is the romantic quest for permanence. The theme may be inspired by Shelley's romantic quest or it may be traced deep into Chinese tradition—to Ch'ü Yüan's passionate search for his unattainable Ideal Beauty on earth and in the supernatural world. In these quest poems, Hsü uses a number of recurring images—a mountain peak, a star, the moon, a child—to symbolize permanence.

WITHOUT TITLE   (1925)

It is your duty, you, the shins and ankles of the mountain
     pilgrim,
To suffer the pain of thorns! Look back at the path that
     you've traveled;
See the mottled bloodstains on clumps of grass and scattered
     rocks.

[20] David Perkins, *The Quest for Permanence*, p. 140.

In the gloom of evening, remember the marks made by
  your coming.
Hold off stroking your wearied limbs. Your final goal
Remains among the mountain ranges encircled by clouds.
The silent evening mist, far from the foothills and the
  wood's edge,
Slowly and tidelike drowns this wild plain, this wasted sky.
Your small solitary shadow faces the dark blind road ahead,
Like the ship that has lost its compass in the fury of the
  sea.
And there is the terror of the dark night, the bone-chilling
  howls of wolves,
The foxes' cries, the hawks' screams, and coiled snakes
  among the tangled grass.

To retreat? The night has swallowed the bloodstained
  traces.
To fall? Who is to take over this burden of cowardice?
Surge forward, surge forward; dash asunder this sinister
  darkness.
Dash asunder all fear, fluctuation, cowardice, and pain.
The bloody trampling on the pointed thistles,
The sharp claws of crouching beasts, the writhing vipers
  in the underbrush.

Oh surge forward, courage; courage of the soul is the
  secret of victory.
See, at this moment when you decide to lose your life,
The thick fog already gives way to the steadfast light of
  heaven.
A curve of jadelike moon peeps through the clouds'
  openings,
And through the gauze-curtained window is seen the
  lovely smile of Beauty.
This is the acclaim of inspiration, the most gracious gift.
There the highest peak, your most desired high peak,
Now emerges before you, lovely as a lotus bud,
In the azure sky, in the moonlight, beautiful and sublime—
Mountain pilgrim, this miracle is the reward of your

pilgrimage!

The unusually long lines in this poem (eleven to fourteen characters per line in the original), together with the heavily stressed nouns and the density of imagery, produce a leaden, laborious movement of the pilgrim's ascent to the pinnacle. Here again the natural setting projects the poet's inner torment during the spiritual ascent. The pilgrimage to the mountain may be interpreted, too, as a metaphorical vehicle for the creative process. Hsü's dark strain is vividly implicit in the animal and birds of prey images (the serpents, hawks, and wolves). His mingling of abstract with concrete images is pronounced, and so is his skill for reinforcing a weaker, less tangible sensation with a strong kinesthetic or motor image: "dash asunder this sinister darkness" or, "the bloody trampling on the pointed thistles." The poem ends in a lyrical outburst as the poet anticipates the fulfillment of his desire to reach the peak and to see the moon emerging through the clouds like an exquisite lotus bud.

Chu Hsiang, a poet-critic, in his review of Hsü's first publication of verse criticized Hsü's faulty syntax and awkward phrasing.[21] In "Without Title" such faults leap to the eye. The opening two lines of the poem—"It is your duty, you, the shins and ankles of the mountain pilgrim, / To suffer the pain of thorns!"—in the Chinese (原是你的本分，朝山人的脛踝，這荊刺的傷痛) are clumsy and syntactically poor. Hsü occasionally omits verbs or part of a compound word: "Oh surge forward, courage; courage of the soul is the secret of victory." The defect here is not obvious in English translation. The use of *yung* 勇 "courage" in the phrase "courage of the soul" sounds abrupt and jarring to ears accustomed to the normal compound of *yung ch'i* 勇氣 or *yung kan* 勇敢, "courage." The phrase reads more like an English translation than an original. The same flaw appears in the use of *wen* 溫 "warmth," in place of its common compound *wen*

---

[21] Chu Hsiang, "P'ing Hsü Chih-mo te-shih," [Review of Hsü's collected poems], *The Short Story Magazine* 17, no. 1 (1926):1–11.

nuan 温暖 "warmth," below:

> Rarely is the night so serene,
> 難 得, 夜 這 般 的 清 静,
> Rarely is the stove so warm.
> 難 得, 爐 火 這 般 的 温.

Wanting to preserve the same number of characters as in the preceding line, Hsü omitted the second character of the compound.

Another flaw is Hsü's overfondness for inversion, which often results in awkwardness and affectation:

> Facing her, I turned my body around.
> 向 着 她, 我 轉 過 身 去

And

> Fluttering in the green grass, her pure white attire.
> 在 青 草 裏 飄 拂, 她 的 潔 白 的 裙 衣.

These defects fortunately are not so prevalent in his later works. In general, Hsü has an admirable command of his language, including the vernacular, the classical, and even some local dialects, which he explores with deftness in poems such as "A Golden Trace of Light" and "Peaceful Circumstances."

The romantic-quest theme is explored in quite a different mold in "Go Away, World, Go Away" (1925):

> Go away, world, go away!
> I stand alone on the lofty mountain peak;
> Go away, world, go away!
> I face the infinite blue canopy of sky.
>
> Go away, youth, go away!
> And be buried with the sweet grass of the valley.
> Go away, youth, go away!

Throw your sorrow to the crows of the darkening sky.

Go away, country of dreams, go away!
   I have scattered the jade cup of imagination.
Go away, country of dreams, go away!
   Smiling, I accept the congratulations of winds and
     waves.

Go away, all in all, go away!
   Before me is the lofty peak piercing heaven.
Go away, all in all, go away!
   Before me is the infinite Infinity!

The same symbol of the mountain peak recurs in this exuberant lyric of a mystical union with nature. The poem, though not innocent of triteness and banalities ("infinite Infinity"), vibrates with romantic abandon; it is a psalm of joy, celebrating the power, mystery, and beauty of nature. Hsü believed nature to be one of the two greatest teachers of mankind, the other being life itself. In this poem he seeks union with nature in order to forget all the pains and sorrows, worldly aspirations, youthful delusions, and torments of the soul. Like a true Taoist poet, he desires to "transform into dust, the formless dust, / Following the Creator's wheel, onward, onward."

In his search for the realization of his ideal, Hsü is determined to sacrifice everything, even life. He once wrote: "The religious ascetics sacrifice themselves for the principles of goodness; the scientists sacrifice themselves for the principle of truth; the artists for beauty. The outcome of all these sacrifices is this culture of ours."[22] This strong conviction is reflected in "Seeking a Bright Star" (1925).

I ride on a limping blind horse,
   Spurring it on into the dark night;
   Spurring it on into the dark night,
I ride on a limping blind horse.

[22] Hsü, *Hsü Chih-mo ch'üan-chi*, 3:178.

I dash into this long dark night,
  Seeking a bright star;
  Seeking a bright star,
I dash into this vast darkness of the wild.

Exhausted, exhausted is my riding animal,
  Yet the star remains invisible;
  Yet the star remains invisible,
Exhausted, exhausted is the body on the saddle.

Now the sky reveals a crystallike radiance,
  An animal falls in the wild;
  A corpse lies in the dark night,
Now the sky reveals a crystallike radiance.

Hsü uses here the enclosure pattern of the quatrain form that he favors for his shorter lyrics. The rhyme scheme of *a b b a, c d d c, e b b e, d e e d,* is honored throughout the poem. In this reflective piece, Hsü seems to think in Platonic terms of the permanence to which he aspires. Like all Platonists, including Shelley, he habitually symbolizes this transcendental reality by an image of light. The star, with its associations of steadfastness, permanence, and something beyond the world of flux and mutability, became Hsü's persistent symbol of man's aspiration for the Absolute. For the imperfect perceptive power of men to penetrate Truth—the star that shines eternally in the sky, though invisible to human eyes during the day—Hsü uses the limping blind horse. The dark night and the wilderness represent the searcher's spiritual state of mind—his utter aloneness in his quest for truth. The poem ends with the ultimate revelation of the star and the death of the apocryphal horse and the seeker, the supreme sacrifice every devotee of truth should be willing to make.

The symbol of the star appears in another poem, "I Have One Love" (1925?).

I have one love—

I love the bright stars in the skies,
I love their radiance;
    There is no such divine light in the world.

On a cold late winter evening,
On a lonely gray early morning,
On the oceans, on a mountaintop after the storm—
    There is always one star, a myriad of stars!

Friends of grass and flowers by the hill stream,
Joy of small children on a high tower,
Lamp and compass of travelers,
    The eternal spirit shines miles, miles away!

I have a shattered soul,
Like a heap of shattered crystal,
Scattered among withered grasses of the wild—
    Drinking every sip of your busy sparkle.

Life's icy coldness and tender warmth
I have tasted, I have endured;
The autumn crickets cry under the steps; at times
    Have caused my heart to ache, forced my tears to fall.

I lay bare my naked heart,
To offer my love to a skyful of stars;
Let life be illusory or real,
Let earth exist or be destroyed.
    There are always the bright stars in the infinite void.

These stars are conceived as something to be sought for their own sake. They are desirable because they are an integral part of nature, which is good and beautiful, like the small flowers and grass by the hill stream; because they are the "joy of small children" and the "lamp and compass" of weary travelers on the dark journey of life; and above all, because they offer something permanent to us who live in a mortal world of constant flux.

In many of Hsü's works, the themes of love and faith occupy a place at least as prominent as that of the romantic-quest themes. One of Hsü's symbols of love and faith is the child. He may have been inspired by Wordsworth's concept of the child as being "possessed by certain essential truths which are lost as we grow older," or by Shelley's child symbol of love that has in it "a strong power to convert or transform things evil or ugly."[23] Hsü's concept might also be traced to Lao-tzu's comparison of the cultivated sage with an infant. Whatever the source, his own words remain the most pertinent. In one of his talks to a group of young students, Hsü told a story about a child planting flowers on the sandy beach and pointed out its significance:

This is not only a beautiful but a powerful symbol, because it tells us that the fountain of creativity lies in our simple faith within ourselves. This simple, pure, and spontaneous genuineness is the most permanent thing in life: no one can scorch it, no winds can blow it down, no waves can wash it off, no darkness dim it. The flowers planted on earth may be destroyed, but the "Truth" in the child's love for flowers and his faith in planting them has a life that is eternal and infinite.[24]

The child is the central symbol in "There Is Thee in His Eyes" (1926?).

I climbed over countless mountain cliffs,
Thorns tore my clothing;
I gazed beyond the distant skies—
O God, I see Thee not!

I dug under the thick crust of earth,
Disrupting the old homes of snakes and dragons;
I cried in the bottomless pool—
O God, I hear Thee not!

[23] David Perkins, *The Quest for Permanence*, pp. 74, 155.
[24] Hsü, *Hsü Chih-mo ch'üan-chi*, 3:176.

> I saw a small child by the roadside,
> Lively, lovely, and clad in tattered clothes,
> Calling to his mother, his eyes gleaming with love—
> O God, Thou art in his eyes!

In "On the Train" (1926?) it is the sudden bursting forth of a child's song that transforms the dreary scene:

> Suddenly from the dark corner a song
> Rises: like a mountain stream, like a morning bird, honey-
>   sweet, clear and high;
> Like a blaze that illuminates the entire desert,
> Its straight golden flame shining in the remote valley.
> .   .   .   .
>
> She sings and sings till every place on the way is filled
>   with light,
> And the bright moon and stars tumble out from the
>   clouds.
> Flowers, lanternlike, vie with each other on the branches,
> And the splendid grass roots gently shake the blithe green
>   fireflies!

The child's song is like the song of Keats's nightingale; it enables the passenger to forget "the weariness, the fever, and the fret" of the fatiguing journey. And like Shelley's skylark, the song of the innocent child has a transcendental quality that transports its listeners to a world far removed from reality. It is something the human soul is forever aspiring to attain—that sudden vision of encountering grace and truth. For the description of the song, Hsü combines elusive sensory images (blaze, flame, moon) with more tangible subjects (desert, flowers, green grass) to gain solidity for his ethereal vision.

In "The Wide Sea" (1926?), the poet compares himself with a child determined to translate his vision of truth into reality:

I do not need the wide sea,
I have no wish to fly a large kite
To tease all the winds in the sky;
  I only want a whole moment,
  I only want a dot of light,
  I only want a thread of opening—
  And like a small child crawling
  Before a window in a dark room,
  I look toward the western horizon for that eternal
    thread of
Opening, one dot of
Light, one whole
Moment.

Hsü's idealism and individualism, naïve as they seem to be, are inspired by a compassionate intelligence and an intellect conscious of reality. His Shelleyan vision of the "white radiance of eternity" is the more comprehensible to us because it grew out of his realization of the "dome of many-coloured glass," which remains beautiful and good in spite of its "stain." As one of his reviewers rightly pointed out, Hsü, though dedicated to the "search of the sublime and the ecstatic, something above the ordinary," was never "of the other world."[25] His Confucian background may account for the strong strain of stoicism and moral sense that runs through his works. His constant assertion of man's lack of moral strength and faith within himself is eloquent testimony to his Confucian heritage. Like Wen I-to, Hsü was obsessed with the world's wrongs. This obsession became the more accentuated because he felt himself, with his imperfections, to blame for them.

Hsü's desire to come to grips with actuality, however painful, is conveyed in his more realistic poems of social significance, such as "Serves You Right, Beggar!" (1925?):

  "Kindhearted ma'ams and charitable masters,"
    The north wind like a sharp knife pierces his face;

[25] Kai-yu Hsu, trans. and ed., *Twentieth Century Chinese Poetry*, p. 71.

"Please give me a little of your leftovers."
   A lump of blurred black shadow presses close to the
      gate.

"Have pity, my prosperous master, I am dying of hunger."
   Inside the gate are laughter, a red stove, jade cups.
"Have pity, my blessed master, I am freezing of cold."
   Outside the gate the wind mocks, "Serves you right,
      beggar!"

Like the beggar, I am but a heap of trembling black
   shadow,
   Wriggling like a worm on the front street of humanity;
Like him, I only want a bit of warmth and sympathy,
   To shield what's left of my maimed body.

But there is only the tightly closed heavy gate: no one
   cares!
On the street, only the wind's mocking, "Serves you
   right, beggar!"

In this modified sonnet it is the abstract theme of the suffering
of humanity, not of any one particular person, that Hsü attempts to elucidate. For that reason, no naturalistic description
of the beggar is supplied; he is "a lump of blurred black shadow," or "a heap of trembling black shadow/Wriggling . . . on
the front street of humanity." The image of the black shadow,
vague and abstract, is joined with the weight of the images
"lump" and "heap"; the solidity of the front street is combined
with the abstract term "humanity." This welding of two contrasting elements is characteristic of Hsü.

   Related to this poem in theme but more successful in method
is "A Picture of Happy Poverty" (1927?).

There is a large pile of newly dumped garbage before the
   lane.
Probably it is from behind those vermilion gates.
They are not all ashes. Still some good cinders left.

Not all bones. There is marrow in them;
Perhaps there are even slivers of meat.
There are rags and untorn newspapers;
Two, three lamp wicks, a few cigarette butts.

This garbage pile is a gold mine.
It is full of crouching gold diggers:
A squadron of dirty rags, tattered pants and jackets,
One, two, countless humped backs.
Young girls, middle-aged women, old grandmas are all
    there,
One hand clutching a basket, the other holding a tree
    branch,
Their waists bending low, not a cough, not a chatter;
No argument, only silent poking and picking from the
    pile,
Poking in the front, poking in the back, poking from both
    sides;
Shoulder to shoulder, head to head, poking and picking.
Grandma finds a strip of cloth. What a fine piece of cloth!
Some are collecting cinders, a ground filled with cinders.
"Mother," a girl shouts, "I found a piece of fresh meat
    bone!
    We can cook it with bean cakes. Won't it be nice?"
One file of rags, like a moving merry-go-round lantern,
Going around and around and around.
The middle-aged women, the young girls, the grandmas,
There are also a few yellow dogs mingling in their midst
    to add to the gaiety.

The ironic overtones of this poem with its surface levity are
beautifully sustained from the initial line to the end. The casual
conversational cadence is in keeping with the loose poetic structure and fluid movement. The narrator of the poem, observing
from afar this little picture of "happy poverty," never intrudes
with didactic comment or sentimental moralizing. Again, the
element of abstraction is registered in the very title and in the
portraiture of the characters. Except for the little girl, the

dramatic personae are more phantoms than full-bodied beings: Hsü is portraying the poverty-stricken mass of humanity, not its individual members. The poem ends with the familiar Chinese lantern; its associations of festivity and gracious living subtly recall the life "behind the vermilion gates," where the garbage came from. The comparison of human characters circling around a garbage pile with paper figures moving involuntarily inside a lighted Chinese merry-go-round lantern is both dramatic and exquisitely realized. This is not a bitter or despairing poem, nor is it sentimental, though it could easily have degenerated into sentimentality in less expert hands. The narrator offers no resolution, sounds no indignant protest; he supplies only the detached observation of a bystander. Beneath the seeming indifference, the almost whimsically playful surface, however, one senses a delicate pathos, a poignancy of feeling, and a profound awareness of the world's wrongs.

Hsü Chih-mo has been described by Robert Payne in *The White Pony* as "the brilliant expounder of a culture he had derived from Cambridge," but his indebtedness to his own tradition was equally vital. With sensitiveness and skill he blends the East and West, the conventional with the new; the result is a poetic voice that is at once familiarly captivating and refreshingly different. He opened up fresh thematic and technical possibilities for the new poets of China. Hsü Chih-mo may not have been the most original or the greatest poet of his generation, but he was certainly one of the most thoroughly romantic.

Feng Chih (1905–)

A native of the northern province of Hopeh, Feng Chih attended Peking University and went abroad after his graduation. He studied German literature and philosophy at Heidelberg, and became particularly fond of the poetry of Goethe, Hölderlin, and Rilke. His translation of Rilke's sonnets was highly praised as belonging to the best achievements of modern Chinese poetry.

Feng's publications are few. In 1927, before he went abroad, his first volume of poems, *The Song of Yesterday*, appeared; it was succeeded by another, *The Northern Wanderings*, in 1930. Then came the sonnets of 1941, which mark the high point of his poetic career. His last collection, *Poems of Ten Years*, contains his postwar work (1947–57). In this latest volume, written exclusively "in praise of the Communist party of China and the great events that occurred under the leadership of the Communist party . . .,"[26] one finds no trace of the poetic voice that speaks with such insight and artistry in the sonnets.

In the preface to his *Selected Works* (1955), Feng Chih expressed regret over his slim creative output. Certainly he was not a prolific writer, but in the little he produced there are signs of a rare poetic gift. His essential poetry is of an introspective, private nature, poetry that reaches out for values and metaphysical assurances. Although Feng was living in an era of overwhelming political and social upheaval, one seldom finds social sloganizing in his early work. There are few overt statements or comments on the problems of his day. In the same preface Feng Chih wrote his own criticism of these early works: "What these poems expressed was a narrow emotion: the sorrows of an individual. If they do contain significance of any sort, it is the frustration of youth after the May Fourth Movement that may be discerned from them."[27] In an article that appeared in the Communist literary journal, *Wen-i pao*, in 1958, Feng Chih further criticized these poems as

> Pale and without vigor,
> Dark and without luster,
> Dry and without blood and flesh.

This apologetic tone and the severe self-criticism are not unexpected from a poet who now exists in a climate that extols

---

[26] Feng Chih, *Shih-nien shih-ch'ao* [Poems of ten years], p. 2.
[27] Feng Chih, *Feng Chih shih-wen hsüan-chi* [Selected works of Feng Chih], p. 1.

collectivism.

Like Hsü Chih-mo, Feng Chih wrote in a strongly romantic vein. The themes of the short lyrics and ballads that comprise the bulk of his works in this period revolve around frustration, loneliness, nature, death, love, and other familiar subjects of universal appeal.

THE SNAKE   (1923?)

My loneliness is a long snake,
Quiet and speechless.
If you happen to see it in your dream,
Oh by no means be startled.

It is my loyal companion,
Its heart suffers from burning homesickness:
It yearns for that lush plain,
Those crow-black strands of silk on your head!

And like the moonbeams, lightly
It will pass by your side
To steal your dream for me,
A dream that is a flaming crimson flower.

Feng Chih, because of his concern with the formal aspects of poetry and his extraordinary success in using the sonnet form, has been classified as a Formalist poet like Wen I-to and Hsü Chih-mo. "The Snake," written in the stanzaic mold, demonstrates his preference for a more formal poetic structure; his felicitous handling of alliteration and rhyme (both internal and end) enriches the verbal texture of the verse. The lush images are reminiscent of Wen I-to's imagery. Like Wen, Feng habitually combines old images (the crow-black strands of silk as a metaphor for the beloved's hair) with his own more daring yet accurate images (the snake and the flaming crimson flower). His fondness for landscape images, which are important in his sonnets, is already present in his use of the "lush plain." One of the constant problems for a poet is the expression of abstract ideas in concrete terms. Many romantic poets were content to state these thoughts abstractly, with the result that their poetry too often deteriorated into vagueness and generalities. Feng Chih was among the few who were able to escape this pitfall by approaching the problem in terms of concrete physical symbols.

Traces of past lyrics and historical allusions are found in some of Feng's works: for example, the cries of the cicadas and crickets in "The Rainy Night," and the proud lady who loves to hear the sound of tearing silk in "What Can Make You Happy?" Although there are moments when the poetry is burdened with excessive emotional weight, in general these early lyrics display the poet's sense of classical balance and the reticence which characterize his later works, especially the mature sonnets.

Feng's long narrative poems share with his short lyrics some of the same distinctive qualities: the sensitive artistry, the verbal delicacy and subtle touch, the fondness for romantic settings welded with a respect for classical balance and harmony. These early narratives ("The Flute Player," "Tapestry," and "The Silkworm Horse") show Feng's remarkable mastery of the ballad form and reveal many common ballad features, such as the romantic love theme and exotic staging, the strong folk flavor, the dramatic presentation, and the expansive use of dialogues, refrains, and supernatural elements.

For "The Flute Player" (1923) and "Tapestry" (1924), Feng employs the popular ballad stanza of four lines, rhyming mostly *a b c d*; but for "The Silkworm Horse" (1925), he uses the stanzaic pattern of eight lines, with the exception of the last three stanzas, each of which contains four lines. The poems vary in length, and rhyme is often approximate, a liberty allowed in the ballad meter.

Of the three, "The Silkworm Horse" has a special appeal because of the strange story of the ballad itself. At the end of his poem Feng uses an extract from the *Sou Shen Chi* to explain the background of the tale:

According to legend, there was a silkworm maiden, Ts'an Nü, whose father was kidnaped; only the father's horse remained. The mother said, "To whoever can bring back the father I shall give my daughter in marriage." The horse heard this. It broke away the halter by which it was tied and galloped off. In a few days the father returned riding on the horse. The mother told the father about her promise but he refused to give the daughter to the horse. The horse roared furiously and the father killed it. Then he skinned the horse and left the skin to dry outside the courtyard. The skin suddenly wrapped around the girl and disappeared. Later the girl was found on a mulberry tree, transformed into a silkworm.[28]

Feng Chih dramatizes this ancient legend in the form of a song sung by a minstrel to the girl who tends the silkworms. He has eliminated the role of the mother.

> When the spring clouds color the sky's rim,
> When the red flowers are in bloom along the stream,
> When love within my heart becomes a flame,
> I walk softly toward her window.
> I say, "O maiden, the silkworms have just begun their
>   first sleep;
> Your love, has it ever felt weary?
> If you weep upon hearing my song,
> You need not lean out of your window to ask who I am."

> At that time when the years were truly old and
>   distant,
> On the road, a few carts; over the water, no boats.
> Oh, those old and distant years
> Have given me so much sorrow, so much grief!
> There was a poor girl, young,
> With no mother and her father far away from home.
> At the time of parting, the father said to her,
> "Take good care of these fields."

[28] Ibid., pp. 36–44.

In the courtyard there stood a white steed.
The father with his eyes on his daughter, his fingers
    pointing at the steed, said,
"It will willingly help you to plow the fields.
It will always be your loyal companion."
The daughter did not understand the meaning of
    parting.
She did not know where her father had gone—to the
    land's end or to the sea's edge?
There was still the same wind, still the same rain.
But the fields, they were more wasted every day.

"O father, when will you come back?
Separation is indeed like a vast boundless sea.
Horse, could you take me to the other shore
To find my father's smiling face?"
She gazed at the faded flowers, the withered leaves;
And gently she stroked the steed's mane.
"If only there was a fine youth,
He would surely be willing to search everywhere for
    me!"

She spoke within her heart.
Over the horizon floated the sun, almost setting,
Like a smiling youth
Stirring before her.
Suddenly a loud clear cry
Woke her from her daydream.
The steed had already plunged toward the distant
    plain,
As the floating image vanished before her eyes!

When the soft warm willow catkins gather into clusters,
When the colored butterflies flutter in the air,
When the flame is ablaze in my bosom,
I walk softly toward her window, whispering,
"O maiden, the silkworms have just begun their third
    sleep,
Your love, has it ever felt weary?

If you weep upon hearing my song,
You need not lean out of the window to ask who I am."

The thorns spread over the fields and gardens,
Sorrows held her days and nights.
And before her deserted window,
There were only a few noisy sparrows.
One day, as she leaned against the window, lost in
    thought,
On the road the dust started to rise in the distance
(She had long since abandoned this dream,
This dream had gone beyond her dream).

Oh now the dust was rising in the distance.
The steed returned with her lost father!
The father rode on the back of the steed.
The neighing of the horse was a melodious song!
The father kissed the daughter,
The daughter gently brushed away her father's travel
    dust;
But the horse only knelt by her side,
Soaked through with sweat.

The father was calm as the vast sea,
The daughter, a clear radiant moon;
The moon, having drowned in the deep bosom of the
    sea,
Had dissolved all the sorrows of the world.
But the horse, kneeling by her bedside,
Wept silently throughout the night.
His eyes were like two shining lanterns,
"O maiden, for you I have gone to the far end of the
    world!"

Petting the horse's head, she said to him,
"You'd better go to the fields to work!
Don't act so foolishly;
Beware, father might kill you!"
The steed refused to eat fresh hay,

Nor would he take clear water.
He either gazed at her face and sighed,
Or fell into half sleep by her side.

When the yellow *miwu* plants wither,
When the sea swallows robed in black are flying everywhere,
When the dying flame within my heart still flickers,
I walk softly toward her window, saying,
"O maiden, the silkworms have just begun their spinning,
Your love, has it ever felt weary?
Oh, if you only weep upon hearing my song,
Then you need not lean out of the window and ask who
    I am."

In the dark night, empty and desolate,
Outside the window the storm was raging;
And on the wall was hung a horse's skin.
It was her only companion.
"O dear father, tonight
Where are you in your wandering?
You killed the steed,
And I am left alone and afraid!

"O dear father,
The lightning flashes, the thunder roars,
And you have deserted your daughter.
Oh how fearful, how lonely and sad I am!"
"Dear maiden,
Don't feel lonely or sad, and please have no fear!
I shall keep your body away from harm,
I shall take care of you through eternity."

From out of the horse's skin sounded these solemn
    words.
Her heart trembled, her hair quivered,
The lightning pierced through her body,
The skin quickened and stirred with the thundering;
With the wind it moaned sadly,
With the rain it cried sadly,

"I shall take care of you through eternity,
If you only would rest in sleep now!"

In a wink of time, there emerged the image of the
   youth,
In a wink of time, the steed wildly charged into the
   distance:
And in that instant before the earth crumbled,
The horse's skin tightly wound round her body!

"Maiden, my song is not yet sung to its end.
Alas, the string is broken;
I fearfully sit before your window,
To continue the last part of my song."

In a wink of time, all winds and rains were stilled.
The bright moon had consumed the thunder and
   lightning,
The steed's skin wound round the girl's body,
Suddenly the two were transformed into a cocoon,
Silk-white as snow under the moon.

The legend has been interpreted conventionally as the sacrifice made by a devoted daughter, and the girl is regarded as a
symbol of filial piety. In Feng's version, the girl assumes a much
more important position: it is the desire to please her and to do
what she wishes that motivates the steed's action. Moreover, it
is her failure to respond to love that leads to the ballad's sur-
prise denouement. By this change, Feng made romantic love
the central theme for his work. Unrequited love is subtly implied in the devotion of the minstrel to the girl who tends the
silkworms and serves as the larger framework for the main love
story. The two stories are linked by the image of the silkworms,
a conventional symbol of self-consuming passion in traditional
poetry as seen in Li Shang-yin's famous line, "The spring silkworm only stops its spinning when dead." In concealing the
outcome of the minstrel's love for the girl, Feng offers room

for imaginative speculation after the violent ending.

The poem has weaknesses: overuse of repetition, uneven poetic quality, stereotyped dialogues, and flaccid rhythm. Its strength lies in the skillful blending of human and supernatural elements, in the hauntingly mysterious atmosphere so well maintained throughout the poem, and in the suspense that holds the reader's attention to the very climax. The ballad has a sophistication that does not violate the basic simplicity of the form. It contains a more suggestive imagery and a more complex emotion than one ordinarily finds in the folk ballad. In this particular piece Feng Chih has written a modern poem which possesses not only the diction and rhythm of the medieval folk ballad, but its mentality—its awed violence, mystery, and the thrill of the supernatural.

In contrast to these romantic narratives, Feng Chih wrote one long realistic poem, "Northern Wanderings" (1928), a chronicle of his impressions while journeying to Manchuria. Departing from his familiar modes (ballads, lyrics, and sonnets), Feng uses a free-verse form with irregular verse lines and a rhythm of slightly heightened speech. The poem is divided into twelve sections: "Prelude," "Departure," "On Board the Train," "Harbin," "The Park," "Café," "Mid-Autumn," "Cathedral," "Autumn already . . . ," "Pompeii," "Memorial Service," and "Prologue." Each section deals with a particular aspect of the arduous journey, and ends with the plaintive refrain of how "dark and cold" everything is. The entire poem is a painful account of the traveler's response to the ugliness, vulgarity, and lonely tedium of life in a corrupt urban society. The tone of weary resignation, mingled with nostalgia and regret, reflects this response. Echoes of other poets seem abundant here. The conversational lyricism, the use of contrast and juxtaposition, the depiction of the most appalling aspects of a metropolis, and above all, the bleak view of the modern world betray the influence of the author of *The Waste Land*. "Northern Wandering" embodies Feng Chih's full consciousness of the contemporary world's spiritual malaise. Like T. S. Eliot, all Feng can see during his trip is "an endless stretch of waste land" where "not a single flower can ever bloom, no spring can survive. . . ." Set against the background of remembered beauty and grandeur is the cheap café, the deserted cathedral, and a wintry park in Manchuria's great metropolis, Harbin, a city which is neither East nor West, a city in which there are

> Beastlike motor cars
> Marauding in the streets,
> Bony horses pulling broken carts,
> Shrieking with their necks outstretched.
> Jewish banks, Greek restaurants,
> Japanese drifters, White Russian brothels,
> All gather in this strange place
> With complete complacency.
> Rich Chinese merchants
> With their fat smug smiles,
> Concubines in outlandish foreign clothes,
> Pasty-faced youths in their melon-shaped caps,
> . . . .
> And prostitutes harboring poisonous germs
> Gaudily strolling on the streets.
> Am I wandering in hell?
> Sinking deeper and deeper at every step,
> . . . .
> The sky is permeated with darkness and cold.
> . . . .
> I stroll in front of the cathedral,
> But God has long lost His dignity.
> The bells sound stricken in the sunset
> As if uttering, "My glory has long vanished."
> Only a poor musician plucking a broken string
> Begging alms from the passers-by.
> . . . .
> This is a sick place,
> The sound of sickness fills every corner;
> No bright clouds fill the skies,
> Only gray ones, dark and cold, dark and cold.
> . . . .

Here sins are deeper than Pompeii's,
Here people are seducing their wives,
Here people are cheating their lovers,
Here men only see gold and silver;
Here men are clothed in germs.
Here daughters curse their loving mothers,
Here men corrupt their own grandchildren.
Not a speck of truth can be found here.
There are only paper flowers, rouged red lips,
Not one single star can be seen,
Not a little bit of innocence.

.   .   .   .

Look at these men and women cuddling together
In this last twilight of the universe,
Hastening to their final destruction, like old Pompeii.

.   .   .   .

Tomorrow, all is changed to dust and ash.
Sun and moon have lost their luster, only darkness and
    cold.

Feng Chih is a lyric poet of simple sensuous verse and a bal-
ladeer of genuine distinction, but as a sonneteer in modern
Chinese verse he is unsurpassed. The sonnet is a compact form
concerned with a single thought or emotion. Normally limited
to fourteen iambic lines, it is divided into two distinct portions:
the major division or the octave, consisting of eight lines, and
the minor division or sestet, consisting of six lines. There are
two outstanding sonnet patterns: the Petrarchan and the
Shakespearean. The former, also called the Italian sonnet,
originated in Florence in the twelfth century and was later
perfected by Petrarch. Its rhyme scheme is *a b b a, a b b a, c d c,
c d c.* The Shakespearean sonnet has three quatrains and a couplet at the end, with a rhyme scheme of *a b a b, c d c d, e f e f, g g.*
But fidelity to these models, especially to the rhyme schemes,
is seldom complete. The variations are so numerous that the
force of a model is hardly recognizable at times.

Like Hsü Chih-mo, Feng Chih adopted the external form of

the foreign model. Although he does not follow the strict iambic pentameter lines, he remains faithful to a completely balanced sonnet form consisting of two quatrains and two tercets. Feng uses both short lines (six to eight syllables) and long lines (nine to twelve syllables). His rhyme schemes are also more flexible. Usually he uses four sets of rhymes (often approximate) for the quatrains and another one or two sets for the tercets. He likes to end the sonnet with the rhyme used in the first quatrain in order to effect a closer unity of the two divisions.

The celebration of great men has been a common theme for sonnets in European literature. Likewise, Feng Chih wrote several sonnets in praise of his "heroes": the well-known educator and scholar in modern China, Ts'ai Yüan-p'ei; the illustrious contemporary writer, Lu Hsün; and two of his favorite poets, Tu Fu and Goethe, as well as the noted impressionist painter, Vincent Van Gogh. All are written in a tone of quiet admiration, almost reverential at times, and they are given a sense of immediacy and intimacy by being addressed directly to the deceased. There is tenderness without sentimentality. The language is plain and conversational, now and then highlighted by the imaginative forging of metaphor and simile.

Sonnet XIV. VAN GOGH
Your passion strikes fire wherever you go.
You set a bouquet of yellow flowers ablaze in the sun,
And kindle the darkly somber yews.
Under the fiercely burning sun,

The passer-by also becomes a flame,
Calling and appealing to the heights.
But a small solitary tree in early spring,
A small courtyard of a prison,

And men peeling potatoes with bent heads
In a dark room: all these
Are like ice frozen in eternity.

Among these you have painted
Drawbridges and light boats: did you wish
To ferry over some unfortunate passengers?

This impressionistic sonnet with its ecstatic play of light
would have pleased Van Gogh, whose intense vision is recaptured here. The desolation of the poor is the more moving when
contrasted with the vibrant yellow flowers and the yew trees
ablaze under the sun. Feng's recurring image of fire or flame
symbolizes passion and the enduring essence of life. The pensive
rhetorical question at the close reflects the poet's own profound
feelings toward the poor and the desolate, the disinherited and
unfortunate inhabitants of the earth.

Sonnet XII. TU FU

You suffered and endured starvation in deserted villages,
You thought often of death in the ditch,
Yet you still go on singing sad songs
For the magnificent defeat of men:

Young men died, wounded on the battleground,
Bright stars fell on the horizon,
Ten thousand horses vanished in the clouds.
To these you dedicated your whole life.

Your poverty sparkles and shines
Like the tattered garment of a saint,
And even the bare thread that now remains

Holds the infinite power of God.
All crowns before its radiance
Appear the more pitiful in their countenance.

Not only to accept and endure the terrors, the sorrow and suffering in life, but also to rise above them and praise them—this
accomplishment is the glory and triumph of Tu Fu, and is the
deeper meaning painfully gleaned from Feng Chih's experience

of war and its terrible waste. This sonnet recalls Rainer Maria Rilke's lines from the *Duino Elegies*:

> For beauty is nothing but the beginning of terror we can
>   just barely endure,
> And we admire it so because it calmly disdains to destroy
>   us.
> Every angel is terrible.[29]

The image of the tattered garment of a saint with its reference to Christ is both apt and imaginative; Tu Fu was traditionally known as the *Shih Sheng*, the Poet-Saint.

The sense of loss brought forth by the seeming meaninglessness and emptiness of our lives invokes Feng Chih's query into the ultimate truth of life:

> Sonnet XV
>
> Behold this caravan of horses
> Bringing merchandise from faraway places,
> So does the water washing up mud and sand
> From some unknown distant land.
>
> The wind from a thousand miles away
> Has carried back the sighs of another country.
> We have crossed so many mountains and rivers,
> Holding them for a moment, losing them in another.
>
> Like a bird soaring high in the sky,
> Seeming to rule supreme,
> Yet forever filled with a fear of loss.
>
> What, then, is the truth?
> From faraway lands nothing can be brought,
> From here nothing can be carried away.

Many of Feng Chih's sonnets are moments or scenes of meditation which the poet with great artistry fashions into concise

---

[29] Rainer Maria Rilke, *Duino Elegies*, p. 3.

memorable lines that convey his innermost thoughts. One persistent theme in these sonnets is the fundamental unity of creation, the oneness of man and the natural universe, strikingly set forth in Sonnet XVI:

> Standing side by side on this high mountain peak,
> We become the boundless distant landscape,
> We become the broad and open plain before us
> And the crisscrossing paths upon the plains.
>
> What roads, what waterways are not related?
> What wind, what cloud do not echo each other?
> The cities, the hills, and the water that we have passed
> Are now all within us.
>
> Our growing, our grieving,
> Is a pine on a certain hillside,
> A mist over a certain city.
>
> We follow the winds, we follow the flowing water,
> Becoming the crisscrossing paths on the plains,
> Becoming the passers-by on the paths.

Like Rilke, Feng is especially fond of using landscape images. The crisscrossing paths, the waterways, the plain become the symbolic prospect of the poet's inner life. Underneath a multiplicity of correspondences the poet finds unity. Baudelaire's influence seems to be mingled with that of Taoism here. The same theme, the same contemplative tone and nature imagery come to the fore in Sonnet XVII, but here there is an added sense of human relatedness and a belief that in the human mind the past comes to join the present:

> You once said that I love to gaze at the plain,
> Its many small paths so full of life.
> The footfalls of many nameless passers-by
> Have trodden such lively pathways.

So too on the plains of our mind,
There are many winding small paths;
But those who have once passed on them
Are now forever gone, no one knows where.

The lonely children, the white-haired couples,
The young men and women,
And the friends now dead, all of them, for us

Have once walked along these pathways:
In memory of their footfalls
Let us allow no weeds to grow on these small paths.

Implicit in this sonnet is Feng's concern with the continuation of meanings from the past into the present and on into the future. The sonnet illuminates the interrelation of all time and the existence of a timeless instant that transcends the temporal.

Feng Chih is deeply conscious of the aloneness of men. The soul is solitary; "every man is an island" holds just as much truth for him as "no man is an Island, entire of itself."

Sonnet VII

In the warm sunshine,
We come to the countryside,
Like separate rivers
Merging into one vast sea.

There is the same warning
Within our hearts,
The same destiny
On our shoulders.

We share the same God
Who cares for us all.
But when the dusk falls,

These parted roads
Again draw us back to ourselves,

And again we become separate rivers.

Here Feng seems to say that the eternity of man is found not only in the merging with the continuous life of the universe but in his own individuality. Solitude is as inevitable a human condition as fellowship.

In Sonnet V, "Venice," Feng Chih adds the warm touch of fraternal love to his personal theme of man's solitude. But again the basic aloneness of the individual is stressed, for when night comes, man has to face the dark alone.

> I can never forget
> That water-city in the West.
> It is a symbol of life—
> The gathering of thousands of solitudes.
>
> Every solitude is an island,
> Every island has become a friend:
> When you shake my hands,
> It is like a bridge across the water;
>
> When you smile at me,
> It is as though on the opposite island
> A window is suddenly opened.
>
> But wait till the night is deep and still,
> Only the closed window is to be seen,
> And on the bridge there is no trace of men.

In Sonnet XVIII Feng Chih expresses the idea that our lives are woven with the familiar and the strange; the past as well as the future is an integral part of our present:

> We often spend an intimate night
> In a strange room; how it looks
> During the day, we have no way of knowing.
> And of its past and future, we know even less.

The plain stretches endlessly beyond our window,
We vaguely remember the road on which
We have come in the dusk. That is all we know.
Tomorrow we leave; we shall not return.

Oh close your eyes! Let those intimate nights
And strange places be interwoven in our hearts:
Our life is like that plain beyond the window,

And on the misty plain, we recognize
A tree, a flash of light from the lake. And in its infinity
Are hidden the forgotten past and the dimly seen future.

Death holds no horror for the philosopher-poet. Feng Chih accepts its imminence as just another phenomenon of change in the universe and anticipates its coming with serenity. He probably has derived this wisdom from the Taoist philosopher Chuang Tzu, who believes that "things are under different species. They undergo changes from one form to another. Their beginning and end are like a circle, no part of which is any more the beginning than another part. This is called the Evolution of Nature."[30] Feng explores this theme of change or transformation time and again in his poems.

Sonnet II
Whatever may be shed from our bodies,
We let it turn to dust:
We prepare ourselves in this life
Like trees in autumn. One by one

The trees entrust their leaves and, later, flowers
To the autumn winds, that they may freely stretch
Their bodies in the cold winter. We too must prepare
Ourselves in nature; like the cicada,

Who throw their dead husks in mud and earth,
We prepare ourselves for

[30] Yu-lan Feng, *A History of Chinese Philosophy*, 1:226.

Our forthcoming death, like strands of melody

Shed from the body of music,
Leaving the hollow husk of song,
To be transformed into veins of silent blue hills.

Even the most insignificant events in our lives may hold an infinite wealth of meaning if we look deeper beneath their surface:

Sonnet XXVI

Day after day, we take the familiar path
To return to our dwelling place.
But in the forest are hidden
Many small paths, deep and strange.

Walking on a strange road, we are afraid
Lest we go too far astray, lost on our way.
But unexpectedly through the openings of trees
We suddenly come upon our house,

Like a new island rising above the horizon.
There are so many things around us,
Begging us to discover them:

Never think that all is already known;
When you touch your hair and skin at the time of death,
You may yet ask, "Whose body is this?"

If the early Feng Chih is essentially a romantic lyricist, the later Feng, as revealed in these sonnets, is a poet of rare sensitivity and meditative strength. He has the incomparable gift of endowing the commonplace with freshness and projecting universals out of the tedious routines of life. The sonnets have intellectual and spiritual validity as well as great artistry. Feng Chih belongs to the company of celebrated meditative poets that includes Rilke and, in his own tradition, Wang Wei.

5

The Symbolists

While the Formalists were brightening the poetic scene with their lute music, a new group of poets, the Symbolists, tried to impress their audience with exotic melodies. Li Chin-fa, its founder, elicited dismay and admiration by his shorthand kind of verse—elliptical and idiosyncratic—which frequently defies deciphering. Li came close to being a decadent; his poetry is weighted down with an obsessive feeling of ennui, of world-weariness, if not perverse sensuality. He sought to penetrate to the mystery of beauty and existence by way of symbols. Tai Wang-shu, a gentler and more musical Symbolist, strove to capture elusive moods by means of Charles Baudelaire's theory of *correspondances* between the senses. Although their influence on the native poets was hardly comparable to that of their counterparts abroad, they nonetheless left their distinctive mark on modern Chinese poetry.

Li Chin-fa (1900–)

Little is known of the life of Li Chin-fa, the founder of the Chinese Symbolist school of poetry and the "poet eccentric" of his generation. The fact that most of his collected poems are unavailable today makes any study or appraisal of his poetry exceedingly difficult.

A native of Kwangtung province, Li, as a young man, traveled in Europe in the twenties. During his stay in France, he became interested in French Symbolist poetry, which he sub-sequently introduced to China through his many translations and his own Symbolist poetry. After the twenties, he wrote more essays than verses. His last volume of collected works, *Tunes of Strange Lands* (1942), shows a shift toward a more conventional mode of expression. His other works include three volumes of poetry: *Light Rain* (1925), *I Sing for Happiness* (1926), and *The Long-Term Visitor and Hard Times* (1927). These highly unorthodox poetic products have shocked and baffled readers with their seemingly disjointed structures, medley of enigmatic images, and private symbolism. Nevertheless, they represent one of the three major schools of modern Chinese poetry in the twenties and early thirties.

Like his French predecessors, Li Chin-fa aspired to a new form of poetic expression, the invention of a special language of private symbols which would "alone be capable of expressing his unique personality or feelings." To evoke and intimate rather than to state directly was a primary aim of the Symbolists. "Difficult and odd" as it has been called, Li's poetry pointed "a new direction to the new poets in China in the 1920s."[1] It is the most defiant departure from tradition, and at the same time the most daring innovation, in the course of modern Chinese poetry.

Chu Tzu-ch'ing, the critic-poet, made the following observation on Li's symbolistic technique:

Li's poetry has no tangible organization. One may understand it in parts, but when the parts are put together, the meaning is lost. He is not concerned with meaning but in expressing sensibilities or feelings. His poems are like many small and big beads with the connecting thread deliberately hidden by the poet, who expects the reader to supply the missing link. This is the technique employed by the French Symbolists, and Li is the first to introduce it into modern Chinese poetry.[2]

[1] Kai-yu Hsu, trans. and ed., *Twentieth Century Chinese Poetry*, p. 161.
[2] Chu Tzu-ch'ing, ed., *Chung-kuo hsin-wen-hsüeh ta-hsi* [Compendium of modern Chinese literature], 8:7–8.

Chu cited Li's assertion of his primary aim in poetry: "to express the mocking mystery and mournful beauty of life" by means of suggestion, images, and symbols.

Su Hsüeh-lin, another contemporary commentator, singles out four characteristic features of Li's poetry: (1) vagueness and obscurity, (2) a supersensitivity in expressing "the true color of psychic art," (3) a deep sense of melancholy and decadence, and (4) exoticism. Speaking of Li's poetic techniques, she is impressed by his "extraordinary power of conceptual association," his "device of personification," and his "method of condensation"; these techniques she describes as the "secret of Symbolist poetry." She complains, however, that Li tends to overcondense, a flaw that renders his poetry awkward to read and incomprehensible.[3]

A recent reviewer of Li's poetry, Kai-yu Hsü, writes:

> Li Chin-fa . . . has acknowledged his debt to Verlaine and Mallarmé, but in his effort to deal with life only through symbols and images, he appears to have gone even farther than his French mentors. He seems to have assumed that outside of the world of impressions, which he captures with his symbols, no meaning exists. He presents a series of pictures, without so much as a string to thread them together for the benefit of the reader. If the reader fails to integrate the fragmentary pictures—some brilliant, some dull, some utterly incomprehensible—into a meaningful whole, Li declines responsibility by saying that life and reality are themselves fragmentary. . . .[4]

Some of the typical Symbolist techniques—suggestiveness, analogy, compression, stress on musical effects, synesthesia— are equally important in traditional Chinese poetry. Poets like Li Ho and Li Shang-yin of the late T'ang dynasty (tenth century A.D.) are particularly noted for their exploitation of these techniques. Their difficulty is none other than the familiar modern one of obscurity. Harold Acton, in his introduction to

---

[3] Ibid., pp. 29–30.
[4] Hsu, trans. and ed., *Twentieth Century Chinese Poetry*, p. xxix.

modern Chinese poetry, makes the perceptive observation:

> . . . the Confucian ancients, who never consciously allowed themselves to be swept away by impulse, . . . told of their emotions and experiences "not directly but allusively, under the guise of flower or bird." Hitherto evocation and suggestion had been, paradoxically, the most conspicuous features of Chinese poetry. As an aesthetic principle Verlaine's *"Pas de couleur, rien que la nuance"* was more Chinese than French in its general application.[5]

Indeed, a large body of Chinese traditional lyrics shares the Symbolists' devotion to subtleties of effect that are, in fact, often inherent in the language itself. It is precisely through these more familiar means that a fellow Symbolist, Tai Wang-shu, achieved his brand of symbolistic poetry and escaped the harsh criticisms heaped on Li Chin-fa.

In illustrating other parallels between the traditional Chinese poetry and the French Symbolist poetry, Robert Payne's comparison of Tu Fu with Baudelaire is illuminating:

> If one could compare Tu Fu with anyone—though he is incomparable—it would be with Baudelaire, for his strange suggestive images derived from poverty and spiritual exhaustion. He has Baudelaire's power of evoking the real terrors, the long nights, the cruelties, the starvations, the miseries of the common people; and there are lines of Baudelaire that read like translations of Tu Fu.

Payne concluded his comparisons of the two poets by saying:

> And like Baudelaire, too, he was possessed of an extraordinary tenderness and sensitivity, especially toward suffering, while at the same time and almost in the same breath he could evoke a sense of majesty and dignity and regal splendor. There were two worlds, and yet they were not incompatible: there was splendor in poverty and in death, and there was misery enough in the royal palaces

---

[5] Harold Acton and Ch'en Shih-hsiang, trans., *Modern Chinese Poetry*, p. 19.

during the wars. He described a princess: "her dignity so flaming that it burned your finger," but almost at the same time he wrote: "Do not let your tears fall.
Pick them up, drop by drop, from the floor.
Even if all your tears are drained away,
Neither heaven nor earth can help you."[6]

In spite of their striking resemblances, there is a fundamental difference between these two geniuses. Tu Fu's sensitivity to "suffering, terror, and death" stems from an intense moral conviction. A Confucian humanist, he accepted life's suffering with typical Confucian stoicism. He did not regard society as hostile, nor did he consider himself an exile as most of the French Symbolists did. Baudelaire, on the other hand, rebelled against the accepted standards. His poetry is a revolt against tradition, an escape as well as a "sacred ritual," a kind of religion to which he dedicated his life and service.[7] "Ugliness, cruelty, self-destruction, terror" are all included in Baudelaire's concept of beauty. His poetry is given "a new dimension, by enabling men to take a bold plunge into infernal depths, from which they could rise upward once again toward the Baudelairian dream of a consoling presence, feminine or divine."[8] It is this aesthetic and spiritual concept of poetry that has attracted moderns such as Wen I-to ("The Dead Water"), Hsü Chih-mo ("The Babe" and others), and Symbolist poets like Li Chin-fa.

In Li Chin-fa's poetry one discovers little concern for the musical quality and richness of sound effects that characterize, for example, the verse of the Symbolist Tai Wang-shu. Li Chin-fa is primarily preoccupied with the darker, harsher, and bolder aspects in symbolism. There is a notable absence of melodious lines so dear to readers attuned to the pure lyricism of old verse. Harsh sound is often employed deliberately to convey his modern sensibility, which is anything but soft and yielding.

[6] Robert Payne, ed., *The White Pony*, pp. 184–85.
[7] Arthur Symons, *The Symbolist Movement in Literature*, p. 5.
[8] Stanley Burnshaw, ed., *The Poem Itself*, p. 10.

It is with a strong sense of gloom and decadence that Li views life.

THOUGHTS   (1925?)
Like spoiled leaves splashing
  Blood on our
    Feet,

Life is but
  A smile on lips
  Of Death.

Beneath a half-dead moon,
  Now drinking, now singing,
    The sound of rent throat
Scatters in the north wind.
    Ah!
Go and caress your beloved.

Open your door and window,
  Make her shy and timid,
    Let road dust cover
      Her lovely eyes.

Is this timidity
And wrath of
    Life?
Like spoiled leaves splashing
  Blood on our
    Feet,

Life is but
  A smile on lips
  Of Death.

In this terse, death-haunted poem, Li combines the sinister and decadent side of Baudelaire with a compression reminiscent of Stephane Mallarmé and some of the traditional Chinese verse. Li also shares Mallarmé's effective distribution of words within the lines and stanzas. The harsh initials of the key words (often alliterative) such as *ts'an* 殘 "spoiled" or "withered," *tsien* 濺 "splash," *tsai* 載 a particle ("now . . . now"), and *lieh* 裂 "split" ("rent" in poem) give force to the images of violence, set the sharply edged tone, and convey the dissonance of the poem. Tension underlies the line immediately following the image of the sound of the splitting throat that scatters in the north wind: one senses a change in attitude toward existence in the commanding "Go and caress your beloved." The development of the next stanza, intuitive rather than logical, gives rise to ambiguity. Usually an open window and an open door with their implications of fresh air and life's force have an affirmative connotation. One anticipates something equally affirmative to follow. But the line that succeeds it, "Make her shy and timid," is negative. Does the road dust then symbolize death inevitable and all-powerful? Or does it refer to the warmth of humanity suggested by the conventional symbol of the red dust for the mundane world in traditional Chinese literature? Li's dualistic feeling toward life and death (humanistic versus fatalistic; affirmative versus negative) is echoed in the fifth stanza. The poem, however, closes with a repetition of the opening stanza, and the poet reaffirms that "Life is but/A smile on lips/Of Death."

In "Tenderness" (1922), Li discloses an ambivalent attitude toward Beauty—she is the object of his love as well as his frustration and despair. The protagonist is irresistibly drawn toward her, but at the same time is mistrustful, conscious as he is of her cruelty and hardheartedness.

> With my rude fingertips
> I feel the warmth of your flesh;
> The small fawn lost his way in the woods;
> Only the sighs of dead leaves remain.

> Your low feeble voice

Screams in my barren heart,
And I, the conqueror of all,
Have broken my spear and shield.

Your "tender glance"
Is like a butcher's warning of slaughter;
Your lips? No need to mention them!
I would rather trust your arms.

I believe in the crazy fairy tales,
But not in a woman's love.
I am not used to making comparisons,
But you do resemble the shepherdess in fiction.

I exhaust all musical tunes,
But fail to please your ears;
I use every color,
But none can capture your beauty.

The subtle placement of the sensuous images in the first two lines with the loss of innocence suggested by the symbol of the lost small fawn is imaginative. The concluding image of the first stanza—the sighs of the dead leaves—with its associations of decay and approaching death adds a sense of futility and inevitability. Unfortunately, the rest of the poem is an eking out of material with banal statements and clichés.

A more successful work is "The Abandoned Woman" (1922?):

Long hair hangs disheveled before my eyes,
Severing all hostile stares of contempt,
And the quick flow of fresh blood, the deep sleep of
    dried bones.
The dark night and mosquitoes arrive slowly together,
Over the corner of this low wall,
To scream behind my clean white ears
Like the crazed winds raging in the wilderness,
Frightening the wandering shepherds.

With a blade of grass, I come and go with the spirit of
   God in the empty valley.
My sorrow can be deeply imprinted only in the brains of
   roaming bees.
Or with the waterfalls, let it be dashed down the hanging
   cliffs,
To be then drifted away with the red leaves.

The hidden grief burdens her every move.
No fire of setting sun can melt the ennui of time
Into ashes, and fly away through the chimney
To color the wings of the roaming crows,
And with them perch on the rocks of a roaring sea
To listen quietly to the boatman's song.

The frail old skirt mournfully sighs
As she wanders among the graves.
Never will there be hot tears
To drop on the lawn
To adorn the world.

In his hideous portrayal of the "abandoned woman," Li
expresses the common Symbolist view of society's hostile and
contemptuous attitude toward the artist. Images of gloom and
violence summon up the Gothic landscape with which the poem opens. The eerie scene is a nightmare of disheveled hair,
blood, dried bone, the dark night and mosquitoes, and raging
winds. This violence is in sharp contrast to the repose that
introduces the second stanza, in which the poet voices his desire to communicate with God in the midst of nature by means
of a blade of grass. The longing for spiritual consolation and release from the weariness and sorrows of life is dramatically
bodied forth in the second and third stanzas. The longing be-
lies the need for emotional and spiritual fulfillment, but remains unfulfilled as the poem closes on a tragic note of hardened
resignation. The reader is left with a profound sense of futility.
   Li's empathic responsiveness to nature is equally apparent

in the prose poem, "Morning" (1927?), which is reminiscent of Arthur Rimbaud's lyric, "Aube" (Dawn). Like Rimbaud's subject, Li's morning is personified as a beautiful woman desired by the poet. However, while the movement of "Aube" is swift and the tone aggressively impetuous, Li's "Morning" is sedate, the tone one of awe and quiet adoration. Morning is recaptured in all her freshness and sensuous beauty in images of color, sound, and fragrance. An aura of mystery and sadness surrounds the poem, especially the last half, when the poet fails to capture the "half-smiling" and "half-solemn face" of his beloved because "the night crow has colored my eyes with deep black and therefore has flown away. The roses have colored your lips with vermilion hues and therefore have faded with the winds. . . ." The poem ends, like Rimbaud's, in disillusionment, for the only means of realizing his desire—to possess nature—is in dream. But nighttime, during which dreams are fulfilled, has "just slipped through the cracks of the door."

The ambiguity of Li's poetry lies chiefly in his use of a private set of symbols which, like those of his French predecessors, are chosen arbitrarily by the poet to stand for special ideas of his own—they are a sort of disguise for these ideas. A good illustration of Li's reliance on private symbolism is "The Expression of Time" (1926?):

1

Wind and rain in the ocean,
Wild deer dead in my heart.
Look, autumn dream has spread its wings and departed,
Leaving behind only this wilted soul.

2

I seek abandoned desires,
I mourn discolored lips.
Ah, in the gloom of dark grass,
The moon gathers our deep silence.

3

In love's ancient palace,
Our nuptials have fallen ill.

Take a discarded candle,
Dusk has shrouded the fields.

4

What do I need at this moment?
As if in fear of being scorched to death by the sun!
Go, the garden gate is unfastened;
The roaming bees have come in winged sandals.

5

I await the waking of dream,
I await my wakefulness to sleep.
But with your tears in my eyes,
I have no strength to see the past.

6

Leaning against snow, you long for spring;
Amid the faded grass, I listen to the cicada's cries.
Our lives are withered, too wasted,
Like a rice field after a stampede.

7

I sing rhymeless folk songs
With my heart keeping the beat.
Entrust your sorrows in my bosom
Where they will be cured.

8

The sleeping lotus in the shade
Cannot understand the glory of sun and moon.
Row your boat to the wide pond,
And let it learn a bit of love in the world of men.

9

Our memories
Are searching for a way home from the wilderness.

In the first stanza, time is compared with "wind and rain in the ocean," elemental and powerful. This image is dramatically juxtaposed with that of the "wild deer dead in my heart" (from the *Book of Odes?*), which has a much stronger emotional force than the image of the "small fawn lost in the woods" (see "Tenderness"). It is a symbol not merely of lost innocence but of lost passion and vitality—the very source of life. The image of the autumn dream having flown away is an extension of the tyranny of time that can even rob one of his spirituality.

The second stanza is a sad lament for the evanescence of beauty, the passing of youthful passion and abandoned desires. It closes with a dreariness and gloom that recall the spiritual state of the "wilted soul" in the preceding stanza. It contains, too, a note of world-weariness, a satiation of all sensual pleasures.

Futility underlies the third stanza as the poet calls for a discarded candle to illuminate the fast-spreading darkness over the palace of love in which the "nuptials have fallen ill," suggesting uncertainty and vague despair.

The swift change of tone and mood in the next stanza is baffling. Is Li alluding to the Greek myth of Phaëthon, who met a fiery death driving the chariot of the sun? If so, does his "fear of being scorched to death" mean his fears of soaring into the realm of pure imagination? Or is he fearful of challenging the forces of nature? The image of the roaming bees with winged sandals presents another ambiguity. The bees, with their sense of instinct, could be a symbol of intuition, the winged sandals possibly an allusion to Pegasus or Mercury. Both images then symbolize the imaginative world of poetry that the poet is urged to follow. This is sheer speculation, and there are other guesses. The second line seems scornful of his hesitation (as if such hesitation were a rather ludicrous fear, especially in winter, the time of the poem). The poet may very well be saying to himself, "I can go, I am free—the bees, like the messengers from the Gods, roam easily and reassure me that I can go too."

The fluctuation between the two worlds (the actual and the ideal, the conscious and the subconscious) is suggested in the opening two lines of the fifth stanza. Too bound by human emotion (the tears in the eyes), he is unable to see the past, to capture the lost memories. Again we are reduced to speculation.

A ray of hope glimmers in the first line of the next stanza, only to be quickly submerged as the poem hits its lowest depth of despair. A sense of tragic waste lies in the stark image of the rice field after a stampede—the wasteland of our human existence. The poem assumes an upward surge of hope in the stanza that follows as the protagonist sings "rhymeless folk songs/With my heart keeping the beat." It ends sentimentally as he asks the "you" in the poem to entrust his sorrow to the poet's bosom where it will receive care.

The human touch deepens as the poet finally denounces a life of seclusion and purity, symbolized in the Buddhistic symbol of the lotus which is asleep in the shade, and therefore cannot understand the "glory of sun and moon." The poet urges, "Row your boat to the wide pond" (the world of human experience) to learn about love, the only consolation and meaning of existence in a life of flux and impermanence. This partially positive view is substantiated in the concluding lines of the poem when memories (subtly referring to the bees' intuitive and unerring sense of direction) are searching a way home from the wilderness.

Li Chin-fa is by no means a major poet, and his achievement is far less impressive than that of his European mentors. Nevertheless, he was the first to introduce the techniques of the French Symbolists into China, and he founded the Symbolist school in modern Chinese poetry. He has combined traditional symbolism with his own private symbols, using the techniques of allusion, suggestiveness, and compression. His poetry is complex and difficult, but at its best it has great subtlety and richness of meaning.

Tai Wang-shu (1905–50)

Like his fellow Symbolist Li Chin-fa, Tai Wang-shu was greatly interested in French Symbolist poetry, which he eagerly studied during his stay in France in the early thirties. Unlike Li, who was particularly attracted to the Gothic qualities of horror and the grotesque, Tai inherited the softer and more musical aspects of symbolism. Following Edgar Allan Poe's theory that poetry should embody an indefinite musicality and vague suggestiveness, he brought to modern Chinese verse a renewed emphasis on the aural values of poetry. A supreme example of Tai's brand of "Symbolist poetry" is "The Alley in the Rain" (1927), the performance that gave rise to his sobriquet, "the poet of the rainy alley."

> Holding an oilpaper umbrella, alone,
> Wandering the long, long,
> Desolate alley in the rain,
> I hope to encounter
> The girl who holds her grief
> Like cloves.

> She has
> The color of cloves,
> The fragrance of cloves,
> The sorrows of cloves;
> In the rain she grieves,
> Grieving and wandering.

> She seems to be in this lonely alley,
> Holding an oilpaper umbrella
> Like me,
> Just like me,
> Silently walking back and forth,
> Cold, lonely, and melancholy.

> Silently she moves close;
> Moving close, she casts
> A glance like a sigh,
> She floats by
> Like a dream,
> Sad, lingering, and faint.

> Drifting by in a dream,
> Like a spray of clove,

She passes by my side;
Farther, farther away she goes,
To the broken hedge walls,
To the end of the rainy alley.

In the sad song of the rain,
Her colors languish,
Her fragrance fades;
All is vanished, even her
Glance like a sigh,
Even her clovelike melancholy.

Holding an oilpaper umbrella, alone,
Wandering in the long, long,
Desolate alley in the rain,
I hope to encounter
The girl who holds her grief
Like cloves.

This haunting lyric embodies some distinctive features of symbolism: suggestive indefiniteness, musical nuances, synesthesia, and the intermingling of the imaginary with the real. Tai creates an atmosphere permeated with effeminate charm, languorous grace, and mellifluous music that is worthy of his poetic guide, Paul Verlaine. The poem is tinged with a melancholy almost cosmic in its pervasiveness. The adroit repetition of particular words, sounds (the *l*'s and nasals), and phrases enhances the dreamlike quality of the poem. So does the interplay of the diverse sense impressions of "color of cloves," "fragrance of cloves," and "the sad song of the rain," lines that recall Baudelaire's "Comme de longs échos qui de loin se confondent/ . . . Les parfums, les couleurs et les sons se répondent."

This Baudelairean emphasis on synesthesia again appears in Tai's "A Little Song" (1936), a poem that expresses the French poet's concept of correspondences that "exist between the visible and the invisible, between matter and spirit."[9]

---

[9] Ibid., p. 8.

The bird, tired of singing, hides its beak in bright
   plumage;
Little soul of song, where have you gone soaring?
Withered blooms, petal by petal, yield to dust.
Little soul of aroma, where are you lingering?

They cannot be in purgatory, no!
Not these fine, fine little souls.
Could they then be in heaven, in paradise?
Shaking his head, St. Peter denied it.

No one knows where they are, no one;
The poet only replies with a smile.
There is something which harmonizes the air
In the eternal universe of his heart.

Tai's graver and heavier approach in "In the Sunset" (1927?)
is in keeping with the unsettling gloom.

Evening clouds scatter brocade in the skies,
The creek trickles gold at dusk;
My long thin shadow hovers on earth,
Like the solitary soul of an old tree on the hill.

The distant mountains turn purple from mourning
The end of a bright day;
The fallen leaves yet dance in joy to greet
The robe's edge of dusk, that spread of clear breeze.

The scent of antiquity steals out from the graves
To spin a magic spell on bats above a withered branch.
They whisper softly and intimately without end
While winging low in the evening mist.

Night secretly returns from the sky's end,
I alone lingeringly wander;
Within this solitude of my heart
All grief, all mirth are dissolved, dissolved.

The irregular verse lines, the varied caesuras and rhyme patterns, the run-on lines—all contribute to the conversational tone, the leisurely tempo, and fluid movement of the verse. The imagery is predominantly visual: its colors are alternately dazzling and haunting, its outlines now blurred, now clearly defined. To enrich the musical nuances, Tai resorts to an adroit intermingling of open (*wan, wo, shang, chang*) and closed (*chin, li, shu, mu*) vowels, of full (*chin, chin*) and slant (*shang, ling*) rhymes, as well as the felicitous echoings of alliteration (*tsai, ts'an; chien, chi*) and assonances (*shui* and *liu; hsiang* and *chien*). Balance of line is at times achieved by antithesis, as in the second stanza.

In "A Sonnet" (1927?), Tai, by the same means of imagistic and tonal effects, conjures up the atmosphere of mystery that has such irresistible fascination for symbolists.

> Light rain drizzles on your long flowing hair,
> Like small pearls dropped among dark seaweeds,
> Like dead fish tossed upon the waves,
> Shimmering in an air of sadness and mystery,
>
> Seducing and bringing my dejected soul
> To rest in the realm of love and death,
> Where the air is golden, where the sun gleams purple,
> Where pitiful creatures weep tears of joy.
>
> Like a black cat, old and all bones,
> I yawn and wilt away in that mystic light,
> Pouring out my every pride, false or true.
>
> Then I shall follow it, faltering in the light mist,
> Like the pale-red wine foam floating in an amber glass,
> Hiding my love-filled eyes in the darkened memories.

Part III: 1937–49
and After

6

The War Period and the Rise of "Proletarian" Poetry

The Sino-Japanese War (1937–45) caused a dramatic change in modern Chinese poetry. With the very existence of the nation threatened, it was only natural that poets should respond with a more realistic outlook, a harsher, more vigorous tone, and a toughening of imagination. It was equally inevitable that the sweet, mellifluous "flute music" should give way to the stirring but often sadly moving war songs of Ai Ch'ing or to the boisterous drumbeat verses of T'ien Chien—the two most popular representative poets of this turbulent era on the eve of revolution. For the first time in their short history, the new poets were united in serving one common cause—a war of resistance against the foreign enemy. Patriotic themes, realistic content, heroic temper, and romantic idealization of war incidents became the features of the day. Too often these products of war are written with more sentiment than artistry; their topical interest and emotional appeal are quickly lost when read out of context. The best poems are those in which the broad patriotic notes and the poet's personal vision are imaginatively interfused, as in Ai Ch'ing's poignant impression of war seen in the death of the young bugler.

Although the war itself produced no masterpieces, it provided the larger setting for the Yenan Forum on Arts and Literature in 1942, where Mao Tse-tung pronounced the literary principles of proletarian literature. The new literature was to be "scientific" (antifeudal and antisuperstitious), "national in character and form," and of service to the "mass"—the worker, the peasant, the soldier. This literary standard, propounded to guide Communist writers in wartime Yenan, foreordained a proletarian literature totally subservient to the political demand of the Communist party.

Ai Ch'ing (1910–)

Ai Ch'ing (pen name of Chiang Hai-ch'eng) was one of the outstanding poets in Communist China before he fell into disfavor with the party in 1957. He was born in 1910, the oldest son of a landed gentry family in Chekiang province. Like Wen I-to, his early ambition was to become a painter, and in the late twenties he went to France to study art. During his stay there he became interested in poetry, particularly in the works of Walt Whitman, Émile Verhaeren, Sergei Esenin, Vladimir Mayakovsky, and of Rimbaud and other French Symbolists.

Soon after his return to China in 1932, Ai Ch'ing was arrested and jailed by the police of the French Concession in Shanghai for "harboring dangerous thoughts." During his imprisonment (1932–35?) he wrote some of his earliest poetry, including his first major triumph, "Ta-Yen-Ho" (1933), a long narrative dedicated to the peasant wet nurse in whose humble home he had spent his early childhood. The poem is a tender, poignant, often sentimental account of the tragic life of his nurse, who was a victim of the old society. Despite the poem's protests of social injustice, Ai Ch'ing's attitude is not that of vehement indignation or political fervor, but of genuine sympathy, understanding, and affection. Other characteristic features of his works are also noticeable in this early poem: the Whitmanesque free verse and reliance on repetition, an intermixture of the literary and the colloquial, the simplicity and clarity of treatment, and a fidelity to details, as well as a love for the common people and a profound understanding of their suffering. The last three stanzas of the poem are:

> Ta-Yen-Ho has gone with tears in her eyes!
> With more than forty years of life's humiliation,
> With countless bitter sufferings of a slave,
> With a few bunches of straw and a four-dollar coffin,
> With a few square feet of burial ground,
> With a handful of paper money ashes,
> Ta-Yen-Ho has gone with tears in her eyes.
>
> This is what Ta-Yen-Ho does not know:
> Her drunken husband is already dead,
> Her eldest son became a bandit,
> Her second son died in the smoke of gunfire,
> Her third, fourth, and fifth sons
> Pass their days in the scorns and abuses of masters and
>   landlords.
> And I, I am writing curses for this unjust world.
> . . . .
> Ta-Yen-Ho, today your child is in jail,
> Writing this song of praise dedicated to you,
> Dedicated to your purple soul beneath the yellow earth,
> Dedicated to your straightened arms that used to carry
>   me,
> Dedicated to your lips that kissed me,
> Dedicated to your gentle mud-black face,
> Dedicated to your bosom that had nursed me,
> Dedicated to your sons, my brothers,
> Dedicated to everyone on earth
> Who resembles my nurse, Ta-Yen-Ho, who loved me as her
>   very own.

Ai Ch'ing's love for the humble people is rivaled only by his deep love of country and the past. In the well-known "North-land" (1938), written while he was traveling to northern China after his release from prison, Ai Ch'ing recaptures the bleak appearance and mood of the landscape:

That's right,
The North is sad.
From beyond the pass, the blown-over
Desert winds
Have rolled away the Northland's greenness of life
And the glory of day.
A spread of dustlike grayish yellow
Is covered with a layer of clinging dust-fog.
The shrill cries flung over from yonder horizon
Bring terror
And frenziedly
Sweep over this vast land:
The barren wilderness,
Frozen in the chill winds of December;
The villages and hills, and the riverbanks;
Crumbled walls and deserted tombs—
All are shrouded in sadness, the color of earth.

. . . .

The North is sad.
Its thousand-mile Yellow River
Rumbles with its muddy waves
To flood the vast Northland
With calamities and misfortunes;
Generations of wind and frost
Have etched out
The immeasurable Northland's
Poverty and hunger.

And I,
This rover from the South,
Love this sad Northland.

. . . .

In this ancient, loose, soft, yellow earth
That we are now treading
Are buried the bones of our forefathers.
They cultivated this land;
Several thousand years ago,
They battled the blasts of nature
To defend this land.

Now they are dead.
They have bequeathed us this land—
I love this sad country,
Its vast bony land
Has brought us a simple, homely idiom
And a generous manner.
I believe this idiom and manner
Will endure on this great earth,
Will never be destroyed.
I love this sad country,
This ancient, aged land,
This land
That has sustained the world's oldest,
Most hard-working people,
Whom I love.

The language is plain, the use of metaphors accomplished; the tone, though deeply moving, is well controlled; and no obtrusive impassioned outcries mar the underlying reserve of this nostalgic poem.

After the outbreak of war, Ai Ch'ing wrote a great deal of war poetry. These works lean toward propaganda and journalism, especially the antifascist poems with their feverish declamations in a Mayakovskian vein. The better ones, however, have originality and depth; they express intense emotion, often bordering on violent indignation or hatred, and gain their impetus through powerful imagery, symbolism, or personification:

Are we not
Crucified on the cross
In our own generation?
And this cross—
Is it any less painful than
That borne by the man from Nazareth?

The hands of the enemies
Have placed crowns of thorns on our heads.
The dark red blood dripping

> From our pale white thorn-pierced forehead
> Can never state to the full
> The sorrows and anger in our bosoms!

It is interesting to note the religious motifs in Ai Ch'ing's works. Christian symbols and quotations from the Bible frequently appear in his early verse. They are not used for mere external ornamentations, but for the deeper symbolic meanings that are crucial to the themes of the poems. In the lines above, Ai Ch'ing identifies the suffering of the whole Chinese race with that of Christ. In another early work, "The Death of Nazarene" (1937), Christ is a symbol of the betrayed, the martyred; he is the savior of mankind whose death is a promise of "the kingdom of heaven" (the revolutionary ideal) to come. Ai Ch'ing is one poet who has meaningfully and creatively incorporated Christian symbols into his poetry—a practice inspired by Western poetry.

The best of Ai Ch'ing's imagery has a concreteness and illumination that recalls the splendid imagery of Tu Fu. In "Snow Fell on China" (1937) he wrote:

> The wind
> Is like a grief-stricken old woman,
> Closely following.
> She stretches out her ice-cold claws
> To clutch and tug at the clothes of passers-by.
> She utters words as old as the land,
> And mumbles without stop.

The poet's fondness for strikingly bold—and often bizarre or morbid—imagery is abundantly evident in his earlier works, perhaps because of his close contacts with French Symbolist poetry in this period. In Marseilles, "the native place of thieves and bandits," the trucks on the bumpy streets "stumble and hobble like drunks." The sun at high noon is "an eye hit by wine poison,/Shooting out muddled anger/And grief. . . ." The dirty hemp cargo is the color of the "gray spittle of a consumptive." Ai Ch'ing's feelings toward Paris are more complex: love and hate, repulsion and attraction are all intermingled. The city is alternately addressed as "vigorous, healthy, and full of magnetism" and "the gorgeous, licentious maiden, the beautiful prostitute."

In a less daring vein, there is the recurring image of deformity: "The dried pond is like the blind eye of our earth." The poet's sorrow and joy in a big city (Marseilles) is like "a lone camel crossing a wind-swept desert." Many of Ai Ch'ing's patriotic poems gain strength from their metaphors and symbolism. A good example of such a poem is "He Has Risen" (1937):

> He has risen
> From decades of humiliation
> From the very edge of the deep pit dug by his enemy
>
> Blood drips from his forehead
> Blood drips on his chest
> But he is laughing
> He has never laughed like this before
>
> He is laughing
> His two eyes staring ahead and gleaming
> As if seeking
> For that enemy who has felled him with a blow
>
> He has risen
> He has risen
> Fiercer than all animals
> More intelligent than all mankind
>
> Because he must be so
> Because he must
> Out of the death of his enemy
> Wrest back his own existence.

Ai Ch'ing uses no punctuation in this piece, a practice he may have learned from Guillaume Apollinaire, who believed that punctuation is superfluous. The absence of punctuation does not impair the clarity of the poem because the verse length and caesuras are arranged to provide the necessary breaks and rhythm. "The Beggar" (193–) is another poem without punctuation. The last two stanzas read:

> In the North
> The beggars with fixed gaze
> Stare at you
> They watch every move of your eating
> Even the way you pick your teeth with your fingers
>
> In the North
> The beggar stretches out his relentless hands
> The crow-black hands
> To beg for a single copper
> From anyone
> Even from the soldier who owns not a single copper.

In the preface to his volume of selected poems published in 1951, Ai Ch'ing wrote, "Being born and raised in the country, I was once fond of Esenin's nostalgic lyrics about the old village."[1] Like the Russian poet, Ai Ch'ing draws on his genuine affection for the small village in composing many memorable lines. Ai Ch'ing also shares Esenin's lyrical gift and melancholic strain. His sensitive evocations of the countryside are full of picturesque details and local color; they reveal the poet's true impressionistic feeling for nature and deep compassion for the peasants. Some typical passages are these excerpted from his long poem, "In Dedication to the Village" (1942), the title poem of his collected works published in 1945:

> I recall the wooden bridge over the small creek near the
>   village:
> Because of its burden, it has thinned into a mere skeleton.

[1] Ai Ch'ing, *Ai Ch'ing hsüan-chi* [Selected works of Ai Ch'ing], p. 9.

Its long skinny legs stand bare in the water all year long,
To let the villagers pass back and forth on its bony hunched
    back.
. . . .
I recall the simple crude huts in the village:
They huddle closely together like people shivering in the
    cold.
. . . .
I recall the oldest woman in the village—
Since she first married and came to live in the village,
She has never left.
She has never seen a sailboat,
Not to speak of a train or a steamboat,
Her sons and grandsons have all died,
But she alone still proudly lives on.
. . . .
I recall the village peasants burdened by constant labor,
Their faces wrinkled and darkened like ancient pines.
Their backs, weighed down daily by heavy loads, are
    now the shape of bows.
Their eyes are dulled and blank with endless disappoint-
    ments and sorrows.

The poem closes with a characteristic note of protest and hopeful anticipation for the future. Despite some remarkable sections, the narrative suffers from too much repetition—a flaw Ai Ch'ing shares with Kuo Mo-jo, possibly because of their common source of influence, Whitman. But Ai Ch'ing's emotional restraint frees him from Kuo's bombast and romantic excess.

Ai Ch'ing won recognition with the publication of his immensely popular "He Died a Second Time," written in 1939. Like the heroes of many war poems, the central character is a common soldier. This twelve-part unrhymed narrative poem is in Ai Ch'ing's customary free-verse form. The opening section, called "The Stretcher," depicts the peasant-soldier, seriously wounded, being taken to the hospital. In the second part, "Hospital," the scenes are well drawn. The mood is heavy, the imagery sometimes gruesome:

We put on cotton jackets with red crosses embroidered on
    them,
We lie in bed, we lie in bed.
We watch countless bodies eaten up by molten metal and
    poisonous gas.
Every man, his eyes sunken, dark, and fearful,
His groans perpetual,
Greets the passing of countless days
Like receiving the send-off of numerous black coffins in a
    funeral procession.

The third section, "The Hands," contrasts the "dainty nimble fingers" of the nurse with the rough, coarse hands of the wounded soldier; the hands that used to hold hoe and gun are "now limp" on his chest. The scene shifts as in a motion picture from the almost naturalistic description of the previous section to this dramatic contrast. The poem achieves its structural integrity and conception through a number of such lyrical and dramatic moments.

In the fourth section, "Healing," the soldier is finally well enough to be discharged. He leaves the hospital on a bright spring morning and walks into a street bustling with life. With the recent experience still so vivid in his mind, he suddenly feels alone and tired:

People hurry by,
Only he alone still feels so tired,
Nobody has noticed him—
A wounded soldier whose wound
Has now healed. He is glad.
And more than ever he understands
The deeper meaning of his healing.
Only now does he feel
He is a soldier:
A soldier who is destined to be wounded on the battlefield,
Who must return to the fighting after his wound is
    healed.

A satirical overtone is heard in the fifth section, "The Posture," when Ai Ch'ing expresses his quiet indignation at the indifference of complacent civilians. The poet attains great pathos by means of contrast and irony. The "pitifully shabby" soldier in his dirty uniform is seen walking down the busy street whose "glaring electric lights, modern motor cars, fashionably dressed ladies" daze him. He is seized with a desire to stride forward with pride because "today he is wearing a robe of glory," and he is convinced that only people like him are entitled to such feelings. But instead of pride, a sense of shame assails him as he fears that the crowd might have guessed his "secret." "But of course no one has even noticed him," comments the poet.

"The Countryside" offers a delightful change of mood and scene as the reader follows the peasant-soldier out of the city. Here Ai Ch'ing's descriptions are lucidly simple and idyllic, yet real, conveying the feel of soil and field. The tone is nostalgic, yet free from mawkishness. The lyrical mood has an elegiac quality that recalls some war poems of Tu Fu and Po Chü-i.

The succeeding section, "A Glance," brings the reader back to the stark reality of war when the soldier suddenly encounters another soldier who, disabled by war, has to beg alms for his living. At this "unbearable sight," the protagonist determines "not to return with one leg/To cry before people/And beg. . . ." The ninth and tenth parts, "Exchange" and "Send-off," see the soldier marching off to battle with his comrades amid the cheers of the civilians who had hardly noticed him before.

The contemplation of death provides the theme of "A Thought," a disappointing section. It is flawed by its direct statements, rhetorical rationalizations, and sentimental overtones. Part eleven, "Forward March," is no improvement. It abounds in stereotyped poetizing of patriotic exhortation. The diction is loose and trite, the rhythm flaccid.

If Ai Ch'ing fails in these last sections, he is unquestionably more successful with the concluding part of this work. With pathos and irony, the poet projects his personal vision of war—

its pitifulness and futility—in the poignant death of the peasant-soldier.

> Before long, his comrades
> Again come in search of him
> This must be life's last visitation
> Only on this occasion
> What they bring is not the stretcher
> But a short-handled spade
>
> Without any careful choosing
> They dig a shallow grave
> Near the bank of a river
> Where he once stood guard.
>
> After the dirt mixed with spring grass
> Has covered his body
> All he leaves for the world
> Is one pathetic mound among the many
> That are now spread like stars in the wilderness
> On those mounds
> No one has ever marked the names of the dead
> Even if one does
> What use can it be?

The vision is more compelling because of its simple and direct presentation. Ai Ch'ing is by nature a lyrical poet of impassioned mood. Like most of his long narrative poems, "He Died a Second Time" is essentially lyrical in mood and feeling; it is less a conventional narrative than a series of lyrical fragments. The illuminating images, the dramatic close-ups, the shifting angles of vision all suggest the method of the cinema. The emotions of the protagonist undergo various adventures, not in a conventional narrative sequence but in a montage of images, reveries, dramatic scenes, and reflections. The poem is important in its bold experimentations with new forms, techniques, and methods of presentation.

"The Trumpeter," a shorter narrative also written in 1939, displays better technical control. The structure is more compact, the material handled with greater economy. The poem is associational in method and in its use of natural and sensory details; the fluid movement of the strophes approaches reverie. The description of nature is sensually vivid and imparts a sense of grandeur:

> Outside in the dark
> The dawn has yet to come.
> He is awakened by
> His yearning for dawn.
> He strolls up the slope of the hill
> And for a long while stands in silence,
> Watching the renewal of the day's miracle.
> Evening has withdrawn her mysterious veil,
> Countless weary stars are fading away.
> . . . .
> Dawn, you are the bride of Time!
> You descend on the golden-wheeled chariot
> From the other end of the world,
> Our world greets you
> And lifts your emblem in the East.
> Behold!
> The majestic bridals are consecrated between heaven and
> earth!

The verbal texture of the poem is a happy blend of the prosaic and the poetic characteristics of Ai Ch'ing. The narrative is carried out with remarkable ease by a skillful manipulation of long and short lines, varied caesuras and run-on lines:

> Now he raises,
> Under the clear blue sky,
> The trumpet to his lips
> And blows.
> The trumpet is filled with fresh air from the plains.
> So in gratitude

He sends forth his lively songs across the plains.
In love with the animated dawn
He sounds the melodies—
The music floats out into the distance.
All things in the universe
In their splendor and joy
Receive his summons.

Ai Ch'ing at his best is a poet of originality and power. His primary strength derives from his clear perception, classical rigor, and intensity of feeling. As Robert Payne has observed, "The old elegists would have been able to describe a whole battlefield in terms of a bloodstained flower or a plume of smoke rising from the marsh-grass. Yet they would have found themselves incapable of the impressionistic vision which sees all tragedy in the glint of a blood-smeared face on the reflected surface of the trumpet, as the trumpeter lies dead."[2]

On that smooth bright surface of brass
Is reflected the blood of the dead
And on his pale face
There is also the reflection of the eternally running,
   Advancing army with its weapons,
   And the neighing horses,
   The rumbling carts.
The sun, the sun
Glimmers brightly on the trumpet.
Listen,
The trumpet seems to be still sounding, sounding.

Some of Ai Ch'ing's best "wartime" poems have little direct connection with war. They are short lyrical pieces, well condensed, written in accordance with a more compressed and formal pattern. The mood varies from profound melancholy to ecstatic joy, the temper from austerity to exaltation.

[2] Robert Payne, ed., *Contemporary Chinese Poetry*, p. 22.

THE WINTER POND   (1940)

The winter pond
Is as lonely as an old man's heart—
The heart that has tasted in full the sorrows in life.
The winter pond
Is as dry as an old man's eyes—
The eyes that have long lost their luster through perpetual
   drudgery.

The winter pond
Is as desolate as an old man's hair—
The hair that is ash-white and sparse as frosted grass.
The winter pond
Is as despondent as a grief-stricken old man,
The old man bent beneath the downcast canopy of sky.

In contrast to this somber poem is "The Words of the Sun"
(1942), which sparkles with optimism and hope. The symbol
of the sun is important in Ai Ch'ing's work.

Open up your window!
Open up your wooden doors!
Let me enter! Let me enter,
Enter into your small huts!

I bring you the golden blossoms,
I bring you the fragrance of the woods,
I bring you light and warmth
And the dews all over me.

Quickly arise! Quickly arise!
Quickly raise your heads from pillows,
Open your eyes covered by eyelashes.
Let your eyes witness my coming.

Let your hearts be like small rooms:
Open up their long windows;
Let me scatter the blossoms, the fragrance, the light,
And the warmth, the dews into your hearts' open spaces!

Ai Ch'ing's kinship with the romantic tradition is apparent in his works, especially those that deal with nature. Unlike the conventional poets, however, Ai Ch'ing brings new significance to the phenomena of nature by his innovative treatments and his own immediate consciousness of the present.

Ai Ch'ing joined the Communist party in 1941 after his arrival at Yenan which was the Communist stronghold during the war, and taught at the Lu Hsün Academy from 1941 to 1945. Like many young idealists of this era, Ai Ch'ing was convinced that communism offered the only possible answer to his country's problems. Mao Tse-tung's cultural policies and literary theories made explicit at the forum in 1942 had left an indelible impression on the young poet. Recalling the event, he wrote in one of his essays on poetry in 1950: "We owe our thanks to Chairman Mao for correcting our mistakes in 1942. He pointed out a new direction for us all, that is, art should be joined with revolutionary realism and the revolutionary masses. It should serve the workers, the peasants, and the soldiers; it should please these working people. It should also have Chinese style and Chinese flavor. . . ."[3]

In another essay Ai Ch'ing insisted on the social utility of poetry: "Poetry must become the spiritual and educational instrument of the masses. It must become the weapon of propaganda and an encouragement in our task of revolution." And he then proposed a future course for poetry: "From the revolution in poetry brought about by Whitman, Verhaeren, and Mayakovsky, we must continue our efforts. We must make poetry into something that can adequately meet the needs of a new era. We must employ whatever new poetic forms are most suited to those new needs. . . ."[4]

Like many another "proletarian" poet of this period, Ai Ch'ing tried to reorient himself and his craft to meet these new demands. He studied Marxism and Mao's political doctrines; he went to work among the peasants; he actively participated

---

[3] Ai Ch'ing, *Shih lun* [Essays on poetry], p. 66.
[4] Ibid., pp. 2, 6.

in party projects; and he experimented with numerous folk-song forms. *Wu Mang-yu* (1943), a book-length narrative poem, is a typical product of this period. Wu Mang-yu is the name of Ai Ch'ing's new hero, a peasant whose misery and toil before the Communist "liberation" is contrasted, in great detail, with the comfort and privileges he comes to enjoy under Communist rule. During the course of the story, the peasant becomes a hero· in the guerrilla fighting against the Japanese, a staunch supporter of the Communist cause, and finally a model citizen in his "liberated" village.

The growing vogue for folk literature of wide popular appeal prompted Ai Ch'ing to abandon his rich literary style for one of homely realism. In this long narrative he makes abundant use of folk motifs, including folk themes and balladic rhythms and vocabulary. If the poet achieves, on occasion, the appeal of naïve simplicity and rustic charm, the virtues are too often canceled by the obtrusion of political slogans and didactic messages. As propaganda it might have been effective, but as a literary piece this poem is a pathetic specimen. In the preface to his selected poems of 1951, Ai Ch'ing acknowledged the literary faults of his works written between 1942 and 1945: "In this period, my creative style underwent immense change. I became acquainted with a few heroes from the working class and wrote some journalistic essays. I learned to write poetry using the folk-song forms. Since most of these are mere exercises produced during the process of learning, . . . I decided not to include them in my collection."[5]

When the war ended in 1945, Ai Ch'ing contributed his share of exuberant poems celebrating the newly won victory and extolling the greatness of Mao Tse-tung and Stalin, the two leaders "responsible" for this glorious event. Those poems, as well as a few composed during the war, were collected in a small volume in 1950. Full of stock hyperboles and hackneyed rhetoric, these inflated propagandist verses add nothing to Ai Ch'ing's poetic stature. After the war he devoted a great deal

[5] Ai Ch'ing, *Ai Ch'ing hsüan-chi*, p. 8.

of time to administrative work for the party and to land reform and other movements. The output of his poetry since then has been small and of a generally low quality, as is the case with Communist literature today.

In the mid-fifties, Ai Ch'ing began to be criticized for lacking "political enthusiasm," for his "unhealthy emotions" and "bourgeois individualism." Finally, in 1957, he was purged by the party. The poet's pronouncement of 1939 strikes an ironic note: "The sound of poetry is the sound of freedom. . . . Suppression of people's speech is the most cruel oppression."[6] With this assertion of his independence as a poet and his conviction of the supreme right to creativity, one cannot help wondering about the true motivation of his poem, "On a Chilean Cigarette Package," written in 1954:

> On a Chilean cigarette package
> One sees a picture of the Goddess of Freedom.
> Although she holds a torch in her hand,
> She yet remains a dark shadow;
>
> For serving as a trademark, an ad,
> Let's give the goddess a space.
> You can buy a pack with a few coins,
> After you are through with it, in smoke it's gone.
>
> You toss away the empty package on the sidewalk.
> People step on it, people spit on it.
> Be it a fact, or be it a symbol,
> The Goddess of Freedom is but a pack of cigarettes.

T'ien Chien (1914–)

The son of a landowner, T'ien Chien (T'ung T'ien-chien) grew up in the village of his birth in Anhwei province, east central China. Although he later moved to the city for ten years, it was rural China that provided the source of his early

---

[6] Ai Ch'ing, *Shih lun*, pp. 127–28.

poetry. While living in Shanghai in the thirties, T'ien Chien became an active participant in leftist and anti-Japanese movements, a course which eventually led him into the Communist party. In 1938 he went to Yenan, where he remained until the end of the war.

T'ien Chien's early poetry, published between 1934 and 1936, deals mainly with life in the small village. Realistic in content and basic approach, conventional in form, these early attempts were undistinguished and received little notice from the public. On the eve of the war T'ien Chien abruptly dropped the old form for the "revolutionary style" inspired by Mayakovsky, then the idol of the young leftists in China. The poet's celebrated "drumbeat verse," with its short lines and quick vigorous rhythm, was eminently suited to the tempo of war. Wen I-to, the established poet and critic, hailed him as "the drummer of our age," and a host of young poets rushed to ink and paper to imitate his style. T'ien Chien's drumbeat verse instantly captured the attention of the reading public and won him wide recognition and popularity.

T'ien Chien does not possess Ai Ch'ing's strong affinity with European culture; nor does he have the latter's urbanity and sophistication in themes, diction, and techniques. His poetry, always baldly taut, direct, and full of folk flavor, has its roots in the native tradition of folk literature. T'ien Chien was, too, a product of war, and his major works were composed during the war. Above all, T'ien Chien is a "proletarian" poet who writes what the Communist party dictates and who places his craft at the service of the party: "I am a Communist party member; my duty as a writer is to sing the praise of the proletarian class and communism. This sense of duty was formed early in my mind: I have grown up in the embrace of the party, have been educated by the party and encouraged by my comrades. Therefore, I never waver in my loyalty to them. I am always full of courage and confidence in my determination to serve the workers, the peasants, and the soldiers. . . ."[7]

[7] T'ien Chien, *Hai-yen sung* [Songs of the sea swallow], p. 54.

The poet's numerous political poems with their incitive and propagandist emphasis speak well for these convictions. Undoubtedly it was the revolutionary fervor of Mayakovsky's works that first attracted the young T'ien Chien. In his article celebrating the sixtieth anniversary of the Russian poet's birth, T'ien Chien eulogized Mayakovsky as "the poet genius of the proletarians" as well as the "dear comrade and master of the age" whose "unwavering political enthusiasm and magnificent service to the party and the common masses" should be emulated by every writer. In speaking of Mayakovsky's poetry, T'ien Chien venerates particularly its "revolutionary spirit" and its "simple and healthy speech of the common people"; he further admires its "regular rhythm" and "melodiousness."

At this point, one cannot help questioning T'ien Chien's grasp of Mayakovsky's works. According to T'ien Chien's frank admission, his understanding was inadequate. In the same article, he has this to say about Mayakovsky's influence on him: "Certain comrades think that I had learned from Mayakovsky. It is true that his revolutionary spirit has long inspired and educated me. But whether or not I had learned anything from him, I myself dare not say. Translations of his works have become more available only in very recent times. Before the war, they were exceedingly scarce. . . ."[8] Among the translations accessible to him in 1955, T'ien Chien goes on, were "At the Top of My Voice," "The March to the Left," "It Is Good," "Order No. 2 to the Army of Arts," "An Extraordinary Adventure," "Conversation with a Tax Collector about Poetry," and "Lenin." There is no mention of the remarkable "Cloud in Trousers," nor the brilliant satires—*The Bedbug* and *The Bathhouse*. It is interesting, too, that there is no reference to Mayakovsky's suicide in T'ien Chien's articles.

There is little doubt that T'ien Chien's drumbeat verse was inspired by, if not derived from, Mayakovsky's declamatory style and its "thumping rhythm." Both poets wrote a great many propaganda verses full of buoyant optimism and revolu-

[8] *Ibid.*, p. 82.

tionary ardor. Both shun conventional poetic diction in favor of the plain idiom of the common people; both frequently intersperse slang expressions or folk vocabulary in their verbal texture. But here they part company. T'ien Chien is much more provincial and conservative than Mayakovsky; his language is occasionally coarse but never deliberately vulgar. There are no intricate verbal innovations, no stunning elaborate metaphors or hyperboles such as are found in the Russian master's works. Nor can one perceive Mayakovsky's range and depth of emotions in T'ien Chien's poems. At its best, T'ien Chien's style comes close to that of Mayakovsky in its strong auditory effects and emotional force.

T'ien Chien is not prolific. That his limited output lacks variety of theme is perhaps not surprising for a poet caught up by the exigencies of war. Much of his war poetry is poor in quality and possibly will not survive except for its historical interest. T'ien Chien's drumbeat verses deal mainly with nationalistic and patriotic themes. Their mood is often one of indignation or optimism, untinged with melancholy. The taut verse lines with their halting cadence and metallic ring are perfectly in tune with the throbbing tempo of the poems. His language is starkly plain, stripped of poetic embellishments. Metaphors are sparingly used. Some of his typical drumbeat verses are included in his volume, *To Those Who Fight*, published in 1943.

THE EARTH
This Asian
Soil
Is dyed in
Anger and
Shame.
O tillers of my fatherland!
Leave those dirty ditches
And run-down
Villages!

To the war,

Drive away
The imperialist
Armies.
With our stubborn will
Let's start sowing
Mankind's
New birth!

In the preface to this volume, T'ien Chien summons poets to write "hymns in keeping with the steps of war," hymns that would rouse the people of China "to fight until we are free."

FREEDOM IS MARCHING TOWARD US   (1938?)
A woebegotten
Nation, ah,
We must fight!
In autumn, beyond the window,
Over the fields
Of Asia,
Freedom
Is marching toward us;
Beyond the bloody puddles,
Beyond the dead bodies of our brothers—
A savage storm,
A swooping seagull.

One of the peculiar devices in T'ien Chien's verse is the inclusion of one extraordinarily long line (consisting of two or three phrases, clauses, or even sentences) amid several very short lines (two to three characters in each line) for emphasis and dramatic purposes.

IN THE MORNING WE DO CALISTHENICS   (1937?)
("Get up, get up!" every morning a comrade would blow his whistle and shout.)

The sky
In April

> Is blue;
>
> The park
> In the North
> Is blue;

—On a blue morning, in a blue world, amidst a blue war,
> In the morning
> We do calisthenics.

T'ien Chien strikes a domestic note in the following short verse, "Shoes" (1938?):

> Go home,
> > Tell your woman:
>
> Everyone must come
> > To make shoes.
>
> Make them like those worn by the soldiers,
> Sturdy and big.
>
> So they can cross mountains,
> So they can fight!

In times of war it seems inevitable that love for one's country and its suffering people should invoke violent hatred of the invaders and oppressors. Love and hate became the dual sentiments in T'ien Chien's much admired long poem, "For the Fighters," written after the outbreak of war in 1937. In this work, T'ien Chien uses a swift interchange of short and long lines that bears an outward resemblance to Mayakovsky's "rapid succession of different contrasting meters." Following are some typical passages.

> FOR THE FIGHTERS   (1937)
> One dark,
> Cold night,

The Japanese plunderers
Burst in,
And from our
Arms,
From our
Bosoms
Wrest away our innocent comrades
And locked them within the stockade of tyranny.
Their bodies
Nakedly exposed
Their blazing scars,
Their hearts
Beat
In rage and hatred.
They trembled
In Darien, in the savage camps
Of the Manchurian plains,
Letting those drunken,
Beastly cannibals,
Flashing their knives,
Mock
The wasted lives,
The starved blood.

I

Glorious is the name
People!
Ah, the people,
You stand on the Lo Kou Bridge,
Braving the storm,
Blowing your bugle for attack.
Ah, people,
On this spacious plain of our great earth,
Giantlike,
You boldly stood up!

VI

Where shall we go?
In this world
Where there is no land,
No sea,

No will,
Men are barely
Breathing
In a life that is death!

Today,
Let us die!
Should we die?
No, absolutely no!

We are giants:
To live is to fight;
Noble spirits
Choose death instead of surrender.
Stretch out both your arms
To greet freedom!

Glorious is the name
People!
Ah, the people!
Victory is before us.

People, all you people!
Seize
Our weapons
From the factories,
From the corners of walls,
From the muddy ditches.
Let us attack the murderers!

People! People!
Raise high
Our seared,
Storm-beaten,
Whipped
Workers' hands.
Let us fight!
In this struggle,
It is either victory

Or death!

This long poem is one of the more successful of T'ien Chien's drumbeat verses. Aiming at the depoetization of language, T'ien Chien, like Mayakovsky, reverted to colloquial expressions and phrasings. He boldly introduced a new idiom of short broken lines and isolated single words, stressing both meanings and intonation in order to secure the utmost in auditory effects. The stanzas are highly charged with a rude emotional power. The terse statements and accentuated rhythm produce the challenging effect that T'ien Chien favors. The rhythm, however, breaks away from the other elements in the poem, becomes overstressed, and dominates the poem. This same weakness may be discerned in some of his other works. The poem also suffers from tedious repetition, which only lengthens it without dramatically developing the theme.

One of the most folklike aspects of war is guerrilla fighting. T'ien Chien's short narrative verse, "The Mule Driver" (1943?), presents a folk hero who risks his life smuggling ammunition across the enemy line to the fighting soldiers. In another long balladlike piece, "Jung Kuan-hsiu" (1943?), he tells the story of a suffering old country woman, the "victim" of China's "feudal society." She lives with the family of her drunkard husband until she is finally "liberated" by the Communist army, and she then helps the party fight the Japanese enemies. In this long narrative, not only anti-imperialist but antifeudal sentiments are exploited in accordance with Mao's literary principles laid down at the Yenan forum. About this work, T'ien Chien wrote: "The long poems, 'Jung Kuan-hsiu' and 'Kan Ch'e Chuan,' were written after I answered the call of the party to work in the country. Even though some readers dislike the poems, I myself think very highly of them because they are fully acceptable to the working masses. . . ."[9]

T'ien Chien's attempt to create a work totally comprehensible to the masses can be seen in his consciously chosen devices: the

[9] Ibid.

crude spirited speech of the peasants, the leisurely lilting rhythm of the folk ballad, and the inclusion of popular sayings and coarse humor. This "folksy stylization" lends color and immense popular appeal to a narrative meant to be recited to an unsophisticated audience. Like most party-oriented verse, it is effective as propaganda but deficient in aesthetic appeal.

It is obvious that T'ien Chien's drumbeat style has limitations. It becomes monotonous and loses its impetus when used as an end in itself. On the other hand, the poet has made a revolutionary break with the traditional past; in his best works T'ien Chien has registered the voice of his time and captured the spirit of a war-ravaged age. He is justly called "the drummer of our age."

Kuo Mo-jo (1892–)

Kuo Mo-jo is the only major poet whose career has spanned the entire historical development in mainland China of the new verse, from its nascent state to the present, from romantic individualism to proletarian collectivism. His first poems constitute his most important contribution to the new verse: this "explosive verse" brought a fresh approach and new modes of feeling and expression that are dynamically contemporary.

One of the most celebrated living writers in Communist China today, Kuo Mo-jo is also one of the most versatile. He is practiced in fields as disparate as archaeology, history, poetry, drama, the short story, the essay, the novel, translation, and politics. It was as a poet that he first emerged on the national literary scene. His initial volume of new verse, *Goddesses* (1922), brought him instant recognition and wide acclaim, establishing him as one of the foremost modern poets in the country. Since then Kuo has published seven more volumes of verse, and is still writing today.

It is unfortunate that the great potentiality shown in *Goddesses* has never been fully realized. A large portion of his work, especially his later verse, is disappointingly mediocre. There is

justification in the adverse criticism pronounced by Achilles
Fang: "Humorless sincerity, death-seriousness, even deadly
dullness,—traits one seldom finds in traditional Chinese poetry
—mark Kuo Mo-jo's poetry." But the same critic also re-
marked that "the emergence of Kuo Mo-jo on the Chinese
poetic scene was almost miraculous; it marked the end of tradition."[10] Though one may agree wholeheartedly with the first
half of Fang's statement, exception must be taken to the second
half. Kuo Mo-jo introduced a much-needed element, vitality,
into the new verse, but he did not bring down the curtain on
tradition. Traditionalism continued to play a meaningful part
not only in Kuo's poetry but in the poetry that followed.

  Despite all the defects of which Kuo has been accused, aesthetic or ideological, one cannot completely ignore his prolific
output, his vast range of subject matter, his stylistic virtuosity,
originality, and inventiveness, or the tremendous force and vitality that paved a new avenue for poetry at once affirmative,
exciting, dynamic, and contemporary. As Wen I-to so aptly put
it, Kuo is one truly modern poet "who has grasped the spirit
of the time."[11] And whether one likes or dislikes these works,
he is sure to recognize a genuine poetic gift beneath the surface
of Kuo's best poetry.

  Those who are familiar with the life and poetry of Kuo Mo-jo
cannot fail to mark two important phases in Kuo's long poetic
career: the romantic strain in his earlier works and the proletarian strain that appeared later. These two phases reveal and
in a general way run parallel with the development of the new
poetry. The shift from "romantic individualism" in the early
and mid-twenties to the realistic proletarianism of the late
twenties and after is symptomatic of the growing leftist dominance among the progressive writers in China of that period;
writers who were disillusioned and discontented with the gov-

---

[10] Achilles Fang, "From Imagism to Whitmanism in Recent Chinese Poetry,"
p. 186.

[11] Wen I-to, *Wen I-to ch'üan-chi* [Complete works of Wen I-to], p. 185.

ernment seemed to find in communism the noblest ideal for China.

Born in 1892 in a small town in Szechwan province, Kuo was something of a rebel even in his youth. Among the many instances of this rebellious streak enumerated in Kuo's autobiographical works is an account of his expulsion from school as a result of his constant revolt against authority. This notable trait might explain the immense attraction nineteenth-century English romantics like Byron and Shelley held for him. Their passionate participation in the revolutionary issues of their time must have struck a responsive chord in Kuo, whose own total commitment to the Communist cause in later days displays an interesting parallel. His revolutionary spirit is reflected in many poems, of which "In Praise of the Rebels" (1919) is a supreme example. In it, Kuo sounds his deep admiration for his rebel heroes: Cromwell, Washington, and José Rizal in politics; Marx, Engels, and Lenin in social revolution; Buddha, Mo Ti, and Martin Luther in religion; Copernicus, Darwin, and Nietzsche in theory; Rodin, Whitman, and Tolstoy in the arts; Rousseau, Johann Pestalozzi, and Tagore in education.[12]

In another poem, "The Victorious Death" (1920), Kuo praises the heroic death of the Irish patriot Terence MacSwiney (1879–1920), who starved himself to death in an English prison. To Chinese ears the name MacSwiney in a poem sounds no more odd than, say, "Cromwell" or "Washington." The poem is moving and sentimental, and ends:

IV

Truth shall restore the light by Nature given. And like Prometheus, bring the fire of Heaven!
—Thomas Campbell

The vast ocean is singing its sad and heroic song of lament,

---

[12] José Rizal (1861–96) was a patriotic poet and national hero of the Philippines. He was killed after having failed in a revolt against the Spanish authority that then controlled the islands. Johann Pestalozzi (1746–1827) was a famous Swiss educator who established schools for poor children.

The boundless blue sky is flushed from weeping,
In the distant western horizon, the sun has set!
O heroic death! O glorious death! O victorious death!
O God of Death who loves all! I thank you! You have
    saved my beloved
Warrior of Freedom, MacSwiney, you have revealed the
    greatness of human will.
I thank you! I praise you! "Freedom" will die no more.
The bright moon after the curtain of night has drawn!
    How radiant!

This vast sympathy and love for rebels, revolutionaries, and patriots is equaled only by Kuo's intense love for his own country, a sentiment shared by all young writers of a fiercely nationalistic time. "At the Mouth of the Huang-p'u River" is a short, emotional lyric written soon after his return from Japan in 1921. The diction is simple, the style quietly effective.

O peaceful country!
    Land of my parents!
How fresh and green is the grass along the shore!
    How soft and yellow is the flowing water!

Leaning against the rail, I gaze afar.
    The smooth great plain is like the sea;
But for a few green willow waves,
    There are no cliffs to intrude upon your view.

The small boat rocks above the waves,
    The men seem entranced in a dream.
O peaceful country!
    O land of my parents!

This nostalgic impression of his country is soon shattered as he records his "Impressions of Shanghai" (1921):

I woke from my dream!
What sorrows of disillusion!

The idling corpses,
  The licentious flesh,
 The long robes of men,
  The short sleeves of women,
An eyeful of skeletons,
  A streetful of coffins
Rush in confusion.
I weep,
  I vomit.

I woke from my dream!
What sorrows of disillusion!

Like many children of well-to-do families in the China of his day, Kuo began his formal education by studying the classics in the traditional manner to prepare himself for the civil examination. After the educational system in China was changed, he entered a modernized school. In his autobiographies Kuo admits that during his school years he preferred T'ang poetry to the classics. He mentions, too, his special fondness for the poetry of Wang Wei, Meng Hao-jan, Liu Tsung-yuan, and Li Po, and his dislike of Han Yü's works. In prose, he enjoyed most the highly imaginative poetic style of Chuang Tzu's work. These inclinations indicate an early leaning toward lyrical, romantic, and individualistic literature, which he was later to favor in his writing.

In 1914 Kuo left China to study medicine in Japan. Though he did finally receive his medical degree from Kyushu Imperial University in 1921, he never pursued a medical career. Kuo Mo-jo is said to have undergone a succession of influences in his life, and he himself has lent support to this view. It was while he was a student in Japan that Kuo became exposed to the vast spectrum of Western literature, which was to prove of immense importance to his literary career: "I came into contact with the work of Tagore, Shelley, Shakespeare, Heine, Goethe, Schiller, and, indirectly, the literature of northern Europe, French literature, and Russian literature. These took root in my literary foundation."[13] Of these, Tagore and Goethe exerted the greatest immediate influence. Goethe was to inspire him to compose his own versions of verse plays, and Tagore was partly responsible for Kuo's cultivation of the "fresh and lucid" style of lyrics in his two volumes, *The Starry Skies* (1923) and *Vase* (1924):

> I first came to know the name of Tagore in 1914. In January of that year I had just arrived in Japan. The literary fame of Tagore was very much in vogue then. . . . That September I entered the preparatory class of the first year of high school. I was living with a relative. . . . One day he came home with a few mimeographed sheets in English, saying to me that they were Tagore's "Baby's Way," "Sleep Stealer," and "Clouds and Waves." I read with great amazement. First, these poems were easy to comprehend; second, the poems were fresh and lucid, strange yet lasting. From then on, the name of Tagore became deeply imprinted in my mind.[14]

From this enthusiastic introduction, Kuo went on to read a great deal of Tagore's poetry in English translation. Later, in 1927, he translated parts of Tagore's *The Crescent Moon, The Gardener,* and *Gitanjali,* intending to have them published in China. Because Tagore was not then widely known in China, Kuo's manuscripts were rejected. In his preface Kuo summed up Tagore's philosophy: "I feel the thought of Tagore is that of pantheism. He has merely cloaked with a Western garb the traditional spirit of India. The reality of 'Brahma,' the dignity of 'I,' the gospel of 'love' can be considered the complete thought of Tagore, which is also the philosophy of the Brahman scriptures, the Upanishad and the Vedanta."[15] Tagore's influence on Kuo is traceable in his free-verse form, his lucid and lyrical style, and, particularly, in the implicit pantheism of his

---

[13] Kuo Mo-jo, *Mo-jo wen-chi* [Collected works of Kuo Mo-jo], 7:12.
[14] Ibid., 10:142–43.
[15] Ibid., pp. 144–45.

verse. It was after reading Tagore that Kuo first tried his hand at writing his own new poetry, adopting the free verse in which he was to excel.

In his article on the nature of poetry, Kuo distinguishes two major types of poetry:

> I think the mind of the poet is like a bay of clear water. It is calm as a mirror reflecting the myriad phenomena of the universe. But once the wind rises, the waves start to surge and all the phenomena of the universe move within it. This wind is none other than the impulse and the inspiration of the poet. The risen waves are none other than the emotions of the poems, the phenomena, or imagination. And these, I think, constitute the basic nature of poetry. The great surging waves become the vigorous type of poetry like the poems of Ch'ü Yüan's "Li Sao," Ts'ai Wen Chi's "Hu Chia Shih Pa P'ai," Dante's *Divine Comedy*, Milton's *Paradise Lost*, Goethe's *Faust*, and the songs of Li Po and Tu Fu. The ripples of the small waves become the "quiet and lucid" type of poetry of the "Kuo Sung" of Chou times, the short lyrics of Wang Wei, the songs of Japanese Classical poets—Saigyo, Shonin, and Basho— and the new *Crescent Moon* poems of Tagore. . . .[16]

Although Kuo is best remembered for his robust and "explosive" style—the "great waves" verse—he can be equally at home with the more subdued and reflective kind of lyrics—the "small waves" verse. One early example of this second type is "Egret" (1919):

> O egret! Egret!
> Where have you flown from?
> Whither are you now going?
> Drafting an ellipse against the sky,
> You suddenly swoop down into the sea;.
> Again you soar into the sky,
> Again you swoop down into the sea,
> O snow-white egret,

[16] Ibid., pp. 205–6.

Whither are you truly going?

The single image of the egret swooping against the sky symbolizes the complete freedom of an independent spirit that men
aspire to, but never quite attain. It is the spirit itself that Kuo,
a strong individualist, cherishes. The poem has a serene classical
grace in spite of its kinesthetic effects. The repetition from lines
5 to 8 not only produces a clear vision of the bird swooping and
soaring (the symbolic movement of the poem) but also accen-
tuates the rhythm of that movement.

If Kuo's first poems, written in his explosive style discussed
below, give an impression of power, his quieter lyrics reveal a
more conscious artist and a more subtle craftsman. The lack of
force is compensated for by a better mastery of emotion and
means of expression. In these verses Kuo uses repetition and
parallel constructions and more flexible stanzaic lines and
rhymes to assure the cohesiveness of conventional patterns without destroying their fluidity. The diction is more polished, the
rhythm tighter in these reflective lyrics. Strains of the old poetry are noticeable.

A QUIET NIGHT   (1921)
Soft, soft is the moonlight
Veiling the pinewoods beyond the village.
Round, round are the white clouds through
Which sieve a few drops of stars.

Where is the Milky Way?
Afar is the misty sea fog;
Might there be a mermaid on the shore
Weeping pearls before the moon?

Kuo's use of traditional motifs is often imaginative. In "The
Streets of Heaven" (1921) he successfully weaves into the fabric
the legendary love story of the cowherd and the spinning maid
(two stars in constellations across from each other in the Milky
Way). When the immortal spinning maid was compelled to

leave her earth lover, the cowherd, and return to the sky, heaven took pity and allowed them to meet once a year on the seventh day of the seventh moon.

> The streetlights in the distance have brightened
> Like countless bright stars sparkling.
> The bright stars in heaven have appeared
> Like countless luminous streetlights.

> Surely in that misty sky
> There are lovely streets.
> The items displayed there
> Must be treasures unfound on this earth.

> Look, that shallow Milky Way
> Surely cannot be too wide.
> The cowherd and weaving maid across the river
> Surely can ride their buffaloes to meet each other.

> I think just at this moment, they
> Surely must be strolling along those streets of heaven.
> If you do not believe me, look at the blooming comet.
> It must be the lantern they carry on their walk.

Written in the same lyrical vein is "A Clear Morning" (1920?):

> Over the pond a few new willows,
> Under the willows a long pavilion,
> Within the pavilion, my son and I are sitting;
> Upon the pond the sun and clouds are shining.

> The cock's crow, the birds' call, the parrots' cries,
> Mingling and flowing on like a crystal stream.
> The powdery butterflies flitting hither and thither,
> The mud swallows fluttering thither and hither.

> The fallen leaves swing

And fly into the pond.
The green leaves swing
And frolic with the silver light in the air.

One white bird comes
To dance on the pond.
Suddenly, there's a band of broken jade!
An endless spread of green rushes!

The echoes of traditional lyrics linger in these lines—the treasured traditional parallelism and the conventional nature imagery of the willows, the butterflies, and the swallow. The sudden debut of the white bird creating the scene of "a band of broken jade! / An endless spread of green rushes!" displays not only the poet's classical discipline but also his own in- genuity. The poem is an expression of the familiar romantic love of spring, a favorite with the old lyricists.

Another characteristic feature of Kuo's poetry that is par- ticularly pronounced in his early works is pantheism. Kuo comments:

> Because of my fondness for the works of Tagore and Goethe, I took pleasure in the philosophy of pantheism. Or rather, because of my original leaning toward pantheism, I became especially fond of those poets who shared the same leaning. . . . Once exposed to this philosophy abroad, I rediscovered my earlier love for Chuang Tzu. During my middle-school period, I loved to read Chuang Tzu on account of his free, soaring style. As for the thought it contained, I was very vague about that. Not until I came into contact with the thought abroad did I suddenly reach a stage of illumination and understanding of Chuang Tzu's philosophy.[17]

Reading Chuang Tzu had given Kuo new insights into the philosopher's concept of Tao as innately pantheistic: "Tung Kuo Tzŭ asked Chuang Tzŭ: 'Where is the so-called *Tao*?'

[17] Ibid., 7:58.

Chuang Tzŭ said: 'There is nowhere where it is not.' Tung Kuo Tzŭ said: 'Specify an instance of it.' Chuang Tzŭ said: 'It is in the ant.' 'How can it be so low?' 'It is in the panic grass. . . .' "[18]

This interest and belief in man's oneness with nature figures prominently in a majority of Kuo's verse.

THREE PANTHEISTS   (1919)

I love my country's Chuang Tzu
Because I love his pantheism,
Because I love his making straw sandals for a living.

I love Holland's Spinoza
Because I love his pantheism,
Because I love his grinding lenses for a living.

I love India's Kabir
Because I love his pantheism,
Because I love his making fishnets for a living.

Kuo wrote a considerable number of nature poems, most of which are pantheistic. Like Feng Chih and a host of traditional nature poets, Kuo sought unity of poetic work in the fundamental unity of creation. He has a great need to establish contact with the elements. In many of his nature poems, Kuo glorifies the sky, the sea, the snow, and the earth. To him these are forces not to be feared or conquered but to be celebrated and worshiped. These pieces are often intoned like a prayer, a hymn of praise to the eternal oneness of all creation.

STANDING ON THE EDGE OF THE GLOBE, CALLING ALOUD   (1919)

Countless white clouds rise and angrily surge forth,
Ah, what a majestic spectacle of the Arctic!
The boundless Pacific is gathering all its strength to
    overthrow the globe.
Ah, the mighty waves come rolling and rushing before me.
Ah, the constant destruction, the constant reaction, the

[18] Yu-lan Feng, *A History of Chinese Philosophy*, 1:223.

       constant striving forth!
    Ah, the power, power, the power!
    The painting of power, the dance of power, the music of
      power,
    The psalm of power, and the rhythm of power!

The poem has flaws: the overuse of exclamatory sentences; the poor choice of words in the ending; and a too-great similarity of "music," "psalm," and "rhythm" to convey the scope that has been created. These faults, however, cannot obscure the tremendous energy generated in the poem, the gathering momentum and cumulative force. Within the lines of rhetoric and soaring exaltation, one sees the vigorous and sinewy style for which Kuo is most admired.

    The poem also points to Whitman as a great source of influence in Kuo's poetry. The poetry of Whitman, especially its style, made an immense impression on Kuo when he came across it while studying in Japan. He recollected this unique experience years later: "That completely unconventional style of Whitman is very much in harmony with the stormy and progressive spirit of the May Fourth era. I was totally taken and captivated by his heroic, spontaneous, and sonorous music."[19] Kuo owes an important debt to Whitman and his "volcanic expression of emotion," as Kuo described it after reading *Leaves of Grass*; he has confessed that the best of his own poetry was written under the influence of the American poet:

> I want to say frankly that after the *Goddesses*, I am no longer a poet. True, I have since published many volumes of verse. They have held many people in their spell. But, to me, they lack flavor. Though technically they may be superior, still the volcanic expression of emotion that produced the *Goddesses* was gone. Only some ripples are left after the tide is over. Some may find particular enjoyment from them, but for myself, only poetry written at life's emotional peak is most significant.[20]

[19] Quoted from Kuo's article on the history of his verse writing in Lou Ch'i's *Lun Kuo Mo-jo ti-shih* [Criticism of Kuo Mo-jo's poetry] (Shanghai, 1959), p. 30.
[20] Kuo, *Mo-jo wen-chi*, 13:121.

Many critics and readers would agree with Kuo's own estimate of his poetry. There is little doubt that his most valuable contribution to the new verse lies in that first volume of collected works. Its innovative prosody and method of expression offered to Chinese poetry a tempo and a mode of feeling hitherto unknown.

Like Whitman, Kuo wrote much of his poetry in the free verse then being adopted by many of his contemporaries (Hu Shih, K'ang Pai-ch'ing, and other pioneering poets), but he did not forswear the stanzaic pattern. In general, he has shown a genuine deftness with form. Kuo and Whitman share the same emotional approach to their work; both achieve an immediate effect by the sheer force of their emotional intensity and their "explosive" manner of expression. The language they favor is simple and plain, though highly charged—as of an "enormous power being liberated." Like Whitman, Kuo had a special awareness of modern science. He frequently incorporated his scientific knowledge in his verse in an attempt to enrich and renew the current vocabulary of poetry.

THE SKY DOG   (1920)

Ya, I am a sky dog!
I have swallowed the moon,
I have swallowed the sun.
I have swallowed all the planets,
I have swallowed the entire universe.
I am I!

I am the light of the moon,
I am the light of the sun.
I am the light of all the planets,
I am the light of *X ray*,
I am the total *energy* of the entire universe.

I am flying,
I am screaming,
I am burning,

> I am burning like a fierce fire!
> I am screaming like the mighty ocean!
> I am running like electricity!
> I am running,
> I am running,
> I tear my skin,
> I eat my flesh,
> I chew my heart,
> I am running on my nerves,
> I am running on my spines,
> I am running in my brain.
>
> I am I!
> The I of I is about to explode!

This feverish, semihysterical piece points up some of Kuo's common weaknesses: emotional inflation; lack of syntactical variation, which results in a mechanical rhythm; excess of scientific terminology; and insertion of foreign words to no purpose (both X-ray and energy are in English).

A calmer and more felicitous performance is "Walking through Jurimatsubara at Night" (1920):

> The sea is already deep in sleep.
> Looking afar I see only a white expanse of misty glow.
> I hear not even the slightest whisper of the waves.
> O great cosmos! How sublime, how free, how heroic, how
>   embracingly vital and serene you are!
> Countless bright stars are opening wide their eyes
> To behold this lovely nightscape.
> Countless ancient pines in Jurimatsubara
> Are raising high their arms in silent praise of the universe.
> Every branch of their limbs trembles in the sky,
> Every branch of my nerve fibers trembles within me.

The emotion here is under better control, the pitch subdued and firmly sustained. The mood is almost devotional, evoking a feeling of awe at the immensities of time and space and the sacred mysteries of the cosmos.

A striking contrast to this psalmlike lyric is "The Sea of Bath" (1919):

> The sun is at its zenith!
> The vast Pacific is playing its stately tunes!
> What a panoramic display! What a circular dance!
> I play with the waves in this enormous dancing space!
> My blood and the sea's waves together rise,
> My heart and the sun's fire together burn,
> The dust, the dirt, the chaffs, the husks that I have col-
> lected since birth
> Have been washed away!
> Now I am transformed into a cicada that, having shed its
> shell,
> Is screaming aloud under the fierce sun:
> The power of the sun
> Is going to melt the entire universe!
> Oh brothers, hurry, hurry!
> Hurry and come play with the waves!
> While our blood's waves are still rising,
> While our heart's fire is still burning,
> Let us take this rotten old skin bag
> And wash it completely clean!
> The reconstruction of the new society
> Depends completely on us!

Like some of his other verse in this vigorous vein, "The Sea of Bath" is launched at high pitch and sustained at that level to the end. The device of enjambment is an improved technique acquired by the poet in this period; it offers a needed contrast to the end-stopped lines and relieves the monotony in the over-all movement of the poem. Here again, Kuo combined the freedom of free verse with a patterned effect achieved by his insistence on rhyme. The poem is a unified though somewhat abstract piece with its social and political implications; it is a lyric moment of exaltation as the poet pays homage to the sea.

Kuo also wrote four verse plays in this early period:

It was under the influence of Goethe that I attempted to write verse plays. Not long after I finished translating the first part of *Faust*, I wrote *The Blossom of the Cherry Wood*. *The Rebirth of the Goddess* and *The Tragedy at the Hsiang River* were both written under the direct influence of Goethe. Needless to say, this influence was assisted by the neoromanticism then popular at the time and the "expressionism" then just beginning to rise in Germany. In particular, it was the dislocated and explosive expressionism of the Expressionist school that found a suitable ground in my dislocated and explosive mind. Ernst Toller's *Die Wandlung* and Georg Kaiser's *Die Bürger von Calais* were the works I enjoyed the most. That group of men worshiped Goethe. They took his words, "von Innen nach Aussen" (from within to without), as their motto. And I who had just finished translating *Faust*, part 1, felt a deeper kinship. But this influence was a limiting one which required much effort to cast off in later days.[21]

The subject matter and characters of these plays were derived from either history or mythology. But "plays" is something of a misnomer, for they are merely scenes dealing with particular moments in the lives of the characters. They are very short, crudely executed, and have little dramatic action; the characterization lacks dimension and depth. Kuo admitted that he used his characters as a mouthpiece—an undesirable result of Goethe's influence, he added.

Kuo was later to expand two of the plays, *The Blossom of the Cherry Wood* (1920) and *The Tragedy at the Hsiang River* (1920), into full-length dramas. The former dramatizes the story of Nieh Cheng of the Warring period (403–221 B.C.), who was slain after his failure to assassinate an important official, the enemy of his friend and benefactor. In his later full-length drama, Kuo made Nieh Cheng into a revolutionary hero who rose against the reigning authority—the enemy of the people. *The Tragedy at the Hsiang River* is about Ch'ü Yüan (second century B.C.), a patriotic poet who, victimized by court slander and banished by his prince, drowned himself. Kuo admired the highly imaginative poetry of Ch'ü Yüan; he confessed in his autobiographical works that often he identified himself with this ancient poet.

For the dramatic personae in *The Rebirth of the Goddess* (1920), Kuo adopted two mythological personages, Kung Kung and Chuan Hsü, to symbolize the warlord factions (south and north) who were struggling for control of China after the founding of the republic in 1912. The rebirth of the goddess symbolizes a third China—a China that is "beautiful and peace-loving." The last of Kuo's verse plays, *The Two Sons of the King of Ku Chu* (1922?), deals with two legendary figures, Po I and Shu Ch'i, who died of starvation rather than live under a new ruler after their state fell.

All four plays are mediocre. The dialogues are undistinguished, often flat and obtrusively rhetorical. The emotions are overinflated, the rhythm commonplace, and the tones sentimental. The looseness of structure discourages any real cohesiveness or variation, and the result is sheer monotony. Following is an excerpt from *The Rebirth of the Goddess*:

> The thunder has stopped!
> The lightning has been destroyed!
> The battle of light and darkness is over!
> What of the overthrown sun?
> It is thrown out of the sky!
> Is the body of heaven torn and broken?
> Has the darkness, once driven away, now stolen back?
> What shall be done to the broken body of heaven?
> Shall we smelt some more colored stones to mend it?
> Such colored pieces are of no use now!
> Oh let it be ruined, let's not mend it again!
> Let's wait for our newly created sun to come.
> It will then shine through the world within the sky, and
> beyond the sky!

Kuo's one real triumph is his long poem, "The Nirvana of the Feng and Huang" (1920), which deals with his favorite theme of rebirth. In this virtuoso performance Kuo forges unity from an unlikely diversity of elements: instances of pure lyricism, passages of highly charged dialogues, satire, and moments of great dramatic projection. Though the poem has weak passages and the ending is faulty, it is in general successful. The Buddhist term Nirvana here stands for the rebirth of China after the May Fourth Movement. Merging the archetypal motif of the phoenix with the Marxian ideal of society's rebirth through revolutionary change, Kuo sees a new glorious China rising from its own ashes.

The poem is divided into six parts: "Prelude"; "Song of the Feng" (the male phoenix); "Song of the Huang" (the female phoenix); "Duet of Feng and Huang"; "Chorus of the Birds"; and "Song of Rebirth," sung by the Feng and Huang, which is the finale of the "chorale." The "Prelude" spotlights the stage—the legendary mountain of Tan-hsüeh, where the Feng and Huang were born—and sets the elegiac mood and tone as the hour of death approaches for the two birds. The verse begins on a hauntingly beautiful note as they make their ritualistic preparations. The incantatory movement of the section, created primarily by a varied pattern of parallel constructions, conveys a contemplative spirit.

In the "Song of the Feng" the tone shifts from the subdued to a more elevated level. The pitch is also raised, reaching its peak in the middle of the section as the Feng recounts the darkness, the wretchedness, the evil and suffering of the world; and then it slowly subsides at the close of the song. Parallelism and repetition of words and phrases give emphasis and tightness to lines and stanzas.

The third section, the "Song of the Huang," has a delicate precision, a gentle touch, that offers a striking contrast to the fierce lyricism of the preceding section. A faint note of nostalgia mingles with elegiac pain in tone and mood. The short duet that follows describes the imminent death of the phoenixes. A variation of the theme occurs in the next section, the choral song of the birds (the eagle, peacock, owl, pigeon, parrot, and stork). The voices of these birds represent the various people in society mocking and jeering the dying phoenixes: each rejoices over the death of these magical birds, for each thinks now it can inherit the world. The last song in which the Feng and Huang celebrate their joyous rebirth after their flaming death, starts at a low pitch which rises gradually until it reaches its fully poetic force and dramatic climax at the poem's end. Kuo's mastery of theme is admirable, his control of mood and feeling expert. The poem is as coherently and deftly orchestrated as a musical composition; each movement builds toward the unity and harmony of the work.

THE NIRVANA OF THE FENG AND HUANG
Prelude
On the threshold of the new year, there in the sky
The Feng and Huang fly back and forth.
Singing mournful tunes as they fly away,
Bearing twigs of fragrant wood as they return,
Return to Tan-hsüeh Mountain.

To the right of the mountain is the withered Wu-t'ung
    tree,
To the left of the mountain is the dried-up spring.
Before the mountain is the wide expanse of the sea,
Behind the mountain is the vast dreary plain,
And over the mountain a frozen sky of bitter winds.

The sky is now darkened,
The fragrant wood is now piled high,
The Feng is now wearied from flying,
The Huang is now wearied from flying,
Their hour of death is nearing.

The Feng pecks at the fragrant wood,
Sparks of fire upward dart;
The Huang fans the fire sparks,
Strands of smoke rise upward.

Again pecks the Feng,
Again fans the Huang,
On the mountain the scented smoke swirls,
On the mountain the firelight fills the sky.

The night has deepened,
The fragrant wood is lighted,
The Feng is wearied from pecking,
The Huang is wearied from fanning,
Their hour of death is nearing!

Ah, ah,
Sad, sad are Feng and Huang!
Feng starts his dance, now slow, now high!
Huang starts her songs, now sad, now exalted!
Again Feng dances,
Again Huang sings,
A flock of birds has now flown over
Beyond the sky to attend the burial.

Song of the Feng
Chi-chi! Chi-chi! Chi-chi!
Chi-chi! Chi-chi! Chi-chi!
Vast vast is the universe, cold and cruel as iron!
Vast vast is the universe, rank and filthy as blood!

.   .   .   .

Ah! Ah!
To live within this gloomy, grimy world
Is enough to rust even a diamond sword!
Universe! O universe!
I curse you with all my power!
You blood-besmirched slaughterhouse!
You anguish-filled prison!
You graveyard of shrieking ghosts!
You purgatory of lost souls!
Why do you exist at all?

.   .   .   .

Song of the Huang

. . . .

Ah! Ah!
This misty, drifting life of ours
Is like a deep dream in a dark night.

. . . .

With sleep before us,
With sleep behind us,
We come like a breath of wind,
We come like a thread of smoke.
Coming like the wind,
Going like the smoke,
With sleep that is gone,
With sleep that is to come,
We are but smoke and wind
In that wink of time within the dream.

. . . .

Song of Rebirth

The Cocks:
   The tide of dawn has risen,
   The tide of dawn has risen,
   The light that died is born again!

   The tide of spring has risen,
   The tide of spring has risen,
   The world that died is born again!

   The tide of life has risen,
   The tide of life has risen,
   The Feng and Huang that died are born again!

The Feng and Huang:
   We are born again!
   We are born again!
   The One in All is born again,
   The All in One is born again!
   The All in One is born again!
   We are he, they are me.

O you in me, and I in you,
Therefore I am you.
And you are me:
The fire is Huang,
The Feng is fire.
Oh soar! Soar!
Oh sing with joy! Let's sing with joy!

Now we are fresh, we are pure,
Now we are beautiful, we are fragrant.
The One in All is fragrant,
The All in One is fragrant,
The fragrance is you, the fragrance is I,
The fragrance is he, the fragrance is fire.
The fire is you,

.   .   .   .   .   .

The fire is fire.
Oh soar! Soar!
Oh sing with joy! Sing with joy!

.   .   .   .

Now we are alive, we are free,
Now we are strong, we are immortal.
The One in All is immortal,
The All in One is immortal.
Immortal are you, immortal am I.
Immortal is he, immortal is fire.
   Fire are you,
   Fire am I,
   Fire is he,
   Fire is fire,
   Oh soar! Soar!
   Oh sing with joy! Sing with joy!
Now we sing with joy, now we soar.
Now we soar, now we sing with joy.
The One in All sings in perpetual joy!
The All in One sings in perpetual joy!
Is it you who gleefully sing, or is it I?

Is it he who gleefully sings, or is it fire?
　　It is joy singing!
　　It is joy singing!
　　There's only the song of joy!
　　There's only the song of joy!
　　Oh sing with joy!
　　　Sing with joy!
　　　　Sing with joy!

As early as 1921, in the prefatory poem to *Goddesses,* Kuo had proclaimed himself a "proletarian":

I am a proletarian
Because but for my naked self,
I possess no other private property.
Goddesses was created by myself,
Therefore it may be said to belong to me alone.
But I am willing to be a Communist,
And therefore I am making her public to all.[22]

Later, in 1932, he explained:

Although my political thinking was comparatively advanced, it was not in any way organically related to my literary activity. In the introductory poem to *The Goddesses* I said, "I am a proletarian" and "I would like to become a Communist"; but this was only playing with words, for in reality the very concepts of the proletariat and of communism were still unclear in my mind.[23]

Kuo's interest in Marxism was climaxed by his "conversion" to communism in 1924 after the completion of his translation of Kawajami Hajime's *Social Organization and Social Revolution:*

The benefits that I derived from translating this work are by no means meager. In the past, I was only vaguely resentful of individualistic capitalism and hopeful for social revolution. Now

22 Ibid., 1:3.
23 Translated by David Roy in *Kuo Mo-jo: The Early Years,* p. 143.

with the added light of reason, they are no longer mere emotional reaction. The translation of this book serves as a turning point in my life. It has awakened me from my half sleep, led me out of my indecision, rescued me from the darkness of death.[24]

Kuo's dramatic conversion was basically responsible for the eventual change of position taken by the Creation Society. Founded by Kuo and his friends Yü Ta-fu, Chang Tzu-p'ing, and others—all of them students who had returned from Japan —the Creation Society (1921–29) was an immensely influential organization. Its publications, *Creation Quarterly* (1922–24), *Creative Weekly* (1923–24), and *Creation Daily* (1923), played an important part in the intellectual life of the youth in those turbulent years. It started with the slogan "Art for art's sake" as opposed to "Art for life's sake," the motto of the rival Literary Research Society. The Creation Society's early aesthetic approach to literature was eloquently demonstrated in the works of its members, especially those of Kuo. As Kuo's shift toward Marxism became increasingly pronounced, the society adopted a more socialist approach in literature. In a letter to his friend, Ch'eng Fang-wu, in 1924, Kuo wrote:

Now my concept of literature is completely changed. I feel our problem at present is not one of techniques. The problem lies in whether it is a literature of yesterday, today, or tomorrow. The literature of yesterday was only an exalted object of amusement for the privileged aristocrats in their leisure. . . . The literature of today is the literature of those who are on the revolutionary path: it is the cries of the oppressed, the screams of the desperate, the cursed words of the battling will, the joy of anticipating the revolution. . . . The literature of tomorrow can only arrive after the realization of socialism. And only after this realization can great genius develop freely and fully. And only then when there are no more social classes, no frustrations in life (except the purely physiological kind), can man be restored to his true nature and can literature take pure nature as its objective and can pure

[24] Kuo, *Mo-jo wen-chi*, 7:183.

literature be created. . . . We are men on the revolutionary path and our literature of today can only justify its existence in its function of hastening the realization of social revolution. All art is a reflection of life and only as such is it true literature. This is my firmest belief. Having reached this view of literature, I am able to obtain a clearer understanding of literature, which has also restored my faith in it. Now is the time of propaganda, and literature is its instrument. My past tendency of indecision is now corrected.[25]

Kuo's change of view on literature wrought a subsequent change in his work as well as in his political life. He became increasingly active in the cause of the Communist party. Since the Communists took over the mainland, he has held numerous prominent positions in the party: he has been vice-chairman of the National Committee of the Chinese People's Political Consultative Conference, vice-premier and president of the Chinese Academy of Science, and chairman of the All-China Federation of Literary and Art Circles.

Though Kuo published a considerable amount of poetry in this period—*The Vanguard* (1928), *The Recovery* (1928), *The Sound of War* (1938), *The Cicada* (1948), *In Praise of China* (1958), *Forever Spring* (1959)—most of these later poems are of doubtful poetic value. Many are barely verse, being prosaic, banal, didactic, and tediously propagandistic in character. The best poems add little to Kuo's artistic achievement. The peaks and pinnacles of promise in his earlier works have eroded to small slopes.

It is true that Kuo Mo-jo was among the first to sound the call for a proletarian literature; it is also true that his later conversion to communism appears to be genuine, as is his concern over the plight of the common people of China. Nevertheless, one suspects that Kuo has always remained a romantic at heart, a romantic who embraced communism with the conviction that communism offers an earthly paradise for China, that a new

[25] Ibid., p. 185.

vital literature "can only arrive after the realization of socialism." His proletarian beliefs have a strong affinity, if not analogy, to those characteristic features of romanticism: humanism and idealism. The spectacles of hunger, abuse, poverty, and the exploitation of the poor by the rich haunted Kuo as much as they did Blake, Byron, Shelley, Tu Fu, and Po Chü-i. Like them, Kuo spoke out in bitter social protest. Like them, he aspired to and anticipated a "utopian vision" of a society in which the common people could live in peace and contentment. For the realization of this vision the poet turned to communism, an answer that was almost inevitable as the tides of revolution swept the nation. The forces of external circumstances were such that Kuo could no longer maintain his moral and artistic integrity if he continued to write in his "ivory tower," insisting on "Art for art's sake." In 1928, the turning point after his recovery from a long illness and personal crisis, he wrote of his new purpose in life:

> I believe that there will be no more hindrance from now
>   on.
> I want to sing aloud without restraint.
> I want to wake up our decadent nation, our weakened
>   race.
> I want to sing about the life of the newly risen proletarian.

And in his prefatory poem to *The Vanguard* (1928), he announced:

> These poems may be crude,
> But they are the vanguard of this revolutionary age.
> They were my voice first sounded five or six years ago.
> They were my outcries sounded five or six years ago.
>
> At that time, only a scanty few had resounded.
> Much more was the cold scorn that I received.
> But now I can boldly declare:
> I have already acquired many friends.

"To Encourage My Unemployed Friends" (1923) is an example of this group of verses.

> O my friends, we need not grieve! Need not grieve!
> It is our duty to destroy this hellish devil's palace!
>
> Under this capitalistic system where can we find employment?
> We are only dogs collared to slave for the capitalists!
>
> O my friends, we should congratulate ourselves that we are free!
> We should congratulate ourselves that we are free!
>
> Though our strength may not be able to destroy this hell,
> We can at least walk hand in hand to the Shou Yang Hall.
>
> O my friends, we need not grieve! Need not grieve!
> From now on let us rouse our spirit and vow to destroy
>   this hellish devil's palace!

In "Morning in Shanghai" (1923), Kuo pours out his bitter resentment of the rich and his compassion for the poor:

> The streets' surfaces are not made of cement,
> They are made of the sweat, blood, and lives of the workers.
> Oh the miserably pitiful lives, the miserably pitiful lives!
> Under the wheels of the rich men's motor cars . . . rolling
>   . . . rolling . . .
> O my brothers, I believe:
> Right in the middle of this street, the Bubbling Well Road,
> There surely will be a violent volcanic eruption!

In these poems the heroes are invariably the poor; the villains, the rich. Kuo's feelings for the poor undoubtedly are sincere. Still, one senses a more impersonal attitude in Kuo than in younger "proletarian" poets like T'ien Chien or even Ai Ch'ing. His treatment is more general and abstract: there is no detailed intimate description, nor is there any personla sentiment involved in his portraiture; nobody faintly resembling Ai Ch'ing's nurse in "Ta-Yen-Ho" lives in Kuo's "proletarian poetry." "The Declaration of Poetry" (1928) in particular lacks immediacy, often disintegrating into rhetoric and abstraction:

> You see, I am plain and simple,
> Without any ornamentation.
> I only love those workers and farmers
> Barefoot and naked.

> I am also barefoot and naked.
> I detest that rich class,
> Though they be beautiful and love beauty
> And their entire body is silk, perfume, and gems.

> I am poetry, and this is my declaration:
> My class is the proletariat;
> Though at present I am still not strong enough
> And still need increased discipline,

> It is because I have recovered only recently.
> My spirit is not as robust as before.
> But I hope there will come a day
> When I shall roar like the storm again.

As in most of the poetry written during the war period, including the works of T'ien Chien and Ai Ch'ing, strong patriotic sentiment dominates Kuo's war poems. Themes of war and its ramifications persist in such works as "Song of the War of Resistance," "Sound of War," "The Great Wall of Flesh and Blood," and "Iron Virgin" (1937). Kuo has become more a master of his emotions and of his means of expression; the style is less flamboyant and more restrained. For such poems Kuo chose the stanzaic form, with its more conventional and regular pattern, instead of free verse.

"IRON VIRGIN"

The Iron Virgin was found in Medieval Europe,
A really cruel torture was she.
Her inside was just a box with sharp nails,
But her outside showed the image of Holy Mary.

The Holy Lady was the door of the box,
From behind her breast a spike protruded.
The victim was put inside, and the door, closed,
The long nail thus pierced the victim's chest.

In Manchuria the Japanese had a new invention,
Sharp nails were lined up on the inside of a barrel.
With the victim in it, and both ends sealed,
The barrel was left in the streets to be kicked around.

The torture had no kind looks of the Holy Lady,
But was equipped with such iron breasts as the Virgin's.
The Japanese, they say, just named it Nail Box,
Ah, they surely are good at imitation.[26]

The poem is one of Kuo's better performances of the period.
The diction is pointed and clear, and the treatment of theme
both novel and effective. The emotional compulsion is there
but never allowed to lapse into sentimentality or hysterical
outbursts. The violent imagery is appropriate and essential for
presenting the incident, for transmitting the terror and inhumanity of war, and for revealing the speaker's inner fury,
which is shared by the whole nation.

Despite the seeming hopelessness of the situation during the
dark hours of war, Kuo Mo-jo, like his younger colleagues
T'ien Chien and Ai Ch'ing, remained optimistic, confident that
the final victory would arrive. The concluding stanzas of his
poem celebrating the war of resistance against the Japanese
speaks well for this faith:

---

[26] Kai-yu Hsu, trans. and ed., *Twentieth Century Chinese Poetry*, p. 38.

My fellow countrymen, do not be discouraged;
Let us rouse ourselves; do not be alarmed and frightened,
We will fight our war of resistance for eight years, ten
 years—
Fight till the Japanese imperialism is destroyed.

The final victory belongs to us alone;
O my fellow countrymen, let us raise our voice and shout:
Shout for the rebirth of our national race,
Shout for the heroism of our courageous soldiers.

And in "The Great Wall of Flesh and Blood" (1937):

To love one's native land is the duty of every man.
Everyone should exert his utmost
Especially when the nation has reached that crucial moment
 of life and death.
. . . .
We are no cowards, nor are we arrogant.
But we do believe that we must defeat our enemies.
We must build a new Great Wall with our very flesh and
 blood!

During a heavy air raid in war-torn Chungking that resulted
in the tragic death of over ten thousand people, Kuo wrote the
impassioned lines:

Even the heart is crippled—
Don't you know?
There is only anger, no sadness!
Only fire, no water!
Even the Yangtze and Chialing rivers turn to torrents of
 fire.
This fire—
Can it not destroy that pyramid founded on sins?

When the war was over in 1945, Kuo Mo-jo did not burst
forth singing jubilant songs about the Allied forces' victory. To

a loyal Communist like Kuo the enemies were yet to be van-
quished, the old feudal order to be overthrown, and foreign
imperialists to be driven out of China. Only then could China
have a glorious future.

EXPLAINING THE TWO CROSSES   (1946)
1

A couple of crosses
Represent a double grave.
Down with imperialism,
Down with feudalism,
Let them both be buried together.
It has been over thirty-five years
Since they were married to each other.
What a devoted couple!

2

A couple of crosses
Represent a determined Jesus,
Inviting over two robbers,
Inviting over the Pharisees,
To double the suffering of people.
They've decided to mess around for
    another thirty-five years!
No, China must be liberated.
The glorious future awaits.

7

Poetry after 1949

In 1949 the Communists in one cataclysmic sweep not only obliterated the old political, social, and economic order of China, but ruthlessly altered the course of the arts. Mao Tse-tung's literary principles, propounded to guide the left-wing writers in wartime Yenan, were now cast as infallible rules for all creative artists in mainland China. Literature became totally subservient to the dictates of the party. The main task of writers in the new China was to create a true proletarian literature founded on "socialist realism" and "revolutionary romanticism": they must represent reality in the "spirit of socialism" and explore revolutionary themes in an optimistic and heroic manner. Communist critics insisted on the "correct orientation of literature and art serving proletarian politics, serving the workers, peasants, and soldiers . . . along the road pointed out by Chairman Mao."[1] Under such crippling confines some writers fell virtually silent and some left the country, but most remained to adjust their beat to the flaming tempo of revolution. Their outburst of exaltation filled the air. Established poets like Ai Ch'ing, Kuo Mo-jo, and T'ien Chien leaped to the occasion with joyous song.

IN PRAISE OF NEW CHINA   (1949)
By Kuo Mo-jo
I
The people's China loftily stands in east Asia.
Its million rays of splendor illuminate the skies.

[1] *Chinese Literature* (Peking), 1968, no. 7–8, p. 141.

After insurmountable hardships comes the celebration of
  victory.
Everyplace is red with five-star banners.
  Living things are manifold, products plentiful.
  Workers and peasants are the true masters.
  May our glorious fatherland
  Steadily advance to Utopia.

II

The people are industrious and courageous:
Enforce national defense, revolutionize traditions.
Strong is the leadership of our Communist government,
Herald of the proletariat.
  Industrialization, rainbowlike atmosphere;
  Tillers own their lands, the earth belongs to all.
  May our glorious fatherland
  Steadily advance to Utopia.

III

The people rule, democracy is centralized.
Radiant and clear is our leader's demeanor.
River and oceans overflow with songs of praise.
The Kunlun Mountain looms high above all.
  Many races and tribes are brothers.
  All the country is filled with freedom.
  May our glorious fatherland
  Steadily advance to Utopia.

Hardly a masterpiece, "In Praise of New China" epitomizes
the victory songs that deluged the poetic scene in the years immediately after 1949. Deeply nationalistic, the poem cele-
brates the glory of the long-awaited day, the achievements of
the party, and the leadership of Mao Tse-tung. It reveals, too,
a new kind of sensibility, a collective brotherhood, and a com-
monality of feelings. Kuo, by adopting a formal stanzaic pat-

tern here, achieves a dignity that lifts his verse above many others dealing with the same theme. His greater restraint and his technical proficiency also set him apart.

The jubilant strain continues in this excerpt from "I Remember My Native Land" (1950), written by Ai Ch'ing on the first anniversary of the Communist victory:

> October first, nineteen hundred forty-nine—
> The great day had arrived!
> After decades of struggle
> Chinese people marched under the triumphal arch.
> The five-star banners wave in the Peking skies.
> Beneath them the clamoring cries of the rejoicing crowd,
> The victorious cannons shook the earth.
> The entire world was celebrating the birth of a new China.
> Gone forever is darkness.
> The sun has risen from the East.

Intoxicated with the newly won political victory, proletarian poets like T'ien Chien never cease singing its glory. Even after the first tide of ecstasy had subsided and China entered its construction phase, the same tone, the same ardor, and the same unshakable faith in communism resounded in T'ien Chien's poem, "Song of My Fatherland" (1954):

I

> Fatherland, your blue sky
> And golden earth
> Now are independent and free,
> Out from the dark clouds.
>
> This is a glorious day—
> Mao Tse-tung has mapped the blueprint.
> O fatherland, we rejoice
> And proudly hasten on our way.

II

> The new constitution shines
> On our great nation.

On the tall golden-red pillars
Hang the mighty words of steel.

The entire nation is jubilant,
Determined to walk on one path
For building socialism,
For elevating labor.

III

O fatherland, your mountains and rocks—
They are roaring aloud.
In mountains, by the Huai River,
We now possess a huge reservoir.

On this vast land,
What shakes the mountains and rocks?
Not fierce winds, not thunderstorms,
But the footsteps of the workers.

IV

On our mountains, near the lakes,
Echo the clear songs of construction.
More precious than gems are these songs.
Not for anything will we exchange them.

Fatherland, your vast country
Holds the greatest treasure—
Its name is bravery and hard work.
This is perpetual honor.

V

O fatherland, your people,
Your six hundred million people,
Who for the future of their country
Shall fulfill their sacred mission.

The flag of our Republic rises
High, and ever higher.
Behold, on this great land

The red sun has risen!

Poetry before the Communist take-over had in common an element of exclusiveness, of appealing to the intellectual few. Themes revolved around the lives and thoughts of the bourgeois intelligentsia. All this was radically changed with the revolution. Poets today are constantly admonished to rid their verse of any decaying residues of the bourgeoisie and to depict the lives and character of the new ruling class—the working masses. One notable feature of proletarian verse is the inexhaustible theme of contrasting conditions—the before and after of the Communist "liberation." The erstwhile miserable lot of the poor peasant is endlessly depicted to expose the cruelty and inhumanity of landlords and other exploiters in the old regime. In the following poem Feng Chih, a bourgeois poet by origin, pictures with his usual gentle voice the wretched life of a poor woodcutter in the old society. The poem reveals again Feng's deft use of dialogue, his skill in creating suspenseful atmosphere, and above all his gift of evoking pathos and drama.

HAN PO CHOPPED WOOD (1953–55)

(A Night Dialogue between Mother and Son)

It was the nineteenth day of the first lunar month,
The rain had been falling for days and nights.
Then suddenly it stopped after midnight,
And a bright waning moon emerged.

The entire room was flooded with moonlight.
Startled awake from her dream, the old woman
Woke up her sleeping son. She said,
"There is a man's shadow outside."

Her son replied, "At such a late hour,
How could there be anyone out there?"
"You young people don't know that

This is the spirit of Han Po.

Han Po was a woodcutter and all day long
He chopped wood on the mountain.
He was so deeply in debt to his landlord that
He could never hope to pay up.

Han Po chopped wood all his life
To supply firewood for his landlord's cooking stove;
Han Po chopped wood all his life
To furnish firewood to keep his landlord warm.

But as for himself, he was always
Hungry and always cold.
No matter how bad the weather,
He never neglected his chopping chores.

It was the same kind of night as tonight,
The rain had been falling for days and nights;
On the nineteenth day of the first lunar month,
The rain had changed into a snowstorm.

Han Po froze to death during the heavy storm,
His death went unnoticed for several days.
Later even the rags on his body
Rotted away in the storm.

But his spirit after death
Felt he must keep on chopping wood.
Because he had not a single stitch of clothing on
He could only come out at night.

Every year on the day of his death
There was always moonlight after midnight
To shine upon the mountain
And transform the night into day for him.

Our spring rain here usually lasts
A whole month once it's started,

Except for this one night,
When the rain would stop for half a night."

As she told this story of Han Po,
Sending chills down the listeners' spines,
Outside, in the moonlight,
A man's shadow truly seemed to have appeared.

"Mother," said the son,
"Han Po's death was tragic indeed.
But it was a tale of the past,
It could not happen today."

"In the past, in our village,
Everyone was Han Po.
But today, among us all
There is not a single Han Po.

In the past, there were many Han Po's
Who died of hunger and cold.
To show our sympathy,
We take only half a night's moonlight.

Now in this moonlight
Perhaps it is Han Po's spirit.
He comes not to chop wood,
But to avenge the wrongs he has suffered.

Tomorrow we will fight our landlords.
Han Po will settle his accounts with his.
He will never feel shy again,
He will come out in broad daylight."

Although most of Communist poetry in China centers on the
national scene, it is by no means devoid of international flavor.
After 1949, many veteran writers were sent abroad to satellite
countries as cultural or goodwill ambassadors. A sizable amount
of poetry about these trips has been produced through the years.

Poems range from the purely descriptive to the baldly propagandistic. The themes are mostly those of friendship, unity, and world peace; the tone is often respectful, admiring, and at times not unmingled with awe and reverence.

THE KREMLIN　(1950)

By Ai Ch'ing

During these traveling days,
I often pass through Red Square.
Following the red palace walls,
I walk to the bank of the Moscow River.

Standing by the river I gaze upward.
This is the Kremlin!
A vision in the air,
It is solidly rooted on this earth.

Such magnificent dignity!
Beautiful and serene,
Like a dream,
Yet it is perfectly real.

It stands loftily high
In gleaming splendor:
At dawn clad in colored clouds;
At dusk bathed in setting sun.

It sends out chimes
That fill our hearts with joy.
Day and night it blesses mankind
And guards the world's peace.

With descriptive details, sensuous images, and polished diction, another old poet, Yuan Shui-p'ai, weaves an ornate tribute to the "flowered land of perpetual bloom":

A SONG FOR INDIA　(1953?)

It is a land shimmering in colors.

Everywhere are green-foliaged canopies, bowllike roses.
The peacocks' jade-green plumage gleams in the
  moonlight.
This is the home of the goddess of spring.

It is a land of riches and beauty,
Nurtured by the blood of her heroic sons.
The people there are brave and firm,
Like our own brothers at home.

Our friendship of two thousand years
Can never be marred by time, nor barred by mountains.
Our nine hundred and sixty million people shall live
  together in peace,
Erecting a new monument for the world to witness.

Ah, north wind, blow. Let my songs soar with you,
Bringing the blessings and wishes of Peking
To the willowed banks of the Ganges River,
To the flowered land of perpetual bloom.

When the Korean War broke out in 1950 the entire nation
was mobilized to "resist the United States and assist Korea."
Troops—the Volunteer Army—were dispatched to the Korean
fronts to help the Korean "comrades" in their war against the
"imperialist aggressors." Writers offered their pens to chant the
heroics of the North Korean people, and the North Korean and
Chinese troops. T'ien Chien, the drummer poet, after his visit
to North Korea in 1951, expressed his emotion in

FOR THE THOUSAND DEAD   (1951):

1

O green pinewoods
I ask you,
"My brothers and sisters,
How did they die?"

A gust of wind blows over;

The pinewood gives its answer—

"The robbers chased them
To the sides of the trenches,
The robbers machine-gunned
Them down by the trenches."

2

O brothers, O sisters!
We are separated by a thousand miles;
That isn't far at all.
I came to your graves.

I stand before your graves,
Hot tears gush forth from my eyes;
But before long
Tears have changed to flame.

3

O brothers, O sisters!
I come from China,
Crossing the Yalu River,
To express my grief.

I come from China,
I come to Korea,
Wanting to lift up the fresh blood
To cast the sword of revenge!

An army officer turned to poetry to express "A Soldier's Wish":

You ask what is my wish?
Comrade, my wish is very simple.
It is the same wish of my comrades—
To accomplish heroic deeds in war, and
When I return home after the day of victory,
To wear a medal of liberated Korea.

On July 27, 1953, an armistice was signed, and peace finally arrived. Three days later a group of Chinese Communist officials and writers paid their respects to the North Korean capital. Following is an excerpt from "Pyongyang" (1953) by Yen Ch'en:

> We offer you the highest honor,
> Pyongyang, the city of heroes,
> A priceless bright pearl
> Gleaming on the crown of peace.
>
> A million tons of steely hurricane
> Could not drown you.
> Sky-penetrating fires
> Could not reduce you to ashes.
>
> The dirty hands of Wall Streeters
> Wanted to erase you from the map.
> Your fighting veins throb with mighty power,
> Your stubborn spirit refuses to be cowed.
>
> Pyongyang, I had passed by your war-torn streets,
> Heard stories of your suffering and your heroes.
> Today, I stand on a spread of ruins;
> I see the grandeur of our tomorrow!

In "Peking–Pyongyang" (1953), T'ien Chien pledges friendship between the two nations:

> In this Eastern part of the world
> The lights blaze in the Hall of Benevolence.
>
> The resplendent hall
> Shines on the Eastern world.
>
> Chairman Mao and Premier Kim
> Met in one place,

Two giant hands held tight
Like a bridge.

It is an immortal bridge
Across the great flow.

It crosses the Yalu River,
It crosses our hearts.

So many brave soldiers
Pass back and forth on the bridge.

From Pyongyang to Peking,
From Peking to Pyongyang.

Pyongyang—Peking, Peking—Pyongyang:
Two different places, one ideal.

This ideal is a great wave
Surging and rushing over the East!

Eleven years later Kuo Mo-jo, visiting war-torn North Vietnam, expressed his feelings and hopes for its people in "Heat and Fatigue" (1964). The poem is in dialogue form, compact, straightforward, and bare of metaphors:

—Comrade, are you warm?
—No, I don't feel warm.
—In such a tropical land, how is it that you're not warm?
—Our friendship is warmer than the tropics.
—Comrade, are you tired?
—No, I am not tired.
—At your age, how is it that you're not tired?
—But I am only fifteen years old!

In a form reminiscent of regulated verse is another poem by Kuo, "On the Way to Haiphong" (1964):

> Near every village
> There is a cemetery for war heroes;
> One salutes in deep respect,
> Realizing the hardship of building a nation.
> This is North Vietnam,
> But it is like Korea.
> Oh, the fresh blood of heroes
> Colors red flags everywhere.

A new crop of young poets appeared on the poetic scene after 1949. Though not necessarily proletarian by birth, they are unmistakable products of the newly born state. Aflame with enthusiasm for building a new life under the aegis of the party, they never tire of shouting the achievements of the revolution, extolling their leaders and the working masses at the top of their voices. Reading their verse, one is struck by their boundless exuberance and optimism about China's "magnificent future." Passionate and vehement in tone, energetic in expression, they give ecstatic play to the emotion and aspiration of the masses. Theirs is the clamorous voice of the revolutionary epoch.

In the early period of their poetic activity, from 1949 to 1953, these apprentice bards produced more ditties or jingles than true verse. Even the best were crude exercises displaying meager knowledge of poetic techniques. By the mid-fifties, however, genuinely competent verse began to emerge. If these works suffer from unevenness, raucous exaggeration, and sloganism, they do attain a naked simplicity and sincerity of feeling not to be questioned.

Intensely nationalistic and fiercely loyal to Mao's advocacy of a proletarian literature that is "national" in character, the new proletarian singers draw their chief inspiration from native sources. They borrow copiously from the rich storehouse of Chinese folklore and adopt the experimental verse forms of their immediate predecessors—from the pioneers' free verse to T'ien Chien's drumbeat meter. They even tried to emulate the style of classical verse, after Mao Tse-tung's poems written in the classical *tz'u* form were published in 1957.

Notwithstanding the extent to which their tastes still are guided and influenced by former poets, their verse is of a strikingly different temper. Singers of the social revolution and its goals, these worker-poets derive inspiration from things and places in which their predecessors had discovered no stimulus. Garage and factory, furnace and boiler, iron and steel—never deemed fit objects for poetic treatment by former poets—have become at once the mighty instruments that will help build a new, all-powerful China. Again and again the new bards rhapsodize their beauty and their titanic force. On the one hand they glorify the symphony of machinery; on the other, the greatness of human endeavor, manual or mechanized. Whatever the subject, every line throbs with a genuine ardor.

The drama of industry prompted one worker-poet to write in about 1954:

> In the furnace
>> coal
>>> is blazing red.
> In the boiler
>> water
>>> is fuming.
> The cistern
>> is seething
>>> with steam.
> The whistle
>> shriek after shriek
>>> is calling.
> Latch them up!
>> Comrades,
>>> together
> Latch them up!
>> the boxcars
>>> of socialism.

The factory, an erstwhile symbol of insufferable drudgery, an inferno of despair, is now filled with sunshine in "The Woman Worker Making Light Bulbs" (1953) by Sha O:

> Those flying fingers
> Like colorful skirted butterflies flitting over the flowers
> Rest upon the pistils,
> Tenderly fan them with their wings.
>
> The soft tungsten threads wind around the metal wire,
> Swift as a passing breeze.
> The blue light blinks on and on.
> The slender glass is flaming red plum blossom.
>
> For bringing light to brightness,
> The energy of youth throbs in their hands.
> The golden sunlight streams into the factory.
> With profound respect,
> It praises this skillful worker!

The sound of a factory whistle, no longer the sad wail of yesterday, inspires the clamoring cadences of "The Steam Whistle" (1958) by Li Ch'eng-yung:

> Climbing up the factory rooftop,
> The steam whistle sounds loud and clear.
> How intimate is its cadence;
> Every note moves my heart.
>
> In the past you softly moaned
> The injustice you had suffered.
> Enraged, you screamed aloud.
> Your cries shook the heavenly kingdom.
>
> Now you loudly sing,
> Praising the Great Leap Forward.
> Toward the capital, Peking,
> You send out good tidings.

> Climbing up the factory rooftop,
> The steam whistle sounds again and again.
> How soaring are its tones!
> Every note inspires the hearts of men!

In yet another piece, "Chimneys" (1958) by Li Pao-keng, factory chimneys are depicted with refreshingly novel images:

> Stretching high toward the white clouds,
> The dark smoke swirls into the blue sky.
> What big tree towers as high as you?
> What bamboo is as sweet as you?
>
> You are an iron arm
> Lifting slogans to the skies.
> You are a giant writing brush,
> Painting a fine spring scene of our fatherland.

In marked contrast to the workers' verse, the peasant poetry is of a homespun texture. More often than not, the peasant poets resort to the folk-song meters of all five or all seven characters. They favor the colorful and racy expressions of country folk, the vigorous yet lilting rhythm of ditties with a strong auditory appeal. Intoxicated by the new honor bestowed on them by the new regime and convinced that they have finally overthrown the old corrupt order, the peasants revel in exalting their "living Buddha," Mao Tse-tung, and in celebrating their "liberation" from their oppressors. With equal fervor they sing of the bliss of life in the communes, of the new irrigation systems, of the harvest. Their songs reveal a deep love of their benefactors and an unshakable faith in the future.

One Shantung province rustic compares his benefactor to the radiant sun in "Thousands and Thousands of Feet Long Are the Sun's Rays" (1958):

> The sun is red, the sun is bright,
> The sun's rays are thousands and thousands of feet long.

We now have two suns,
The two suns are not the same.
One sun stations in Peking,
One sun hangs from the sky.
The sun in the sky warms our bodies,
The sun in Peking warms our hearts.

A farmer from Canton chants his devotion to the great Communist party in "They Follow the Party with All Their Hearts" (1958):

A thousand streams flow into the East River,
Ten thousand rivers flow into the ocean,
Three million farmers of the East River
Follow the party with all their hearts.

Electric light inspires one commune member to sing its blessings to the farmer in his poem, "Electric Light Brightens Every Heart" (1958):

Big stars, little stars up in the sky,
Electric light fills the commune.
Look, how many stars are there in the sky!
Look, how many stars are here in our commune!

The stars are many, the ground is bright.
The lights in the commune have lit our eyes.
Grandma sewing at night no longer needs
My help to thread her needle.

The stars twinkle in the skies,
The electric light glows in the commune.
Sister embroidering pretty flowers
Need not rush during the day.

Stars in the skies are as dense as hemp,
The commune's light shines on my family.
Mother, holding little brother,

Studies under the electric light.

Stars in the skies,
Lights hang from every house beam;
Stars are not as bright as the electric light
That brightens every man's heart.

The sight of a pretty coed hauling manure to help the villagers prompted one observer to write "University Student Hauling Manure" (1958):

The magpies on the twigs chatter loud,
Everyone gaily laughs,
Thought some family was greeting a new bride,
But it was a girl student hauling manure.
Grandpa stroked his beard and muttered:
"Me, an old man, lived these eighty-eight years,
But never saw a college miss hauling manure!"

A tractor is the subject of a song called "The Iron Ox" (1963).

The commune has a giant iron ox,
It eats no grass but loves to drink oil;
Its tail drags a "big, big comb,"
To comb the fields smooth and green.

The commune has a giant iron ox,
It still roars after the sun has set;
Ask if it is tired,
All it does is roar.

The soldier-poets, like their worker and peasant comrades, have contributed their share of jubilant songs glorifying the new regime and its great leaders. In addition, they write verses about soldiering—the spirit of adventure, heroism, and intense love of the fatherland. Written in a variety of forms, from folk ditties to regular stanzaic patterns, these poems speak of the defense of the fatherland and the burning desire to "liberate"

Taiwan. With fiery determination and perhaps with more sta-
tistics than art, one soldier of the People's Liberation Army
made a vow in 1956 for the whole nation:

> Six hundred million people solemnly vow
> To liberate Taiwan!
> My heart scorching hot like flame
> Can hardly wait to dash to the battlefield.
> . . . .
> I let out my pent-up hatred
> On the training field,
> Battling the fierce storms,
> Daring the blazing sun.
> Blood reddens my uniform.
> I want to sharpen my skill to kill,
> I want to master the use of weapons.
> Let the five-star banner fly on top of Jade Mountain,
> Let a thousand million Taiwan comrades
> Soon be bathed in the sunshine of freedom and happiness.

Another soldier boldly proclaims in a short folk song, "Three
Atomic Bombs" (1959):

> Dare to think, to speak, to do,
> Are three atomic bombs,
> Blasting open a thousand years of superstition,
> Shattering ten thousand years of inferiority complex.

Following are three poems published in *Chinese Literature*, a
literary journal in English put out by the Communist press for
foreign consumption.

THE HEARTS
OF FRONTIER GUARDS TURN TOWARDS PEKING
(1968)[2]
By Tang Ta-hsien
Fighters' hearts turn towards Peking.

[2] Ibid., pp. 69–70.

Here at the frontier,
 We look up at the Polar Star in the night sky
 And gaze at the clouds above the far horizon
Until, as time goes by,
The green grass where we stand
 Is worn away by our feet.

Fighters' hearts turn towards Peking.
Here at the frontier,
 We write our innermost thoughts on every boulder,
 Carve our love on every tree
Until, as time goes by,
The neighborhood of our red sentry-post
 Can no longer hold all our devotion.

Fighters' hearts turn towards Peking.
Here at the frontier,
 We long to leap on to some scudding cloud,
 To scale some soaring peak.
Time and again,
From the bottom of our hearts
 We make our pledge to you.

Fighters' hearts turn towards Peking.
 No pass, no mountain, can obstruct our vision;
 No sea, no river, sunder our deep feeling,
For in Peking lives
The red sun in our hearts;
We fighters have boundless love for Chairman Mao,
 Are boundlessly loyal to him!

Fighters' hearts turn towards Peking. . . .

I RIDE MY EAGLE TEN THOUSAND LI (1968)[3]
   By Sun Jui-ching
My red-starred pilot's hat neatly set,
Clad in a uniform of olive green,
I'm going on duty for Chairman Mao,

[3] Ibid., no. 10, pp. 60–62.

Singing a battle song, hurrying steps keen.
I climb into the cockpit
With a joyous mien.

I ride my eagle into the sky,
Flying o'er mountains massive and tall.
What does a fighter love the most?
The Chingkang Mountains most of all.
The red flag Chairman Mao raised upon them
Reflects red on earth and on heaven's wall.

I ride my eagle into the sky,
Flying o'er many a river and stream.
What does a fighter love the most?
The Yen River, of beauty extreme.
On its banks Chairman Mao moved his pen of genius,
And revolution's blueprint sprang forth a-gleam.

I ride my eagle into the sky,
Flying o'er cities dotting the land.
What does a fighter love the most?
Peking City, our capital grand.
Loud and clear sing the masses: *The East is Red*,
Chairman Mao on Tien An Men takes his stand.

I ride my eagle into the sky,
Over rivers and lakes I fly.
What does a fighter love the most?
The waters green on Chungnanhai.
There Chairman Mao moves his mighty hand,
And revolution's thunder rumbles nigh.

I ride my eagle ten thousand *li*
Thinking always of Chairman Mao.
Deep are a fighter's emotions,
I love him best, I vow.
The red sun within our hearts
With light the world does endow.

A thousand ditties, ten thousand songs,
Sing of Chairman Mao, so great.
The skies may tumble, the earth may split,
We fighters will never vacillate.
With Chairman Mao we'll go for ever,
Planting red flags o'er the globe in spate.

In the barracks a foot soldier contemplates his mission in life
as he stitches away on his satchel in these lines from "Stitching
the Satchels" (1968) by Chung Tse:[4]

The fiery sun climbs from the distant east
Clothing the barracks with its warm light.
The squad and its leader among the beds
Busily stitch at their satchels with needle and thread.

"Serve the People" beneath our fingers does appear
As needle and thread to follow our thoughts,
"Serve the People" in characters red
To glow and sparkle wherever we go.

Satchel on shoulder, we march away,
Nothing can stop us in a thousand miles.
While marching on the path of revolution
In our satchel we could bear a thousand *jin*.

Proletarian bards of the border tribes are not to be outdone
in singing praise to their new life under their "liberators." Robust, colorful, and at times even candidly naïve, their songs have
a distinctive flavor and captivating charm.

THINKING OF CHAIRMAN MAO (1966)

When I milk,
I think of Chairman Mao:
If it weren't for Thee,
I would still be milking for Pa-i [a rich landlord]!

---

4 Ibid., p. 53.

When I shear,
I think of Chairman Mao:
If it weren't for Thee,
The more fleece I sheared, the more would belong to Pa-i!

When I make a rug,
I think of Chairman Mao;
If it weren't for Thee,
When it was done I would have to deliver to Pa-i!

One poet sings about the abundant production in the communes:

OUR LIVES   (1966)
Formerly the white clouds in the sky
Were more abundant than our herds of sheep,
Now the sheep in our communes
Are more than the white clouds.

Formerly the flowing water in the river
Was more than our horse milk.
Now the horse milk in our communes
Is more abundant than flowing water.

In song after song they chant the wisdom, courage, and greatness of their new leader. One Tibetan bard offers his homage in "Chairman Mao Is Our Beacon" (1966):

One thousand lamps, ten thousand lamps,
Chairman Mao is the beacon of all revolutionary people!

One thousand red flags, ten thousand red flags,
The thought of Chairman Mao is the greatest!

One thousand books, ten thousand books,
Chairman Mao's books are the most revolutionary!

Even forests change into brushes, oceans to ink,
They can never express the liberated serfs' love for
    Chairman Mao!

In the folk song "Our Hopes" (1966) a Mongolian poet sings:

> Men walking in the Gobi Desert
> Thirst for a village ahead;
> Men living in the hills
> Thirst for a clear running stream:
> We Mongolian people
> Long to see Chairman Mao in the capital!

The proletarian poets offer no delicate lyrics, no contemplative sonnets, no enigmatic experimental verse. Their purpose lies not in producing poems of beauty or technical excellence but in service to the state and the working masses. What Mao Tse-tung decreed at the Yenan forum in 1942, and enforced in 1949, continues its authoritarian rule. As the violent tides of the Great Proletarian Cultural Revolution finally receded, Mao Tse-tung, its founder, again emerged victorious after crushing the "capitalist-revisionist counterrevolutionary" forces led by his arch enemy, Liu Shao-ch'i—China's Khrushchev. The victory was grist to the mill of the Communist poet.

A LIVING LESSON   (1969)[5]
By Shih Hsüeh-tung
Lift up your voices and sing songs of praise,
Let iron arms beat the rejoicing gongs,
The workers must exercise leadership in everything,
Let's celebrate; our joy cannot be held.

. . . .

Who says "Exploitation merits reward"?
It's only a fantastical venture
On us shackles to forge.
"Down with Liu Shao-chi!"

[5] Ibid., 1969, no. 1, pp. 71–72.

Show exactly what he stands for—
This our resolve will be.

Him we'll expose, accuse, repudiate
On an ever greater scale,
Flames of hate burning
In the hearts of all.
Let's bury to the last inch
His revisionist educational line
In the overwhelming tidal waves
Of struggle-criticism-transformation,
As powerful as the Yellow River in spate. . . .

Poetry like "A Living Lesson" has traveled a long way from
that of Li Po, who once sang of the Yellow River in "Wine Is
To Be Served":

Do you not see
The Yellow River coming from heaven,
Dash toward the sea, never to return?
Do you not see
Before the bright mirrors in the high hall men mourning
    their silver hairs,
At dawn black silk, at dusk turned to snow?
To have a good life is to enjoy it to the full,
Never let an empty cup face the moon alone!
There must be some use for the talent Heaven granted
    me.
A thousand pieces of gold spent will be back again.
Roast the lamb, butcher the ox, and let's be gay!
Let's drink at least three hundred cups!

Master Ts'en,
Tan-ch'iu my friend,
The wine is here, pray don't stop!
I have a song for you.
Kindly listen with both ears.
Feasting on gems to the sound of bells and drums is nothing

to me!

I'd rather be drunk forever and never wake.

Ancient sages have long been forgotten.

Only the grand drinkers have left their names behind.

Once long ago Prince Ch'en held a banquet in the Hall of
Peace and Bliss,

Feasting his merrymaking guests with wine at ten thousand
gold pieces a quart.

How could a host bewail that he's short of cash?

Just send to the shop for more and keep on drinking.

The five-flower stallion,

The fur coat that costs a thousand gold pieces.

Send the boy to sell them for the best of wine.

Together we'll dissolve the sorrows of ten thousand years!

Selected Bibliography

ENGLISH SOURCES

Acton, Harold, and Ch'en Shih-hsiang, trans. *Modern Chinese Poetry*. London: Duckworth, 1936.

Baker, Carlos H. *Shelley's Major Poetry: The Fabric of a Vision*. New York: Russell and Russell, 1961.

Bate, Walter Jackson, ed. *Keats: A Collection of Critical Essays*. Englewood Cliffs, N.J.: Prentice-Hall, 1964.

Birch, Cyril. "English and Chinese Meters in Hsü Chih-mo's Poetry." *Asia Major* 7 (1959): 258–93.

————, ed. *Chinese Communist Literature*. New York: Praeger, 1963.

Bloom, Harold. *The Visionary Company: A Reading of English Romantic Poetry*. Garden City, N.Y.: Doubleday, 1961.

Brière, O. *Fifty Years of Chinese Philosophy, 1898–1948*. Translated by Laurence G. Thompson. London: Allen and Unwin, 1960.

Burnshaw, Stanley, ed. *The Poem Itself*. New York: Holt, Rinehart and Winston, 1960.

Chow, Tse-tsung. *The May Fourth Movement: Intellectual Revolution in Modern China*. Cambridge, Mass.: Harvard University Press, 1960.

Davis, A. R., ed. *The Penguin Book of Chinese Verse*. Translated by Robert Kotewall and Norman L. Smith. Harmondsworth, Middlesex: Penguin Books, 1962.

Deutsch, Babette. *Poetry in Our Time: A Critical Survey of Poetry in the English-speaking World, 1900 to 1960*. 2nd ed., rev. and enl. Garden City, N.Y.: Doubleday, 1963.

Fang, Achilles. "From Imagism to Whitmanism in Recent

Chinese Poetry: A Search for Poetics That Failed." In *Indiana University Conference on Oriental-Western Literary Relations*, edited by Horst Frenze and G. L. Anderson. Chapel Hill: University of North Carolina Press, 1955.

Feng, Yu-lan. *A History of Chinese Philosophy*. Translated by Derk Bodde. 2 vols. Princeton, N.J.: Princeton University Press, 1952–53.

Fogle, Richard H. *The Imagery of Keats and Shelley*. Chapel Hill: University of North Carolina Press, 1949.

Hawkes, David. *Ch'u Tz'ŭ, The Songs of the South: An Ancient Chinese Anthology*. Oxford: Clarendon Press, 1959.

Hsia, C. T. *A History of Modern Chinese Fiction, 1917–1957*. New Haven, Conn.: Yale University Press, 1953.

Hsü, Kai-yu. "The Life and Poetry of Wen I-to." *Harvard Journal of Asiatic Studies* 21 (1958): 134–79.

————, trans. and ed. *Twentieth Century Chinese Poetry: An Anthology*. Garden City, N.Y.: Doubleday, 1963.

Hummel, Arthur W., ed. *Eminent Chinese of the Ch'ing Period (1644–1912)*. 2 vols. Washington, D.C.: U.S. Government Printing Office, 1943–44.

Karlgren, Bernhard. *Sound and Symbol in Chinese*. Rev. ed. Hong Kong: Hong Kong University Press, 1962.

Kurtz, Benjamin P. *The Pursuit of Death*. New York: Oxford University Press, 1933.

Levenson, Joseph R. *Modern China and Its Confucian Past: The Problem of Intellectual Continuity*. Garden City, N.Y.: Doubleday, 1964.

Liu, James J. Y. *The Art of Chinese Poetry*. Chicago: University of Chicago Press, 1962.

Mayakovsky, Vladimir. *The Bedbug and Selected Poetry*. Translated by Max Hayward and George Reavey. Edited by Patricia Blake. New York: Meridian Books, 1960.

McAleavy, Henry. *Su Man-shu, 1884–1918: A Sino-Japanese Genius*. London: China Society, 1960.

Payne, Robert, ed. *Contemporary Chinese Poetry*. London: George Routledge and Sons, 1947.

————, ed. *The White Pony: An Anthology of Chinese Poetry from the Earliest Times to the Present Day.* New York: The New American Library, 1960.

Perkins, David. *The Quest for Permanence: The Symbolism of Wordsworth, Shelley, and Keats.* Cambridge, Mass.: Harvard University Press, 1959.

Prusek, Jaroslav, ed. *Studies in Modern Chinese Literature.* Berlin: Akademie-Verlag, 1964.

Rilke, Rainer. *Selected Poems.* Translated by C. F. MacIntyre. 2nd ed. Berkeley: University of California Press, 1961.

Roy, David. *Kuo Mo-jo: The Early Years.* Cambridge, Mass.: Harvard University Press, 1971.

————. *Kuo Mo-jo: The Pre-Marxist Phase (1892–1924).* Papers on China, 12. Cambridge, Mass.: Center for East Asian Studies, Harvard University, 1958.

Schwartz, Benjamin. *In Search of Wealth and Power: Yen Fu and the West.* Cambridge, Mass.: Harvard University Press, 1964.

Scott, A. C. *Literature and the Arts in Twentieth Century China.* Garden City, N.Y.: Doubleday, 1963.

Symons, Arthur. *The Symbolist Movement in Literature.* Rev. ed. New York: E. P. Dutton, 1958.

Werner, E. T. C. *A Dictionary of Chinese Mythology.* Shanghai: Kelly and Walsh, 1932.

CHINESE SOURCES (* indicates sources from which poems are translated)

*Ai Ch'ing. *Ai Ch'ing hsüan-chi* [Selected works of Ai Ch'ing]. Peking: K'ai-min, 1951.

*————. *Ch'un-t'ien* [Spring]. Peking: Jen-min wen-hsüeh ch'u-pan-she, 1956.

*————. *Hsien-chi hsiang-ts'un ti-shih* [Poems dedicated to the village]. Chungking: Pei Man, 1945.

————. *Shih lun* [Essays on poetry]. Shanghai: Hsin-wen-i, 1953.

*————. *T'a ssu-tsai ti-er-tz'u* [He died a second time]. Shang-

hai: Tsa-chih, 1953.

*Chu Tzu-ch'ing. *Chu Tzu-ch'ing shih-wen hsüan* [Selected works of Chu Tzu-ch'ing]. Hong Kong: Wen-li, 1959.

*———. *Hsin-shih tsa-hua* [Talks on the new poetry]. Shanghai: Tso-chia ch'u-pan-she, 1947.

*———, ed. *Chung-kuo hsin-wen-hsüeh ta-hsi* [Compendium of modern Chinese literature]. Vol. 8. Shanghai: Liang-yu, 1937.

Feng Chih. *Feng Chih shih-wen hsüan-chi* [Selected works of Feng Chih]. Peking: Jen-min wen-hsüeh ch'u-pan-she, 1955.

*———. *Shih-nien shih-ch'ao* [Poems of ten years]. Peking: Jen-min wen-hsüeh ch'u-pan-she, 1959.

*———. *Shih-ssu-hang shih* [Sonnets]. Kweilin: Ming-jih-she, 1942.

Feng Hsüeh-feng. *Lun-wen chi* [Essays]. 2 vols. Peking: Hsin-wen, 1944.

*Hsü Chih-mo. *Hsü Chih-mo ch'üan-chi* [Complete works of Hsü Chih-mo]. Edited by Chiang Fu-ch'ung and Liang Shih-ch'iu. 6 vols. Taipei: Ch'üan-ch'i wen-hsüeh ch'u-pan-she, 1969.

Huang Jen-ying, comp. *Kuo Mo-jo lun* [Essays on Kuo Mo-jo]. Shanghai: Kuang-hua, 1933.

*Huang Tsun-hsien. *Jen-ching-lu shih-ts'ao ch'ien-chu* [Collected works]. Shanghai: Ku-tien-wen-hsüeh ch'u-pan-she, 1957.

*Hu Shih. *Ch'ang-shih chi* [Experimental verses]. 3rd ed. Hong Kong: Ya-tung t'u-shu-kuan, 1954.

———. *Hu Shih wen-ts'un* [Collected works of Hu Shih]. 3 vols. Shanghai: Ya-tung, 1921.

*K'ang Pai-ch'ing. *Ts'ao-tsai-ch'ien chi* [Grass]. Shanghai: Ya-tung, 1921.

*Kuo Mo-jo. *Mo-jo wen-chi* [Collected works of Kuo Mo-jo]. 17 vols. Peking: Jen-min wen-hsüeh ch'u-pan-she, 1957.

*Liang Ch'i-ch'ao. *Yin-ping-shih ho-chi* [Collected works]. Vol. 16. Shanghai: Chung-hua, 1925.

Liang Shih-ch'iu. *Liang Shih-ch'iu hsüan-chi* [Selected works of Liang Shih-ch'iu]. Taipei: Hsin-lu, 1958.

Mai Jo-p'eng. *Huang Tsun-hsien chuan* [Biography of Huang Tsun-hsien]. Shanghai: Ku-tien wen-hsüeh ch'u-pan-she, 1957.

*Ping Hsin. *Ping Hsin shih-chi* [Collected poems of Ping Hsin]. Shanghai: K'ai-min, 1943.

Shih Chien. *Kuo Mo-jo p'i-p'an* [A Kuo Mo-jo critique]. Hong Kong: Ya-chou, 1954.

Shih Hsüan 1949–1959 [Collection of poetry, 1949–1959]. Shanghai: Shang-hai wen-i, 1960.

Shih Hsüan 1953.9–1955.12 [Collection of poetry, Sept. 1953–Dec. 1955]. Peking: Jen-min wen-hsüeh ch'u-pan-she, 1956.

Shih Hsüan 1956 [Collection of poetry, 1956]. Peking: Jen-min wen-hsüeh ch'u-pan-she, 1956.

Shih Hsüan 1957 [Collection of poetry, 1957]. Peking: Tso-chia ch'u-pan-she, 1958.

*Tai Wang-shu. *Tai Wang-shu shih-hsüan* [Selected poems of Tai Wang-shu]. Peking: Jen-min wen-hsüeh ch'u-pan-she, 1957.

*———. *Wang-shu ts'ao* [Poems of Wang-shu]. Shanghai: Hsien-tai shu-chü, 1933.

* *T'ang-shih san-pai shou* [Three hundred T'ang poems]. Shanghai: Kuang-i shu-chü, 1941.

*T'ien Chien. *Chi chan-tou-che* [To the fighters]. Shanghai: Sheng-huo, 1928.

*———. *Hai-yen sung* [Songs of the sea swallow]. Peking: Pei-ching ch'u-pan-she, 1958.

*Wang Ching-chih. *Hui-ti-feng* [Orchid wind]. Shanghai: Ya-tung, 1928.

*Wen I-to. *Wen I-to ch'üan-chi* [Complete works of Wen I-to]. Edited by Chu Tzu-ch'ing. 4 vols. Shanghai: K'ai-min, 1948.

*Yü P'ing-po. *Tung-yeh* [Winter night]. Shanghai: n.p., 1922.

Index

Publications on Asia of the Institute for Comparative and Foreign Area Studies (Formerly, Far Eastern and Russian Institute Publications on Asia)

1. Compton, Boyd (trans. and ed.). *Mao's China: Party Reform Documents, 1942–44.* 1952. Reissued 1966. Washington Paperback-4, 1966.
2. Chiang, Siang-tseh. *The Nien Rebellion.* 1954.
3. Chang, Chung-li. *The Chinese Gentry: Studies on Their Role in Nineteenth-Century Chinese Society.* Introduction by Franz Michael. 1955. Reissued 1967. Washington Paperback on Russia and Asia-4.
4. *Guide to the Memorials of Seven Leading Officials of Nineteenth-Century China.* Summaries and indexes of memorials to Hu Lin-i, Tseng Kuo-fan, Tso Tsung-tang, Kuo Sung-tao, Tseng Kuo-ch'üan, Li Hung-chang, Chang Chih-tung. 1955.
5. Raeff, Marc. *Siberia and the Reforms of 1822.* 1956.
6. Li Chi. *The Beginnings of Chinese Civilization: Three Lectures Illustrated with Finds at Anyang.* 1957. Reissued 1968. Washington Paperback on Russia and Asia-6.
7. Carrasco, Pedro. *Land and Polity in Tibet.* 1959.
8. Hsiao, Kung-chuan. *Rural China: Imperial Control in the Nineteenth Century.* 1960. Reissued 1967. Washington Paperback on Russia and Asia-3.
9. Hsiao, Tso-liang. *Power Relations within the Chinese Communist Movement, 1930–1934.* Vol. I: *A Study of Documents.* 1961. Vol. II: *The Chinese Documents.* 1967.
10. Chang, Chung-li. *The Income of the Chinese Gentry.* Introduction by Franz Michael. 1962.

11. Maki, John M. *Court and Constitution in Japan: Selected Supreme Court Decisions, 1948–60.* 1964.

12. Poppe, Nicholas, Leon Hurvitz, and Hidehiro Okada. *Catalogue of the Manchu-Mongol Section of the Toyo Bunko.* 1964.

13. Spector, Stanley. *Li Hung-chang and the Huai Army: A Study in Nineteenth-Century Chinese Regionalism.* Introduction by Franz Michael. 1964.

14. Michael, Franz, and Chung-li Chang. *The Taiping Rebellion: History and Documents.* Vol. I: *History.* 1966. Vols. II and III: *Documents and Comments.* 1971.

15. Shih, Vincent Y. C. *The Taiping Ideology: Its Sources, Interpretations, and Influences.* 1967.

16. Poppe, Nicholas. *The Twelve Deeds of Buddha: A Mongolian Version of the Lalitavistara; Mongolian Text, Notes, and English Translation.* 1967. Paper.

17. Hsia, Tsi-an. *The Gate of Darkness: Studies on the Leftist Literary Movement in China.* Preface by Franz Michael. Introduction by C. T. Hsia. 1968.

18. Hsiao, Tso-liang. *The Land Revolution in China, 1930–1934: A Study of Documents.* 1969.

19. Gasster, Michael. *Chinese Intellectuals and the Revolution of 1911: The Birth of Modern Chinese Radicalism.* 1969.

20. Thornton, Richard C. *The Comintern and the Chinese Communists, 1928–1931.* 1969.

21. Lin, Julia C. *Modern Chinese Poetry: An Introduction.* 1972.